**Praise for *Provoking Democracy***

"Yes, democracies need art, especially art the
Levine's shrewd, eloquent, and often enterta
From the controversies swirling around the
and the demolition of Serra's *Tilted Arc* to tl
*Lover* and 2 Live Crew, Levine shows how                                      ...mo-
cracies from its worse excesses – the muting c        ........ voices, the oppression of
majority rule, and the blind conformism of consensus politics. Indeed Levine is
to be commended for negotiating an honorable truce in the culture wars. Her
important new work recognizes not just the right but also the obligations of the
avant-garde to act as a permanent minority working within democratic institutions
to ensure a more open and genuinely plural society."

*Maria DiBattista, Princeton University*

"In these increasingly barbarous times, it is good and refreshing to see work that
stands up for the provocative – and potentially emancipatory – powers of the arts.
Caroline Levine's wide ranging and serious engagement with the question of how
the arts might provoke or even promote democracy, and her realization that this
question is itself fundamental for us, is a timely and much needed rejoinder to the
brutish dimensions of contemporary polities."

*Thomas Docherty, University of Warwick (author of* Aesthetic Democracy*)*

"Caroline Levine's *Provoking Democracy* gives an extremely compelling account of
how Anglo-American law has, in counterintuitive ways, supported avant-garde art,
and why Anglo-American democracies depend, in turn, upon such art, which provides a dissident voice that pluralism and an orientation towards the future demand.
Covering a broad range of topics, from public involvement in decisions about whether
particular pieces of art should be displayed, to the operations of the House Un-
American Activities Committee during the Cold War, to the role of originality in
judicial determinations of what counts as art, Levine's book furnishes ingenious readings of the dynamic interplay between particular figures and events. In the course
of reading *Provoking Democracy*, one is shocked at how the CIA secretly funded the
work of Abstract Expressionist painter Jackson Pollock to promote the ideal of
American freedom internationally at the same time as American publics and media
reviled his painting, but one also laughs at how customs officials categorized Constantin
Brancusi's sculpture *Bird* as a kitchen implement. All of these revelations are con-
veyed in a pellucid and gripping narrative style. *Provoking Democracy* is a book that
anyone interested in democracy or the arts simply must read."

*Bernadette Meyler, Cornell University Law School*

# Blackwell Manifestos

In this new series major critics make timely interventions to address important concepts and subjects, including topics as diverse as, for example: Culture, Race, Religion, History, Society, Geography, Literature, Literary Theory, Shakespeare, Cinema, and Modernism. Written accessibly and with verve and spirit, these books follow no uniform prescription but set out to engage and challenge the broadest range of readers, from undergraduates to postgraduates, university teachers and general readers – all those, in short, interested in on-going debates and controversies in the humanities and social sciences.

## Already Published

## Forthcoming

# Provoking Democracy

## Why We Need the Arts

Caroline Levine

**Blackwell** Publishing

© 2007 by Caroline Levine

BLACKWELL PUBLISHING
350 Main Street, Malden, MA 02148-5020, USA
9600 Garsington Road, Oxford OX4 2DQ, UK
550 Swanston Street, Carlton, Victoria 3053, Australia

The right of Caroline Levine to be identified as the Author of this Work has been
asserted in accordance with the UK Copyright, Designs, and Patents Act 1988.

All rights reserved. No part of this publication may be reproduced, stored in a
retrieval system, or transmitted, in any form or by any means, electronic, mechanical,
photocopying, recording or otherwise, except as permitted by the UK Copyright,
Designs, and Patents Act 1988, without the prior permission of the publisher.

First published 2007 by Blackwell Publishing Ltd

1   2007

*Library of Congress Cataloging-in-Publication Data*

Levine, Caroline, 1970–
    Provoking democracy : why we need the arts / Caroline Levine.
       p. cm.—(Blackwell manifestos)
    Includes bibliographical references and index.
    ISBN 978-1-4051-5926-5 (hardcover : alk. paper)—ISBN 978-1-4051-5927-2
(pbk. : alk. paper)
    1. Democracy and the arts.   2. Art and society.   3. Avant-garde (Aesthetics)—
Social aspects.   I. Title.

    NX180.P64L48 2007
    700.1′03—dc22

                                                                    2006037928

A catalogue record for this title is available from the British Library.

Set in 11.5/13.5pt Bembo
by Graphicraft Limited, Hong Kong
Printed and bound in Singapore
by Markono Print Media Pte Ltd

The publisher's policy is to use permanent paper from mills that operate a sustainable
forestry policy, and which has been manufactured from pulp processed using acid-free
and elementary chlorine-free practices. Furthermore, the publisher ensures that the text
paper and cover board used have met acceptable environmental accreditation standards.

For further information on
Blackwell Publishing, visit our website:
www.blackwellpublishing.com

*For Amanda and Martin*

# *Contents*

# *Figures*

# *Preface*

More than ten years ago, when I set out to write a book about arts controversies, I had in mind a rather different project. I started by investigating the various theories of art that were circulating in the public sphere, considering the ways that journalists, politicians, academics, lawyers, and ordinary people talked about art objects. Drawing on long histories of aesthetic theory and cultural criticism, I set out to articulate the range of philosophical issues implicitly at stake in public battles over the arts. Yet what I discovered surprised me. No matter where I looked, I kept happening on a single clear pattern that shaped every controversy I investigated. Wherever I turned my attention, from battles over arts funding to propaganda to obscenity law, from Britain to the US to Poland to India, from the beginning of the twentieth century to the beginning of the twenty-first, I found the complex and surprising relationship between art and democracy. Rather than investigating specific disputes over particular art objects, located in different historical contexts, I gradually realized that I needed to be able to account for the fact that the same problem kept recurring with surprising persistence. I set out to understand the basic organizing principles – the logic – that structured an array of disparate cases. This project took me far from my own field of aesthetic theory and pushed me into political science, sociology, and law. And it drove me to generate methods for describing patterns of recurrence and return. Ultimately, what emerged was this: a book that follows the strangely paradoxical relationship between art and democracy as it is played out in four contexts: debates over public art; the use of art as propaganda; obscenity law; and the question of originality in customs and copyright disputes.

All of these cases led me to a conclusion that also surprised me. We are used to telling ourselves that the arts need the protection of a flourishing democracy in order to survive. But in fact, the opposite is at least equally true: *democracies require art* − challenging art − to ensure that they are acting as free societies. Democratic citizens have gotten into the habit of believing that theirs are the freest societies in the world. But political theorists since Alexis de Tocqueville have warned that democratic governments can actually work *against* freedom. Intent on imposing the will of the majority, democracies are inclined to repress and silence nonconformist voices. And since majorities can − and do − decide to squelch unpopular expression, democratic societies always run the risk of becoming distinctly unfree societies. So: how can democracies guarantee freedom?

This book argues that democratic states need the challenges to mainstream tastes and values launched by artists in the tradition of the avant-garde. Since the beginnings of the avant-garde in the late nineteenth century, artists have claimed that they are helping to liberate society through their resistance to majority rule. Intent on shocking and unsettling conventional values, they have refused to allow the majority to imagine that its will is either absolute or universal. In the past few decades, artists have proclaimed the death of the avant-garde, but as this book will show, the idea that art represents a struggle for freedom from dominant norms and values remains surprisingly robust and influential. In fact, whenever art works are contested in the public sphere, artists and arts advocates leap to invoke the revolutionary, heroic, marginalized figure of the avant-garde artist and set that oppositional figure against an idea of the "people." Arts controversies for a hundred years have hinged on a struggle between democratic majorities and deliberately provoking outsiders.

Despite the end of the historical avant-garde, then, what I call the *logic of the avant-garde* emerges again and again in the public sphere.

This logic has earned the arts the reputation of being deliberately elitist, difficult, and challenging – and it is this elitism that has appalled populists, who have condemned the avant-garde as anti-democratic. But as I contend in this book, democracies that are committed to the value of freedom actually need the logic of the avant-garde. The art world's anti-majoritarian impulse remains crucial whenever democratic majorities threaten to turn tyrannical. Dissenting and unpopular artists – from Jackson Pollock and Bertolt Brecht to D. H. Lawrence and 2 Live Crew – have allowed democracies to demonstrate their commitments to fostering and protecting marginal voices. And the logic of the avant-garde is portable, elastic – useful in a surprising range of times and places. Indeed, with democracy on the line today, the logic of the avant-garde might once again prove a surprisingly effective force around the globe.

This argument took shape over many years, and I could not have begun to address the questions explored in this book without the extraordinary support of students, colleagues, institutions, and friends. The first version of the book emerged in a seminar I taught at Yale in 1997, and the magnificent intensity of those students has invigorated the project from the beginning. Since that time, my students at Wake Forest, Rutgers-Camden, and the University of Wisconsin-Madison have animated and reanimated the debates with liveliness and keen perception, and I could not have written this book without them. I am especially grateful to Cary Franklin and Amy Johnson, who read and responded to chapters in progress; Gwen Blume, who pursued Richard Nixon in the archives for me; and Jennifer Geigel Mikulay, whose own interest in the subject has made for many a spirited conversation, just as her reading has sharpened and improved my work.

Institutional support has allowed me indispensable time, funds, and collegial exchange, and I wish to acknowledge Wake Forest University's Archie Fund and Rutgers University's research leave program. In the past few years, the University of Wisconsin-Madison has provided a wonderfully hospitable context for my research, teaching, and collegial discussion: I especially appreciate the research time funded by the Graduate School. The Rockefeller Foundation Archives and Marje Schuetze-Coburn of the Feuchtwanger Memorial Library at the University of Southern California furnished me with crucial primary materials. Many thanks to Art Rogers and Scott Vanderlip for generously providing images.

A whole crowd of readers gave their time to making this a better book. I am thankful for the opportunity to present my work at Wake Forest University's faculty colloquium, the Institute for Philosophy and Public Policy at the University of Maryland, the Delaware Valley British Studies colloquium, and the English Department Faculty Draft Group at the University of Wisconsin-Madison. I am particularly grateful for the year I spent at Rutgers' Center for the Critical Analysis of Contemporary Culture, where I reaped the benefits of an exciting – and always bracing – conversation. My deep thanks, as always, go to Carolyn Williams, who not only led our colloquium with striking intelligence, but also gave me the gift of her extraordinary generosity and friendship. The readers who responded to the text for Blackwell provided invaluable suggestions: Bernadette Meyler deserves special thanks for her thoughtful commentary. Jon Connolly and Tom Silfen offered me the benefit of their legal expertise, which I tried my best to absorb. I am indebted to Lew Friedland for his friendly skepticism and for his patient willingness to hash out the details of my arguments. Three perfect strangers kindly agreed to talk to me at length: Laurie Adams, Stephen Radich, and Art Rogers. Most recently, the editors at Blackwell Publishing – Al Bertrand and Emma Bennett – have worked hard to see this book through to completion. And finally, I cannot speak highly enough of Robert Shepard, who exceeded every expectation I had of a literary agent: performing the mingled roles of champion, critic, editor, counselor, and ally with endless cheerfulness and enthusiasm, he made sure that writing, even at its hardest, was never a lonely venture.

When it comes to the task of expressing my thanks to my friends, I find myself faltering. I would be nothing – and nowhere – without them. Jan Caldwell, Rachel Harmon, Louise Keely, Terry Kelly,

*Preface*

Jonathan Marks, Nancy Marshall, Lisa Sternlieb, and Henry Turner offered me captivating conversation, thoughtful guidance, and boundless encouragement. I am so glad and grateful to have Susan Bernstein in my life and want to thank her especially for her writing camaraderie and generous hospitality. Jane Gallop's dazzling warmth and intelligence have brought with them many pleasures – among them, the delicious indulgence of talking about the emotional work of writing books. Rebecca Walkowitz started down the same professional path with me on the very same day many years ago, and I am not sure how I would have managed without her since: from the multiple drafts she has read to the counsel and encouragement she has offered along the way, I see everywhere her steadfast friendship, her wit, her luminous intellect, and her kindness. In their very different ways, two friends – Amanda Claybaugh and Martin Puchner – have had more influence on the writing of this book than anyone. They read, encouraged, disputed, defended, reread, stimulated, soothed, inspired, and advised, and through it all, expressed such utter and unfailing confidence in me, and in the book, that I could not help but keep going. Whatever is best about the work I have done can be traced back to their brilliance and their friendship. This book is for them.

My two extraordinary parents have provided support of every kind – emotional, material, and intellectual. My brother, Peter Levine, provided not only warm hospitality but also thoughtful critique and suggestions. As for my immediate family, I honestly don't know how I came to be lucky enough to share my life with Jon and Eli McKenzie. Jon's creativity and his intellectual sparkle shape every moment of my writing and thinking, and his care and companionship sustain me through everything else. Eli, who came along in the middle of it all, prompts a happiness I never knew existed. I wish I knew how to thank them for the astonishing gift of their laughter, their teasing, their encouragement, and their unwavering love.

# 1

# Democracy Meets the Avant-Garde

*Art is not democratic. It is not for the people.*

Richard Serra

*Mass Culture is very, very democratic: it absolutely refuses to discriminate against, or between, anything or anybody. All is grist to its mill, and all comes out finely ground indeed.*

Dwight Macdonald

What would an "art of the people" look like? In the mid–1990s, two Russian artists, Vitaly Komar and Alex Melamid, proposed a post-Cold War answer to this question. Polling more than a thousand people in each of fourteen countries, including the United States, Russia, Kenya, China, and France, they set out to gauge public opinion on the question of art. They hired professional pollsters who asked participants about their favorite colors, their preferences for landscapes or nudes, abstract or traditional styles, wild or domestic animals. While Americans overwhelmingly preferred fully clothed figures, historical characters like Abraham Lincoln, and realistic-looking styles, more than 50 percent of Russians favored nude or partially naked figures, ordinary people, traditional Russian styles, and rural scenes. In China, the Komar-Melamid survey was one of the first public opinion polls ever conducted. The majority in almost every country preferred light blue to any other color.

Having gathered their information, Komar and Melamid then painted the results. That is, they produced a single painting to satisfy

1

**Figure 1.1** Vitaly Komar and Alex Melamid, *Kenya's Most Wanted* (1994), courtesy Ronald Feldman Fine Arts, New York.

majority tastes in each national group (figure 1.1). The results are pretty comic: a parade of light blue landscapes, sporting recognizably local flora and fauna, highly conventional painterly styles, and hackneyed historical figures – George Washington for the Americans, Jesus for the Kenyans, Mao for the Chinese. But Komar and Melamid insist that they are drawing a serious connection between art and democracy:

> We had this image in Russia of America as a country of freedom, of course, where the majority rules – which in a way is true, because in the election, you can win by sheer majority. So if 20,000 more people voted for you, it means that you are the President. That's why we mimic this in the poll. We trust – it's interesting – we trust this people, we believe that this system, among existing systems, is the best political and social system. We trust these people to vote for the President. But we never trust them in their tastes, in their aesthetic judgment.[1]

2

Comic or serious, Komar and Melamid raise a crucial question. What is the relationship between majority rule in politics and majority rule in matters of artistic judgment? US Congressman Henry Hyde (R-IL) has argued that it is a grave mistake for a democratic government to sponsor art that offends any large number of people: "Public funds, in a democracy, are to be spent for public purposes, not for the satisfaction of individuals' aesthetic impulses. And if the impulse in question produces a work which is palpably offensive to the sensibilities of a significant proportion of the public, then that work ought not to be supported by public funds." Similarly, disgruntled citizens often raise the banner of democracy to voice their dismay at contemporary art. Here's lawyer Peter Hirsch: "Democracy says we are not fools, we are not stupid, we don't like the piece of art . . . [I]n a democracy, why not let democracy rule?"[2]

The question is a good one. Why *not* let democracy rule? Why not let the majority of people decide what they do and do not like in art? This book argues that this is precisely the question that has been at stake in every major controversy over the arts in the past century, from public funding to obscenity and from copyright to wartime censorship. And it makes the case that the solution to the recurring deadlock between artists and politicians is a new and more fundamental set of arguments than those we have become accustomed to. Battles about the arts cannot be put to rest by conventional claims for and against censorship, or by familiar arguments for and against government arts funding. Instead, we need a direct response to the question that implicitly and persistently haunts battles over works of art: namely — what *is* art's proper role in a democratic society?

## The Logic of the Avant-Garde

Speaking out in the *Washington Post* a few years ago, a sculptor named Frederick Hart condemned the contemporary art world, claiming that artists had abandoned their traditional role as servants of public ideals and shared values. In the past, Hart lamented, artists were responsible to society, just as society was responsible to artists, both dedicated to order and purpose, meaning and morality. No longer. For the past hundred or so years, artists had deliberately set themselves against the citizenry, holding public taste in contempt and only too delighted to provoke perplexity, revulsion, and shock:

> Since the beginnings of bohemianism in the late 19th century, rejection by the public has become the traditional hallmark of what comes to be regarded as great art. . . . Every artist worth his salt yearns to create works of art that are (mistakenly perceived, of course) so offensive, so insulting to the public as to earn him a clear judgment of genius for his success at being misunderstood. . . . What is really going on is the cynical aggrandizement of art and artist at the expense of sacred public sentiments – profound sentiments embodied by symbols, such as the flag or the crucifix, which the public has a right and a duty to treasure and protect.[3]

The contemporary artist emerges here as elitist, self-involved, disdainful of national unity, and contemptuous of inherited emblems and values. On the other side is the public, proud of their cultural traditions, cherishing those signs of deeply held feeling which they have inherited from their forefathers.

Surprisingly, perhaps, champions of the art world are inclined to agree. When art is under attack in the public sphere, its supporters typically launch the defense that genuine works of art always and necessarily challenge social and political norms. In 1990, Vaclav Havel, the newly elected democratic leader of then-Czechoslovakia – and practicing playwright – took part in the US culture wars, arguing that it was the artist's *obligation* to upset settled values and conventions:

> There are those around the world, indeed even those in democracies with the longest tradition of free speech and expression, who would attempt to limit the artist to what is acceptable, conventional, comfortable. They are unwilling to take the risks that real creativity entails. But an artist must challenge, must controvert the established

4

order. To limit that creative spirit in the name of public sensibility is to deny society one of its most significant resources.[4]

Despite crucial differences, Hart and Havel reach the same conclusion: contemporary artists feel that they are required to challenge the status quo. Thus a strange consensus underpins the most ferocious debates about the arts. From right-wing politicians to radical outliers, voices across the spectrum tend to agree that artists have every intention of upsetting and unsettling the public.

But artists have not always been defined as adversaries of convention. Hart laments the contemporary state of the arts in part because he longs for a time before an antagonism toward the public defined the artist's role. Hart puts the transition in the nineteenth century, claiming that the battle between artists and the public accompanied the emergence of a new "bohemian" art world. And he is right: the idea that art should challenge mainstream values is not much more than a century old. In fact, although it is possible to find earlier examples of artists who shocked authorities and challenged dominant tastes – Michelangelo, for example, or Goya – it is only since the late nineteenth century that societies began to define art by its rebellious and oppositional character.

Hart calls the shift "bohemian." I prefer to use the term *avant-garde*.[5] Although scholars debate the precise meaning of the term, in popular parlance "avant-garde" has come to mean art that is ahead of its time – shocking, insurrectionary, capable of summoning the future. The term comes originally from a military context – meaning the front line or vanguard. In the mid-nineteenth century, the word "avant-garde" was used almost exclusively to refer to the political radicalism associated with revolutions in Europe. But artists eager to challenge the political, cultural, and social status quo began to adopt the term too, and in France in the 1870s and 1880s the title began to attach to artists more often than to political radicals.[6] The new artists of the avant-garde were a collection of deliberate outsiders – celebrating the margins, advocating an overturning of conventional aesthetics. Specifically, they were reacting to rigidly conservative art sponsored by national academies. They claimed authenticity only for art works that challenged familiar and conventional tastes, art that was embattled, unpopular, marginal, and, above all, new. The military roots of the name "avant-garde" invoked an image of warlike struggle: artists saw themselves not only as innovators, but as warriors against the status quo, doing battle with the present in the name of the future, provoking radical change through rupture and destruction so that a new world could come to take the place of the old. As the painter Giorgio de Chirico put it, "What is wanted is to rid art of everything known and familiar that it has contained up to now: every subject, thought and symbol must be put aside."[7]

Sociologist Pierre Bourdieu argues that the emergence of the revolutionary avant-garde marked a new identity for art. Art became known as a special field, separate from the rest of social life. Artists described their work as an end in itself, pure, free, and supremely indifferent to official accolades and commercial taste. In the words of Italian artist F. T. Marinetti: "We . . . above all, teach authors to *despise the audience. . . .* We especially teach *a horror of the immediate success* that normally crowns dull and mediocre works." He argued that applause was a sign of failure. Similarly, photographer Alfred Stieglitz urged fellow artists to refuse all rewards: "NO JURY – NO PRIZES – NO COMMERCIAL TRICKS."[8] In this new context, the "starving artist" became a heroic figure, deliberately repudiating financial rewards and state recognition, insisting that art could not be subjected to corrupt interests, whether economic or political. Art's new identity, according to Bourdieu, was paradoxical, representing "an interest in disinterestedness."[9] The artist's success was now contingent on failure – the failure to earn the traditional rewards of money, fame, and power. Art, in its very uselessness, seemed liberated from the demands of utility and profit. Artists started to see their role as standing for freedom itself. And ultimately, they imagined, artistic freedom would revolutionize all of life.[10]

Yet, each impulse toward freedom had to be short-lived. No sooner had groups of artists voiced their battle cries against the elite than that very elite hailed them as its cultural heroes – the best representatives of the freedom that their society had to offer. Even the uproariously lawless Dada group seemed in danger of being co-opted by the dominant culture: "The mediocrities and the gentry in search of 'something mad' are beginning to conquer Dada," lamented Richard Huelsenbeck in 1920.[11] And so the avant-garde had to be dynamic, constantly changing to throw off the fetters of dominant norms and values.

Given the constant peril that they would be reassimilated into the cultural mainstream, avant-garde groups turned against the very idea of art itself, casting the traditional practices and concepts of art-making as repressive and conventional. A new kind of "art world" began to take shape to replace the old academic system. Now, little-known groups of artists who had begun at the margins, grandly indifferent to prizes and markets, would garner praise from critics and collectors, gaining ascendancy over more established figures, displacing them as the centers of the art world. But the more such groups won prizes and acclaim, the more their status as perfectly disinterested artists was threatened, and they would soon be displaced by new marginal groups. The insistent marginality of the avant-garde demanded a rapid obsolescence, as each rebellious artist was incorporated into the mainstream and lost ground to the purer artists on the margins. Thus avant-garde movements proliferated, giving way in quick succession: Impressionism, Symbolism, Pointillism, Fauvism, Cubism, Futurism, Vorticism, Constructivism, Dadaism, Surrealism, and Abstract Expressionism, among others. Playwright Alfred Jarry predicted that his own avant-garde contemporaries would be displaced by a new generation "who will find us completely out of date, and hence abominate us." He added: "This is the way things should be."[12] And similarly, here is Marinetti: "When we are forty years old, younger and stronger men will throw us in the trash can like useless manuscripts. We want this to happen!"[13]

Peter Bürger has argued that the defining characteristic of the late nineteenth- and early twentieth-century avant-gardes was their attack on art as a modern institution: avant-garde groups bewailed the separation of art from life and aimed to shift art's liberating energies out of the rarefied sphere of the gallery into the experience of the everyday. But crucially, Bürger makes the case that such protests against the institutionalization of art have now themselves become accepted as art, and so can no longer perform the same critical function that they did a hundred years ago. Thus he claims that we should reserve the name "avant-garde" only for those movements that took shape in the late nineteenth and early twentieth centuries. All later echoes and revivals of their efforts are not really avant-garde at all.[14]

It would certainly be a mistake to assume that contemporary art can be avant-garde in the same way as its precursors. But although it is true that the most intense moment of avant-garde energy came to its end in the first half of the twentieth century, the model of freedom and resistance associated with the avant-garde has remained surprisingly powerful both inside the art world and beyond. The characterization of art as oppositional, rebellious, and liberating persistently reemerges in the most recent debates about the arts, as though all art did still strive to belong to the avant-garde. Thus contemporary society exhibits a deep and longstanding attachment to what I call the *logic of the avant-garde*. This is the logic that comes into play whenever art becomes the subject of controversy in the public sphere: at the heart of arguments about the arts we typically find a shared understanding, as defenders and detractors alike connect the art work to the gestures of avant-garde rebellion, defining art – for better or for worse – as the social force that challenges the status quo in order to usher in a new world. When it comes to shocking contemporary art, commentators often remind us of the avant-garde as the historical origin of such scandals; or they accuse contemporary artists of being boring and out of date, continuing to strike avant-garde postures long after they are able to exert any impact.[15] What I want to suggest here is that we cannot reduce the avant-garde to either a long-gone source or a tired gesture: the logic of the avant-garde is in fact eminently portable, adapting itself to new contexts. Indeed, as we will see, it performs a necessary *structural* function within democratic contexts. Thus despite the death of the historical avant-gardes, the logic of the avant-garde continues, strong and vibrant, into our own time.

We do not have to look far to find art defined as critical, defiant, and challenging. Recently, *New York Times* critic Roberta Smith adopted the classic rhetoric of the avant-garde to defend contemporary art works under attack: "Art's job," she wrote, "is to provoke thought in ways that are difficult to resolve and uncomfortable." Nicholas Serota, director of the Tate Modern museum in London, defended Damien Hirst's *Mother and Child Divided* this way: "For me, the undoubted shock, even disgust, provoked by the work is part of its appeal. Art should be transgressive. Life is not all sweet." Similarly, US Congressman Ted Weiss (D-NY) characterized art by its refusal to allow us to feel comfortable with the status quo: "Artists are society's watchers, critics, and champions. They speak the unspeakable, even if it manifests itself in horrifying, untidy, or esoteric manners. . . . Art that challenges existing prejudices serves a most important function; it helps us to grow and reach a higher state of humanity." And this position is not limited to the bohemian left. "Let us never forget," warned the late Senator Jacob Javits (R-NY), "that one of the greatest works of art mankind has ever produced, Picasso's *Guernica*, is neither likable nor pleasing." Meanwhile, art's detractors point to the same defiance of public taste. As conservative commentator David Gergen puts it, "artists . . . want to engage in the wanton destruction of a nation's values and they expect that same nation to pay their bills." And George Will bemoans the fact that "artists feel entitled to public subsidies, any denial of which is censorship that proves the need to shock the bourgeoisie from its dogmatic slumbers." Popular culture too has taken up the logic of the avant-garde. In Showtime's television series "The L Word," a fictional museum director who has fought protestors and administrators to display a controversial show called *Provocations* explains that the art is important because it brings us to "the edge of our present culture where we stand to face ourselves before we jump into an unknown future."[16] In short, from leftist intellectuals to right-wing pundits, from legislators to television shows, just about everyone in battles over the arts agrees that artists are on the side of critical resistance, inaccessibility, and minority values, while the "public" is on the side of tradition, faith, and majority tastes and preferences. The fundamental disagreement in arts debates centers on the *value* of critical outsiders and difficult challenges, mainstream traditions and popular tastes.

Strangely, the public image of the brave, combative, liberated artist survives despite the fact that most artists working now have deliberately distanced themselves from the historical avant-garde. We might think of artists working in recombinant media, site-specific installations, formalist poetry, popular music, community-based groups, and folk styles: all are producing art that quite purposefully rejects avant-garde claims to radical autonomy and thoroughgoing innovation. It is true, too, that artists who work in traditional styles and affirm transcendent, humanizing values continue to stand for "art" more generally in the minds of many.[17] However, it is a striking fact that whenever art is the subject of controversy, its supporters will argue that art's primary purpose is to displease, disrupt, and offend, and its critics will bemoan the fact that art has relinquished its duty to reflect traditional shared values. Even those artists who seem very far indeed from the historical avant-garde – Jeff Koons, a self-conscious recycler of sentimental kitsch, or the Dixie Chicks, a popular country band – find themselves wearing the mantle of the embattled, marginal artist in public battles over their work.[18]

What I want to suggest is that in every kind of arts controversy, art works under attack have the potential to *become* avant-garde. Here, then, lies the difference between the historical avant-garde and its contemporary manifestation: these days, no matter what the content or intention of the art work, the rhetoric of avant-garde defiance can kick into gear whenever art becomes the target of public controversy. And what I am calling the logic of the avant-garde is, in fact, a certain structural understanding of the role of art in society that almost always forms the backdrop to arguments coming from both right and left, advocates and detractors, art experts and

10

laypersons. The definition of artists as the adversaries of mainstream tastes and values reemerges with quite a startling inexorability, as if the desire for shock and disruption always lay latent even in the folksiest, kitschiest, most self-consciously postmodern of art works.

## Is Art For or Against Democracy?

The critical autonomy and rebellion associated with the avant-garde have come to serve as a kind of default definition of the social role of art. And this means that art's relationship to democracy is vexed and often hostile. Art that intentionally shocks and unsettles majority preferences seems to set itself – quite unflinchingly – against the will of the people. Deliberately defying popular tastes, it appears eminently anti-democratic. And it is true that the historical avant-gardes often expressed a deep antipathy to democracy. Masculinist and anti-Semitic, avant-gardists such as Ezra Pound, F. T. Marinetti, and Wyndham Lewis embraced fascism and expressed contempt for the "people." Others, such as Georg Grosz and John Heartfield, were disgusted by the failures of parliamentary democracy.[19] Meanwhile, stable and longstanding democracies such as the US and Britain are often said to have produced a tamer, less revolutionary, and less innovative art than their more volatile counterparts.[20] The logic of the avant-garde and the logic of democratic politics would appear to have little in common.

But it is equally true that many critical and anti-conventional artists over the past hundred years have made an impassioned claim that their art advances the cause of legitimate democracy. Picasso, for one, refused to allow *Guernica* to return to Spain until democratic institutions and civil freedoms had been fully restored, claiming that the painting belonged to the Spanish people.[21] In another example, in the late 1960s, after two military coups in Brazil, radical theater director Augusto Boal worked to restore democracy in a self-consciously avant-garde way, by inviting his audiences onstage to offer solutions to ongoing political questions.[22] A third extraordinarily

11

influential avant-garde proponent of democracy was German artist Joseph Beuys. In 1972, Beuys was fired from his position at the art academy in Düsseldorf for arguing that anyone should be admitted who wanted to make art. Acting on his famous motto, "everyone is an artist," he intended to bring out the creative potential latent in every person and so to democratize the arts. The education minister responsible for Beuys' dismissal was so afraid of the artist's creative power and global influence that he refused to confront Beuys directly, saying: "I cannot and will not allow myself to be made into an art object."[23] If this episode seems to reveal a familiar gap between art and politics, it is important to note that Beuys not only wanted to democratize the arts, he also wanted to bring art to democracy: a candidate for the German Parliament and a founding member of the Green Party, he sought to incorporate his ideas about a radically democratic culture into parliamentary politics.

Boal and Beuys might seem like relics of the activist sixties, but an artistic commitment to democracy is not limited to the past. To give just one example among many: in 2005, a group called Concerned Artists of the Philippines (CAP) rallied artists, art students, and fellow citizens to put together effigies, posters, streamers, songs, skits, and speeches as part of a street spectacle to protest against President Gloria Macapagal-Arroyo, whose declaration of a state of emergency and attempts to stifle the press seemed like the start of authoritarian rule. They teamed up with fellow artists to form an alliance called Artists for Democracy and the Immediate Ouster of GMA (ADIOS GMA!).[24]

Is the avant-garde for or against democracy? The two sides in arts controversies tend to offer versions of the same arguments over and over again. One camp insists that the democratic state is expressing the will of the people, while elitist art self-indulgently flouts and defies majority tastes and values. The other camp asserts that governments are repressing the people's expression, while rebellious artists are opening new avenues to promote the real welfare of the people. Which camp is right? It is the central contention of this book that both sides of the argument have gotten it wrong.

## Democracy, Mass Culture, and Nonconformity

In order to unpack the complex relationship between democracy and the avant-garde, I want to start by considering one of the most pressing problems posed by democratic governance. Contemporary politicians in democratic states often speak as though the terms "freedom" and "democracy" were synonymous.[25] And it is true that most modern democracies have grown out of revolutionary victories over tyrannical despots and powerful elites. The framers of the US Constitution designed a political structure that would impede the domination of the country by a centralized government. But government is not the only source of power, and the potential for a different kind of tyranny began to develop along with the growth of democratic society. In the nineteenth century, "the people" claimed more influence than ever before, power increasingly dispersed among the many rather than concentrated in the hands of a few. And in this context a new question began to emerge: what if democracy could breed its own version of tyranny? What if "the people" themselves could turn into a kind of tyrant? Political theorists warned that where "the people" are taken to be sovereign, majorities can work to repress and silence nonconformist voices. Thus democratic societies always run the risk of becoming disturbingly unfree societies.

When Alexis de Tocqueville traveled to America in 1829 and 1830, he intended to gauge the success of the new republic – and to see what lessons he could learn from it that might apply to other nations, including his own politically tumultuous France. One fact he noted was that people in the vast territories of America, despite their different histories, had been linked together extremely effectively by new methods of transportation. And alongside faster transport and commerce came inventions of newer, faster, and cheaper methods of communication – including the increasing mechanization of printing methods and the mass production of paper.[26] In this new world, Tocqueville maintained, people who had never met were so well connected to one another that "variety is disappearing from the human species; the same manner of acting, thinking, and feeling is found in all corners of the world."[27]

If mass communication was helpful to democracy in that it allowed people to debate questions of shared concern, to hear distant perspectives, and to make informed decisions, Tocqueville warned that it also brought with it a new danger. As people were becoming more alike, they were also relinquishing the benefits which extraordinary individuals might bring to society – special genius, for example, or uncommon insight – forces which had in the past helped to shape politics, art, and society. The more a common culture was at work, the less people seemed to want to exercise their own intellects to come up with new ideas or arguments not already imagined by the majority. This was true not only for politics, but for religion and art. And so with democracy came mass culture and with mass culture came a decline of great and exceptional goals and talents. "One can foresee that faith in common opinion will become a sort of religion whose prophet will be the majority," Tocqueville wrote. "The spectacle of this universal uniformity chills me, and I am tempted to regret the society that is no longer."[28]

The problem, according to the author of *Democracy in America*, was not democracy itself. The problem was that his contemporaries were confusing *equality* and *freedom*. Equality – the sameness of conditions – was certainly not a sufficient guarantee of a good society; it could be exploited by tyrants, who had in the past ruled by boasting of their capacity to put an end to material inequalities. To counter despotism one needed freedom – which clearly brought with it the potential for violence and strife, breaches with tradition and an embrace of upheaval. But if both equality and freedom were necessary to a great republic, it was not hard to see how one might be purchased at the expense of the other. Equality offered immediate satisfactions but weakened spirits and intellects in the long term; freedom produced immediate excesses but long-term rewards.

The most common modern solution to the tension between equality and freedom has been the development of the liberal-democratic state: a kind of mixed government that relies on popular sovereignty, but also incorporates a range of checks on the majority's will, including an independent judiciary capable of assessing and restricting the laws passed by elected assemblies, and a constitution and a bill of rights to guarantee certain inalienable individual freedoms. In this paradigm, governments restrain equality in the interests of freedom. Challengers sometimes claim that this is a false distinction, since a genuine democracy is one that supports essential freedoms.[29] Others argue that democracy's emphasis on popular sovereignty and liberalism's demand for individual rights are always and necessarily at odds.[30] But what is important for our purposes, here, is that although contemporary politicians around the world on both right and left are inclined to use the words "freedom" and "democracy" in the same breath – as though one followed necessarily from the other – political theorists since Tocqueville reveal how difficult it is to articulate a persuasive and necessary connection between the power of popular sovereignty and the elusive goal of freedom.

Perhaps all of this feels pretty far removed from the question of art, but let us return to Tocqueville's observation that mass communication posed a specific kind of threat to freedom. In the nineteenth century, what seemed clear to Tocqueville was that political institutions were not the only engines of democracy: an increasingly homogenizing *culture* was contributing to an oppressive sense of a dominant majority. A couple of decades later, British philosopher John Stuart Mill argued, similarly, that social pressures to conform could be far more confining than any legal or political regulations, and he claimed that a whole society could suffer terribly from these conformist pressures. In fact, unless societies nurtured and encouraged genius, talent, difference itself, they were destined to a stifling mediocrity.[31] In 1927, John Dewey argued that the "machine age" had produced impersonal and watered-down reasoning processes that prevented the public from acting wisely on its own behalf: "The creation of political unity has . . . promoted social and intellectual uniformity, a standardization favorable to mediocrity. Opinion has been regulated as well as outward behavior."[32] The growing power of mass culture in the nineteenth and early twentieth centuries prompted

15

both an artistic and a political response: avant-garde artists began to distance themselves from popular pressures and mainstream tastes, while political thinkers increasingly articulated the fear that a homogenizing mass culture posed a significant threat to independence of thought – the freedom to articulate critical and dissenting views.

By the 1950s, the rise of "mass culture" had become the target of a debate about the proper culture for a democracy. Many intellectuals in the 1950s defended mass culture precisely on democratic grounds, arguing that it allowed the best cultural expressions to reach the most ordinary people and so raised the level of the "masses," which had never – so they argued – been higher: the "mass media . . . hold out the greatest promise to the 'average man' that a cultural richness no previous age could give him is at hand."[33] The elitism of Tocqueville and Mill, frightened of the brutish and uneducated working classes, seemed to these thinkers like a relic of a more hierarchical aristocratic age, unwilling to share the best of cultural life with the population at large.[34] On the other side, critics maintained that mass culture was so dangerous to public discourse that it ultimately posed a threat to democracy itself. Bernard Rosenberg, one of the editors of the influential anthology *Mass Culture*, warned: "At its worst, mass culture threatens not merely to cretinize our taste, but to brutalize our senses while paving the way to totalitarianism."[35] Famously, the philosophers of the Frankfurt School issued similar alarms about what they called the "culture industry," which, they argued, "has moulded men as a type unfailingly reproduced in every product." According to these theorists, what loomed as a consequence of this endless reproduction of simplistic sameness was the specter of fascism with its pitiless refusal of all outsiders and all dissent: "The ruthless unity in the culture industry is evidence of what will happen in politics."[36]

The countercultural movements of the 1960s disrupted notions of collective uniformity by celebrating marginal identities. And these bore an intriguing new relationship to mass culture: businesses soon picked up on the appeal of rebellious outsiders, willing to buck the system, and began to market their products as liberating, subversive, and nonconformist. What emerged, as Thomas Frank argues, was a new mass culture organized around "hipness" and "cool," valorizing difference and innovation – but as a rationale for ever-increasing consumption.[37] Turning rebellion into a devious kind of conformity, advertising took the edge off the unsettling power of radical and dissenting outsiders.

In the decades to follow, theorists would be divided about the relative merits of mass or popular culture, some arguing that popular culture was liberatory and expansive, reflecting the people's genuine tastes and values, others that it was deadening and sinister, driven by corporate interests and a repressive state. Jürgen Habermas has made the influential case that mass culture has undermined a genuinely democratic public sphere, since citizens now understand themselves not as active, critical participants in a vibrant public debate about collective problems but merely as consumers willing to offer their friendly assent to pre-packaged plans for social action.[38] And Lawrence Lessig has warned that the startlingly successful concentration of the popular media in the hands of a tiny number of powerful corporations has meant a severe limitation on democratic dialogue, innovation, and dissent.[39]

These days, the world wide web has added a new wrinkle to the question of mass culture. Political bloggers across the political spectrum have asserted that their medium undermines the corporate control of ideas, allowing any voice with merit to enter the political debate, thereby allowing the people to elude the manipulative powers of the big media. Thus we are supposedly freer now than ever before.[40] But as Cass Sunstein argues, an oppressive common culture in the age of the internet may no longer be the greatest threat to public discourse; more dangerous now is the increasingly effortless act of *filtering* – the decision to expose ourselves only to sources and kinds of information selected in advance. Filtering is perilous for democratic societies because it allows citizens to make the decision to expose themselves only to what they *already* know: to listen only to like-minded people, to come across only topics of prior interest, to encounter only views already held in advance. The rise of popular conservative and liberal bloggers seems to support this hypothesis. Reading only those blogs that we already agree with, we are forced to encounter no innovation and no surprise. And so filtering works against the "unplanned, unanticipated encounters" that are crucial to a recognition and understanding of difference and plurality. Sunstein asks us to consider "the risks posed by any situation in which thousands or perhaps millions or even tens of millions of people are mainly listening to louder echoes of their own voice."[41]

On the one hand, we face the dangers of standardization, and on the other we confront the perils of fragmentation. But the results are curiously similar: both standardized and fragmented societies are confining because they prevent us from encountering new and challenging people and perspectives. If this sounds like an idealizing or utopian position, Sunstein argues on market grounds – using statistical evidence – that both homogenization and filtering produce not only the social pressure to conform, but also startlingly high degrees of error and poor judgment. It turns out that most people are willing to agree with those who are around them even when the evidence contradicts their own sense of what is right. Thus bureaucracies, communities, courts, and even businesses profit from plurality and friction: "The highest-performing companies tend to have extremely contentious boards that regard dissent as a duty."[42]

This paradoxical conclusion – that outliers and nonconformists benefit insiders and majorities – has gained some support among political theorists in recent years. These thinkers have criticized the mainstream of democratic political theory for assuming that the goal of proper political deliberation is the achievement of consensus: "the elimination . . . of dissonance, resistance, conflict or struggle."[43] They have begun to embrace dissent as a necessity – and a value. In the words of Chantal Mouffe: "What is specific and valuable about modern democracy is that, when properly understood, it creates a space in which . . . confrontation is kept open, power relations are always being put into question, and no victory can be final. . . . [S]uch an 'agonistic' democracy requires accepting that conflict and division are inherent to politics and that there is no place where reconciliation could be definitively achieved as the full actualization of the unity of 'the people.' "[44] It is not that consensus disappears; only that too strong an embrace of consensus runs the risk of authoritarianism, the quelling of a range of perspectives in favor of a single dominant view. Mouffe urges us to recognize both the inevitability and the benefit of ongoing struggle, diversity, and contest. Similarly, Jane Mansbridge argues that even the fairest of models of consensus always involves coercion: since genuine unanimity is rare, collective political decision-making ultimately closes down conflicting and dissenting views in favor of a specific course of action.[45] For a range of recent theorists, then, it is crucial to begin to embrace "oppositional consciousness," and not just for those on the margins. As Mansbridge puts it, "We have only recently come to understand how hard it is to resist the dominant ideas of one's time."[46]

Valuing anti-conventional resistance as the guarantee of a range of values – freedom, vitality, progress – theorists from Tocqueville and Adorno to Mouffe and Mansbridge resolve the longstanding tension between an egalitarian society and a potentially volatile freedom by arguing that the defiance of the mainstream enriches the mainstream. We all benefit, so the argument goes, from bracing challenges to entrenched and dominant perspectives. But a practical problem remains: how can we keep both established and emerging democracies vigorous with new ideas without fragmenting into an array of hostile camps? What would guarantee the ongoing creation of plural, various, enlivening views even when they ruffle the mainstream? Ideally, presumably, we would encourage the development of societies that would refuse both standardization and fragmentation, while accommodating opposition as a value. In short, *lively, energetic dissent should be integrated into the mainstream of public life.*

How might this happen? As we have seen, the power of mass culture has emerged as central to the question of dissent in political democracy. One might even say that modern democratic politics and mass culture are indistinguishable: it is impossible to discuss

19

democratic deliberation and participation without considering the ways that values, opinions, and arguments circulate through the social body. Perhaps even more importantly, we cannot conceive of a large and complex "social body" in the first place without being able to imagine and represent it.[47] Anthony Arblaster argues that liberalism's long tradition of understanding reasoned debate as the most crucial element in political deliberation may miss the significant force of imagination.[48] There is certainly an argument to be made that mass culture not only disseminates ideas and information but proffers images that circulate widely and influentially, persuading us that our world looks like *this* rather than like *that*, helping to produce our sense of a "common sense" and a "mainstream," which may in turn – as Sunstein's statistics suggest – powerfully shape our values, our choices, and our sense of what is possible. Indeed, although I am drawing on Sunstein's argument here, I want to differ in one crucial way: while Sunstein argues that dissenting views are crucial because they help us to sort through good and bad information, I would argue that dissent is essential, too, because it offers alternative *images* of what is and what could be. If imagination can act as a powerful political force, producing our sense of the collective, then mass culture is an instrument of democracy not only because it allows us to be in contact with one another, to share views, and to deliberate, but because it gives shape and specificity to our images of "the people." The popular media therefore become responsible for our sense of how close we are to social norms and majority values. They provide an understanding of what qualifies as mainstream information, argument, and image, against which we measure our own views and aspirations.

This might seem an obvious claim, but it points to what might come as a surprising conclusion: namely, that both mass culture and the avant-garde defiance of mass culture are inextricably bound up with a set of ongoing political questions about the success of democracy. That is, we may not be able to think about the relationship between liberty and equality without first considering the standardization of mass culture and the freedom to reject mainstream values; similarly, we may not be able to address the tension between social consensus and freedom of expression without addressing the cultural routes by which societies come to share core values and to enable dissent. The three institutions at stake here – mass culture, avant-garde art, and modern democracy – are all intertwined; all three developed out of nineteenth-century struggles over the power of "the people," and together, these three institutions pose fundamental questions about democracy's workings: how do we know what the will of the people really looks like, and does that will necessarily indicate the wisest, fairest, freest course for societies to take?

It is in the context of debates about the character of a properly democratic culture that the logic of the avant-garde comes to play a powerful social role. While large, modern democracies rely on mass communication to guide public decision-making, while also persistently debating the extent to which mass culture really reflects the will of "the people," the avant-garde sets itself up as the permanent cultural minority, questioning *both* the values of the majority *and* their expression through mass culture. Fearful of mob rule, the avant-garde refuses social pressures to conform; skeptical of the culture industry and its willingness to normalize images and ideas that happen to suit the interests of a few powerful corporations, the avant-garde refuses the passive consumption of popular culture by introducing an array of startling alternatives. Thus although strange and difficult art has often been called elitist, it might make more sense to call it *alternativist*. The logic of the avant-garde rejects popular pressures toward standardization rather than "the people" per se. And while a range of other social institutions prize dissent and deliberation as crucial to their pursuit of their own core values – we might think of religious associations, the press, racial and other identity-based political groups – the avant-garde, I would argue, holds a special place in democratic society: it is that cultural institution that is *defined* by its resistance to the mass, the mainstream, the majority. Its core value is identical with dissent itself.

Of course, one might argue that the avant-garde is so alienated from mass culture that it has little to do with enriching mainstream

21

discourse, and emphatically refuses to take part in public life. Both artists and their detractors have claimed as much many times. But let us return, for a moment, to the particular logic of avant-garde opposition. Avant-garde artists typically assert their defiance of the mainstream in the name of the future. They must constantly shift and move forward because every existing gesture is in danger of becoming accepted, normalized, familiar. And it is this *temporality* of the avant-garde, I would argue, that has a particularly valuable role to play in the context of a potentially coercive mass culture. After all, if particular voices or perspectives are taken up by the mainstream, then those voices are not dissenters for long: eventually they become comfortable and common and do not necessarily encourage debate and further innovation. But on the other hand, if all dissenting voices remain too marginal, then it becomes impossible for the majority to imagine and propose genuine alternatives to prevailing beliefs and values, and the dissenters may well be inclined to feel increasingly isolated and alienated. What is crucial about the logic of the avant-garde is its perpetual movement between inside and outside, present and future, mainstream and margins. That is, the avant-garde defies the majority in the name of freedom from social pressures, but knows full well that that very gesture of defiance may well one day become the norm. If this sounds perilously like Thomas Frank's culture of consumerist "cool," the logic of the avant-garde might be described as an effort to outrun cool, perpetually to find the outside of popular appeal, that which resists integration and incorporation. Indeed, the logic of the avant-garde has an endlessly dynamic relationship to mass culture: dependent on mainstream media to define its posture of opposition, it is also quickly reincorporated into the mainstream and must constantly find new ways to generate dissent. Sergei Eisenstein's politically radical techniques of montage in cinema, for example, broke up linear sequences in favor of startling juxtapositions that were intended to provoke audiences to feel the impact of social collisions and contradictions; but when advertising picked up techniques of montage, it was difficult to continue to claim it as a radically unsettling technique.[49] From the point of view of avant-garde artists themselves, the moment that their work becomes mainstream or fashionable it loses precisely the critical edge that makes it valuable in the first place. But the incorporation of their dissent into the mainstream does not put an end to their work; to the contrary, it only incites the artist to create new tests, new challenges. On the one hand, the avant-garde engages the majority by refusing it; and on the other, it sees itself as eventually assimilated, incorporated into the life of "the people." And this constant movement back and forth between majority and minority perspectives is exactly what makes it an effective instrument of democracy: the logic of the avant-garde, we might say, involves the *perpetual and dynamic process of challenging the mainstream to incorporate difference and dissent.*

At this point, we may return to Komar and Melamid, that pair of Russian artists whose idea of a democratic art meant – however tongue-in-cheek – pleasing the largest number. In light of the brief history of democratic theory I have traced here, their idea of majority rule emerges as dangerously narrow, willing to overlook the most recognizable threat to freedom that comes from democratic governance: the pressure to conform. In a world where dominant groups hear their voices in every medium, and minorities turn to niche channels and servers to air and reaffirm dissenting views, it is the avant-garde that insists on putting pluralism and dissent itself at the heart of public discourse. And so, if democratic government is invigorated by challenges and experiments, if a vibrant, ongoing diversity is the sign of freedom, then it is not majority taste but defiant, rebellious, unorthodox expression that represents the best, most valuable art of the people.

## The Institutionalization of the Avant-Garde

We might agree that it is important for a democratic society to permit and even invite dissenting viewpoints, but how does an unorthodox voice come to speak out? What makes it possible for the plural perspectives of the avant-garde to enter the public arena? In a historical moment when the local contact of small communities has yielded almost entirely to mass media and the vast and anonymous throng of society, it is almost impossible to hear the sound of a lone voice. A solitary writer or artist might be impatient to comment on contemporary life, but her perspective will remain obscure, perhaps altogether invisible, until she finds a way of gaining access to the public sphere. To make a work of art one needs materials – paint and canvas, a camera and darkroom, a computer. To develop a work of art one needs time – freedom from other kinds of labor and responsibilities. To present a work of art to the public, however limited, one needs space – access to the walls of a gallery or a page in a circulating publication. And to enter the public sphere one needs an audience – not only viewers or readers but also, typically, published responses and critical evaluations. And all of these require a measure of economic independence. Indeed, although artists have been quick to proclaim their freedom from normalizing pressures and commercial values, they have been dependent on a certain necessary infrastructure. And I want to suggest that this infrastructure allows us to reevaluate the role of the artist as revolutionary outsider. Up to this point, I have been arguing that democratic societies need the bracing challenges of anti-conventional art to guarantee dissent and plurality. But the reverse is also true. Even the most defiant and unruly artists often end up relying on precisely the social institutions they typically scorn – the market, the press, established arts organizations, and most of all, governments. Although artists frequently decry the state as ignorant and powerfully repressive, liberal-democratic states have been surprisingly hospitable to art works that reject the people on principle. Refusing to let art works be burned or torn down by outraged majorities, state institutions have frequently protected the most unpopular art in the public sphere. Thus, for more than a century, the avant-garde has carried on an uncanny – and often unwitting – alliance with democratic states.

This alliance has been contingent on the fact that artists are not such radical outliers as the avant-gardists were led to believe. Sociologist Howard Becker argues that the production of any work of art involves not only artists and audiences, but also critics and practitioners willing to debate what art is. Thus part of the very making of art involves a set of definitions, inclusions, and exclusions: "what is and isn't . . . art, who is and isn't an artist."[50] To claim an object *as art* has been especially difficult since the emergence of the historical avant-garde movements, which repeatedly asserted that the only genuine art was the type that smashed conventions and assumptions associated with past art forms. But in such an unpredictable context, how can anyone ever satisfactorily define art? Sociologists like Becker suggest that a field of art − a relatively coherent if loose collection of academics, critics, and artists themselves − emerges precisely to thrash out the limits of the field itself. In other words, what is known as the "art world" − with its experts, practitioners, funding bodies, publications, and exhibition spaces − exists in part simply to define its own borders, to separate outsiders from insiders, art from non-art. Implicitly, even art's outcasts and discards are implicated in the larger system, and are capable of challenging the system by redefining the limits of the field.[51] Certainly in the past century or so the field of art has continually defined and redefined itself, engaged in an ongoing and always contested process of including and excluding particular figures and styles.

Following Becker's analysis, I want to suggest that the logic of the avant-garde itself can best be understood as a social *institution.*[52] Sociologists, political scientists, and economists typically define institutions as "legitimized social groupings" that share three major characteristics: they are reasonably stable over time, transcending specific participants; they are self-regulating, encoding expectations for continuity that help to enforce compliance over time; and they are relatively autonomous, having their own goals, standards, and procedures, which may be reshaped by external social pressures, including fellow institutions.[53] Continuous, organized, self-governing, and prescriptive, institutions might seem like the very antithesis of the spirit of the avant-garde. And yet, despite its desire to be radically outside of the social order, the logic of the avant-garde does take shape as a social institution, reappearing with surprising regularity over time, and supported and legitimized by fellow institutions. And so to claim that the logic of the avant-garde is an institution is to draw attention to a certain paradox at its heart: despite its aim to disrupt settled norms and routines, it is itself highly organized and self-regulating.

Even the most anarchical of the historical avant-garde movements struggled to institutionalize themselves, and they relied on the very institutions they most scorned in order to do so. Consider, for example, Dada, which aimed at liberating people from all "rules, precepts, money, and critical praise," celebrating "the freedom not to care a damn about anything."[54] The Dadaists saw themselves as helping to drive away "a tottering world in flight," and prompting all laws to "wither away."[55] The movement tried to undermine the very conception of art itself: "we spoke not of art but of anti-art; art as an 'industry' having lost all meaning for us."[56] And Dada claimed that anyone – everyone – could become a Dadaist: this was not an art world but a new way of life.

In practice, however, even Dada depended on the processes of institutionalization. The most basic element was the power that came from numbers. Typically, avant-garde artists established small networks. But how and where does one convene a number of like-minded people? The first Dada association was founded in 1916 in Zurich. Neutral Switzerland in the middle of the war brought together a range of disaffected characters, all in flight from other parts of Europe. According to one of the early Dadaists, Hans Richter, "the peculiarly claustrophobic and tense atmosphere" of Zurich was essential to the formation of the initial Dada group: "It was here, in the peaceful dead-center of the war, that a number of very different personalities formed a 'constellation' which later became a 'movement.'"[57]

If the great European war assisted in the formation of Dada, so did the local Zurich business scene. In order to gather kindred spirits together in the city, the artist Hugo Ball struck up an arrangement with the owner of a local bar. He promised the owner that he would boost his sales in beer and sausages if the owner allowed Ball and his associates to stage a series of events there. On financial grounds, Ball's "Cabaret Voltaire" was certainly a success, since the bar owner reaped the profits of Ball's scheme.[58] And the venue allowed Dada to begin to cohere as a group. Although the Dadaists themselves did not work for profit, then, they relied on the forces of the marketplace to establish themselves as a movement.

The publication and circulation of the name "Dada" was crucial to bringing attention to the group's attack on bourgeois society and the art world. Before the Cabaret Voltaire, the artists who would later become Dadaists worked in isolation and garnered little public attention. But as soon as they joined forces, gave themselves an intriguing name, and produced events that caught the attention of the press, they became a phenomenon. "It did not take many articles in the papers to make people talk about Dada," wrote one of the participants.[59] Indeed, the Dadaists were no innocents when it came to publicity: they sent out press releases, performed in public halls and galleries, and deliberately caused a stir in public venues. They also developed their force as a movement by persuading preexisting institutional structures in the art world to house and publicize them: the small literary magazine, *Littérature*, in Paris, became a way of disseminating Dada poetry; and Alfred Stieglitz's gallery, *291*, in New York, became the space where New York Dadaists, including Marcel Duchamp and Man Ray, gathered and showed their work.

Thus Dada, though it noisily declared its freedom from all social organizations, rules, and regulations, took shape as a recognizable, autonomous movement by relying on the marketplace, the political scene, the press, advertising, and established arts institutions. The Dadaists' attack on the art world had little force until they used the existing arts infrastructure to make an impact. Paradoxically, then, the force of Dada's anti-institutional agenda depended on its successful institutionalization.

Dada is one example among many. All of the historical avant-garde movements cast themselves as outsiders, as the enemies of the law, the state, and the market; and all of them implicitly relied on their enemies to launch their assaults on the status quo. And given their covert dependence on social norms and established organizations, artists who proclaim their freedom have always been vulnerable to accusations of failure and hypocrisy. Writer Margaret Spillane condemns the art world for its "restricted notion of who its audience needs to be, and its equally troubling lack of alarm at who is being left out of the art-making, -consuming, and -rewarding tracks."[60] According to painter Jessie Gray, art can look all too much like party politics: "whoever is in office seems to do all the talking"; power lies in "the small but tightly organized and very controlled clique of galleries, curators, and critics. They all write about each other, recommend and promote each other, and . . . they sit on each other's boards and advise and give grants and monies to each other."[61] The art world, as any struggling artist will tell you, is hardly a free-for-all. And so, while artists for a hundred years have claimed to stand for freedom, the field that recognizes them as artists and therefore allows them to become visible as practitioners of their art is a field clearly governed by normalizing pressures and social organizations – including schools, galleries, theaters, universities, publications, prizes, peer review committees, critics, festivals, and funding sources. In this context, it has been easy enough to dismiss artists, with their rhetoric of freedom, as disingenuous and self-serving.

But this tension is a logical outcome of the history of the avant-garde. It is not possible to imagine an art so free that it ceases to engage with existing norms in the field of art; indeed, it is impossible to produce anything that can exist *as* art without a self-regulating art world willing to define it. But equally, after the emergence of avant-garde experimentation, it has become impossible to separate art from the impulse toward freedom. So: where does this leave us – with a painful sense of art's inadequacy and the inevitability of artistic hypocrisy? Not quite. To see the arts as only enemies of legal norms and regulatory controls, as only rebellious and subversive, is to miss the normalizing forces that shape the institutional character of artistic production and dissemination. And yet to see the art world as wholly beholden to insiders and elites, organized around cliques and fads, is to miss the ways that the values of defiance and subversion continue to shape artistic production and reception.

I want to suggest that there are two ways in which the avant-garde continues to pose and develop the question of freedom, despite its own institutionalization. Firstly, art cannot work outside of institutional structures because it has become virtually impossible to find the "outside" of modern institutionalization. According to Cass Sunstein, for example, the idea of expression entirely free from state constraints is a myth:

> Suppose, for example, that you would like to publish something in the *Washington Post* or in *Time* magazine. Perhaps you believe that one or the other has neglected an important perspective and you would like to fill the gap. If you request publication and are refused, you are entirely out of luck. The most important reason is that the law has created a firm right of exclusion – a legal power to exclude others – and has given this right to both newspapers and magazines. The law is fully prepared to back up this right of exclusion with both civil and criminal safeguards.[62]

Given a social and legal context in which broadcasters and publishers are licensed and protected at taxpayer expense, "free" speech only ever happens in a highly regulated public sphere. Thus no one in the media can be genuinely opposed to government regulation as such, only to specific regulations that seem particularly onerous.

If there are no opportunities to speak publicly outside of institutional structures, the art world cannot claim an absolute freedom. But it *can* claim to be that institution that has repeatedly challenged the dominance of other institutions: the state, the courts, the church, educational systems, media, museums, corporations. Indeed, artists have deliberately tested the limits of freedom that are specific to modern democratic regimes: the restrictions and hierarchies brought about by capitalist economics, the rule of law, and the force of majority values.[63] Artists have also been quick to spot failures on

29

the part of democracies to live up to their ideals, and thus have been, as arts advocates have often argued, champions of freedom within democracy, willing to cry out when governments have seemed to overstep their bounds. Artists have thus routinely explored the question of freedom *within* the constraints of modern democratic institutions.

Artists not only work within institutions in order to interrogate and unsettle them: my second point is that their freedom to do so is guaranteed by precisely the very states they critique and despise. It is true that popularly elected officials have called for clamp-downs on the arts many times in the past century. And even in the very recent past, contemporary democracies, including the United States, India, Australia, Italy, and Poland, have witnessed a number of successful attempts to censor art in the name of "the people."[64] This is a very real danger. But popularly elected officials are not the only agents of the democratic state. In fact, modern democratic governments are not single institutions but complexes of overlapping institutions – including executives, courts, and bureaucratic agencies. And for good reason: the separation of powers into different groups that check and balance one another is intended to ensure that neither the majority nor a particular elite will achieve total or tyrannical control of a nation's governance.[65] But what this means is that some parts of the democratic state are precisely intended to work *against* the impulses of majority rule by populist politicians. And so it turns out that certain bodies within liberal-democratic states – including the courts and state bureaucracies – have been strongly inclined to support the challenges launched by artists.[66] Indeed, if we take into account all of the overlapping institutional bodies that make up democratic governments, it becomes clear that liberal democracies have done more to protect the subversive rumblings of the avant-garde than to stifle them.

My focus here will be largely on the US and Britain, but the analysis, I hope, will have implications for democracies worldwide. As the following chapters will show, Anglo-American courts turn out to have an especially generous relationship to the avant-garde.

Famously, of course, artists have strenuously objected to obscenity, copyright, and flag burning laws as repressive enemies of free expression. But this familiar story turns out to be surprisingly misleading. Traditionally, one of the most significant institutional checks on mob rule in democratic states has been the judiciary. As Tocqueville puts it, "the power granted to American courts to pronounce on the unconstitutionality of laws still forms one of the most powerful barriers that have ever been raised against the tyranny of political assemblies."[67] Working against the tastes and preferences of a volatile electorate, the courts have taken seriously the task of protecting unpopular expression, often overturning repressive statutes passed by legislators in favor of rebels and dissenters. The fact that the judiciary is unelected means that it has sometimes been understood as undemocratic, but the courts share with the art world a remarkably analogous democratic function: set up to counter the tyranny of the majority, they are similarly dedicated to the protection of minority and marginal perspectives. And so, as we will see, artists have surprisingly often won their case in court, regularly seeing their works accepted and legitimated by the courts. And even more surprisingly, artists on trial have also repeatedly managed to *change* the law, persuading the courts to recognize new rules for art.[68]

But if the distribution of power between the arts and the law is so unequal, how is it that artists – who are so often dismissed as marginal, arcane, and hopelessly impractical – come to effect changes in the law, that massive structure that underpins and enforces power relations? The answer is that the playing field is rather more level than artists have acknowledged. If we see artists as lone outsiders, struggling against the institutions of legal power, the battle looks unequal indeed, but if we understand the "art world" and the law as internally mixed and necessarily contestatory social bodies, they come to share two crucial patterns. Both the avant-garde and the judiciary are not only counter-majoritarian in spirit: they are specifically counter-majoritarian *institutions*; both respond to expressions of majority will with an assertion of their institutional independence. Secondly, both art and Anglo-American common law are dynamic institutions with a strikingly similar relationship to history. Though the law is often seen as conservative and repressive, while artists cast themselves on the cutting edge, both artists and common-law jurists actually favor a balance of innovation and tradition.

Let me address these two shared patterns briefly here, though they will become clearer in the chapters that follow. Firstly, far from understanding artists as radical individuals struggling to free themselves from social norms and regulations, Anglo-American courts are inclined to recognize the art world as a fellow institution. For example, by law, art cannot be defined or understood adequately by either the "average" person or by legal professionals. As the US Supreme Court put it in 1966, when deciding an obscenity case against the renowned eighteenth-century novel *Memoirs of a Woman of Pleasure*: "We are judges, not literary experts or historians or philosophers. We are not competent to render an independent judgment as to the worth of this or any other book, except in our capacity as private citizens. . . . If there is to be censorship, the wisdom of experts on such matters as literary merit and historical significance must be evaluated."[69] The courts thus maintain that a proper judgment of literary value depends on specialized knowledge, and must be spoken for in the legal process by recognizable delegates. What is an expert? It is up to the lawyers in any given case to establish an art expert's qualifications on the stand. Most often, witnesses declare their years of formal training, their publications, gallery shows, commissions, or prizes. In the process, the courts honor art's professionalization: its specialists, its organizations, its official judgments. Indeed, far from imagining artists as marginal, treacherously subversive, and beleaguered, the judiciary typically casts the art world as a self-regulating network of organizations, much like the law itself, reliant on recognized authorities and training, traditions and ceremonies, practitioners and theorists, certificates and diplomas. And there is certainly some truth to this characterization: as we have seen, given its complex of intertwined organizations and procedures, the "art world" can be seen as a powerful infrastructure that enforces norms and hierarchies, develops trends, and encourages certain voices while excluding others.

But the courts have not only understood the art world as institutionalized and self-organizing; they have recognized the particular value of art inhering in its *resistance* to majority tastes and values. From obscenity to copyright, the courts have protected artistic expression on the grounds of its challenges to the status quo. And so if we understand the courts and the art world as more similar than different – both self-governing institutions, both committed to unsettling the tyranny of the majority – it is not surprising to learn that the Anglo-American judiciary has helped the arts far more often than it has harmed them.

One might argue, of course, that the courts should not be concerning themselves with art at all. But this proposal is difficult to put into action, because in order to allow art to have complete freedom, the law still needs to draw boundaries between what is art and what is not, between what is free from regulation and what is not. If the courts had to steer clear of anything that called itself art, all kinds of acts of violence and domination might earn legal protection under the cover of art. And so the problem is this: how can the law leave art alone unless it defines art, first, as a legal concept? Or to put this another way: even when the courts are trying to leave art alone, they are posing complex and difficult questions about *what art is*. And when it comes to putting those questions on the stand, the law does not try to define art in the abstract, but rather turns to the art world's authorized experts to define and articulate its current aims and values.

While I do not mean to claim that the art world and the law are equally powerful social bodies, I do want to suggest that art is not so powerless as artists would have us believe. And this is not only because of the role of experts in the courtroom. A more subtle kinship also links the specifically Anglo-American tradition of common law with the project of the avant-garde. While statutes passed by legislators often express the values of the majority in a particular time and place, common law binds itself to tradition. At first glance, common-law adjudication, defined by its appeal to historical precedent, might seem fundamentally conservative, since it involves reaching back into the past for guidance. But common law allows for transformation as well as tradition.[70] Common-law adjudication struggles to relate each new case to cases before it, but it always acknowledges the possibility of the new, the potential for each example to demand a departure from past principles. Cases that do not conform easily to previous standards prompt the courts to forge combinations of existing case law to establish new precedents. And Anglo-American law specifically makes space for artistic innovation, supporting the understanding that a vibrant democracy needs the new. As the following chapters will show, obscenity, customs, and copyright law have *all* come to protect innovative expression in the name of a healthily plural society.

Meanwhile, avant-garde art is more indebted to tradition than artists have been inclined to admit. While rebellious avant-garde artists may always claim to reject the past, their very insistence on breaking from previous art forms ties their rebellion to a history of art-making. As Bourdieu puts it, "Absolutely nothing is more connected to the proper tradition of the field, including the intention to subvert it, than avant-garde artists who, at the risk of appearing as naifs, must inevitably situate themselves in relation to all previous efforts at overtaking which have occurred in the history of the field."[71] Paradoxically enough, what defines the avant-garde is a *tradition of innovation*. Tied to the past in the very effort to split from it, avant-garde art inevitably binds its radical newness tightly to a sense of artistic tradition. It is true, too, that the avant-garde's rebellious gestures can take place *as art* only in an existing institutional field, marked by existing structures of professionalization and recognition. And so, although the law has emphasized its conservatism and the avant-garde its subversiveness, in fact both the avant-garde and the common law contain within them a balance of tradition and innovation. And this particular model of history shared by Anglo-American common law and the art world has contributed to the surprisingly cordial, if unacknowledged, relationship between the courts and the avant-garde. Thus, if we continue to imagine that art is subversive and heroic while the law is normative and repressive, we mystify both – and do neither justice. I propose, instead, to show that the art world and the law share a deep value: a commitment to institutionalized dissent.

The judiciary is not the only arm of the democratic state that sets itself against the tyranny of the majority: state agencies and bureaucracies in the past century have also worked to protect art from the power of popular dislike. I hope, then, that it is becoming clear why I suggested earlier that the two most familiar positions in debates about the arts are mistaken. Firstly, the "state" is not necessarily the enemy of art, fearful of artists' emancipatory energies, always seeking to quell their challenges in favor of a more conservative status quo. While it is true that populist politicians in democracies have tried to subdue and silence the subversive energies of artists more than once, liberal democratic governments have ways of counteracting groundswells of mass culture. As networks of institutions, democratic states include counter-majoritarian bodies that often work hard to preserve a special place for artistic nonconformity in the public sphere. Thus despite the avant-garde's challenge to majority values, democracies have not been inclined simply to capitulate to popular outcry. And the courts, far from repressing and subduing art's energies, have been especially powerful supporters of art's role in the social world, frequently protecting art against the power of majority tastes and values.

But the other side has been wrong, too. Though it may well be the case that the arts are often deliberately elitist and exclusive, this minority status does not render art anti-democratic. Indeed, it is precisely by virtue of art's marginalized position that it plays a particularly valuable role in a democratic society. In the most repressive moments for democratic states in the twentieth century, when free speech was threatened and calls to unanimity and a common culture seemed to triumph over marginal and minority voices, art continued to stand for a crucial and longstanding democratic value: the importance of minority voices and the benefits of pluralism.

35

# 2

# The People v. the Arts

*Taking a poll is no way to judge whether a work of art should survive.*
Claes Oldenburg

In March of 2006, an award-winning theater production that had enjoyed a successful run in London was scheduled to open in New York. *My Name is Rachel Corrie* is a one-woman play based on the diaries and emails of a young American activist who attempted to save a Palestinian home from destruction by Israeli soldiers. She was bulldozed to death in the process. Seen by some as pro-Palestinian propaganda and by others as a brave and truthful account of an individual woman's experiences, the play sparked intense debate well before its New York debut. So passionate was the dispute, in fact, that after consulting with an array of unnamed groups, the New York Theater Workshop abruptly decided to postpone the show.[1] The most immediate cause of this controversy was the intensity of the conflict over Israeli-Palestinian relations, and the vexed role played by an art work that commented on those politics in a powerful way. But there was another question at stake here. Katherine Viner, one of the play's co-editors, accused the theater company of consulting certain community groups and overlooking the opinions of others: "I think that for example some Jewish groups were polled and some Arab-American groups weren't. It's very confusing who was polled and who wasn't."[2] The New York Theater Workshop asserted that they did no "polling" at all: what they conducted was rather a standard "process of research" to "understand the depth of the cultural and political issues surrounding the play."[3] Viner claimed that even this kind of community research was peculiar to the US: "in Britain . . . when we do plays, political plays . . . we don't really believe in consultation. We think the plays are works of art and stand on their own feet."[4] Whether or not the NYTW was guilty of conducting covert opinion polls, the very anxiety this provoked is intriguing. Why did the question of polling come up at all in a debate about a theater production? What Viner objected to was very specific indeed: the notion that art might not be autonomous enough to stand on its "own feet," but might find itself answerable to opinion polls, backroom lobbying, and community approval – answerable, in other words, to democracy.

This chapter suggests that Viner was right to be anxious. When we worry about the kinds of societies that clamp down on artists, we probably first think of totalitarian and fundamentalist regimes: Nazi Germany, where "degenerate art" was torn off the walls of museums; Stalinist Russia, where artists were expected to produce art works that fit the strictest propaganda needs; Afghanistan under the Taliban, where two ancient Buddha figures were destroyed, judged offensive to Islam. But though we might like to think of democratic states as the best sanctuaries for artists and the best protectors of free expression, there is no guarantee that democracies won't exercise their own kind of tyranny. When public pressure to destroy art works grows powerful in democratic contexts, the pressure of majority loathing can become strong enough to choke artistic expression.

The historical avant-garde, with its deliberate attacks on mainstream tastes and values, incited violence more than once. The Armory Show in New York in 1913 was the first major exhibition of European avant-garde art in the United States, and it so scandalized American viewers that Marcel Duchamp's *Nude Descending a Staircase* had to be protected by guards. When Stravinsky's *Rites of Spring* opened in Paris the same year, audiences jeered and threw objects at the orchestra. A few years later, architecture and design coming out of the Bauhaus School in Germany seemed so unsettling that the institution had to be moved from volatile Weimar, hub of the new German democracy, to the sleepier

37

town of Dessau. As avant-garde art work grew more and more visible, public outrage intensified, and passionate voices repeatedly called for the extinction of the new art. The pattern became predictable: artists produced radically new and unsettling work; the public reacted with indignation. Mocking this familiar round of shock and outrage, the Cologne Dadaists actually provided hatchets to visitors to their exhibition so that they could smash the works of art on show.

Predictable though it might have become, the urge to destroy works of art did not end with the historical avant-gardes. Democratic societies, as we will see, have shown themselves quite persistently capable of squelching works of art. From the turn of the twentieth century onward, representatives who claim to speak for "the people," enraged by artists who flout tradition and offend belief, have repeatedly taken matters into their own hands – vandalizing, stealing, bulldozing, suing, and voting art objects into oblivion. I want to suggest here that the will of the majority and the deliberately minoritarian avant-garde are *structurally opposed*, which means that they are destined to come into conflict as long as the logic of the avant-garde is active in democratic contexts. But this formulation is clearly abstract. So how exactly do particular democratic societies imagine, define, and enlist a sense of "the people's will"? How do they respond to art's challenging marginality? And in what ways can and should democracies address the structural tension between the two? This chapter shows the serious consequences of the very idea of popular sovereignty whenever the artistic avant-garde is under attack for its refusal to capitulate to popular taste. And it suggests that it might be wise to be on our guard against the pressing dangers posed by democracy and revealed by the logic of the avant-garde.

## The Artist as Minority: Jacob Epstein and the Fascists

There once was a sculptor of mark
Who was chosen to brighten Hyde Park;

> Some thought his design
> Most uncommonly fine,
> But more liked it best in the dark.
>
> *Punch* (June 3, 1925)

In 1922, friends and admirers of a novelist and naturalist named William Henry Hudson gathered in London. Best known for his novel *Green Mansions*, Hudson had also written an extraordinarily popular ornithological guide, *The Birds of London*. After Hudson's death, his fans decided to build a memorial to him in one of London's best known public spaces – Hyde Park. The newly formed Hudson Memorial Committee agreed to invite the renowned sculptor Jacob Epstein to design a medallion depicting Hudson to adorn a new bird sanctuary in the park.

Epstein was famous for rejecting traditional styles in art. A relative newcomer to England, he was born to Jewish parents in New York, and then studied art as a young man in Paris. From the start, his work invited controversy. In 1908, a series of his statues for the British Medical Association building in London brought charges of obscenity, and he provoked a new scandal in Paris in 1912 when authorities declared his memorial to Oscar Wilde indecent, and covered it up so that the public would be protected from the shocking display. Epstein's 1920 statue of "Christ" then upset conventional viewers by refusing traditional Christian iconography, and indeed his unfamiliar, experimental style startled many, who called it "hideous," "barbaric," "grotesque," and "repulsive." An artist who attacked established conventions on all fronts, Epstein was often associated with the avant-garde.[5] And yet a growing number of voices also began to consider him the best sculptor in England. John Middleton Murry, a fiery critic of the period, wrote: "There is much, and there is room for much, controversy as to who is our best painter; but there is none on the question who is our best sculptor. News editors, newspaper readers, cognoscenti . . . are in agreement that Epstein is – the real thing."[6] The Hudson Memorial Committee chose Epstein because, they said, they were "really anxious to give the Nation a dignified piece of art."[7]

**Figure 2.1** Jacob Epstein, *Rima* (1925), Hyde Park, London, courtesy Royal Parks.

The committee's proposal was at first rejected by the Office of Works because portraits of non-royal personages are not allowed in the Royal Parks. But since the government approved "imaginary figures," the Hudson Memorial Committee suggested an image of Rima, a character from *Green Mansions*.[8] Epstein duly produced a new sketch and a plaster model, and the committee submitted the plan, which was soon accepted by His Majesty, King George V.[9] Work began immediately, and the piece was triumphantly unveiled on May 19, 1925 (figure 2.1).

Such a hue and cry followed the unveiling that over two hundred articles and letters about *Rima* were published in London newspapers in 1925 alone.[10] The conservative tabloid, the *Daily Mail*, led the onslaught, but there were also caricatures of the work in magazines, spoofs on stage in one London theater, petitions to remove the sculpture, two debates in the House of Commons, and even a fight between Epstein and one of his detractors in a London restaurant. All over the British Isles reporters were outraged by the intrusion of Epstein's work into the public sphere: "That isn't Rima," exclaimed the *Yorkshire Evening Post*. "That's the soul of a . . . poulterer's wife being conducted to hell by two frozen hen turkeys."[11] Epstein's crime in this instance was not obscenity, or offense to religious tradition. *Rima* posed a different kind of threat: "a danger that if such things are encouraged or allowed to remain in our midst . . . the world will be made hideous."[12]

"Hideousness" might seem like an unreliable category, dependent on shifting and unpredictable personal preferences, but as the controversy unfolded it became clear that it had everything to do with the avant-garde's break from traditional expectations about beauty. Letters to the press repeatedly bewailed Epstein's rejection of recognizable artistic styles, and particularly his refusal to imitate nature faithfully: they complained of the "malformed" figure of Rima, and declared that she was flanked by birds "unknown to the ornithologist."[13] On May 25, 1925, an angry citizen wrote: "God forbid that Woman's form shall degenerate into such an unshapely mass. If this crude representation is called artistic perception, then what can be called ugly?"[14] The twisting of natural and familiar shapes was fast becoming the hallmark of the new art. The *Daily Mail* editorial page argued that *Rima* was simply its most prominent illustration: "a conspicuous example of the modern cult of ugliness."[15] As the debate wore on, "pretty" became a synonym for conservative, realist art; "ugly" for the avant-garde break from tradition.[16] Strikingly, even Epstein's admirers relied on the opposition of pretty and ugly. The *Daily Mail* art critic praised Epstein for taking "no notice of the public craving for prettiness."[17] And the *Daily News* made a similar case, saying that Epstein "has made no concessions to any popular desire for what is merely agreeable."[18]

If the tabloids claimed to represent a mass public, and Epstein's champions stood for the marginalized and shocking avant-garde, the official institutionalization of English taste was housed in the Royal Academy of Art. Slow to enter the battle, the Academy's first volley was a powerful one. In November of 1925, the President of the Royal Academy drew up a petition demanding to have *Rima* removed.[19] This petition called itself an "artists' appeal," and claimed to speak for English art. Epstein's supporters immediately launched a counterattack, which they claimed was far more representative of "artistic and intellectual endeavour" than the first petition.[20] Who really spoke for the art world? The Royal Academy held official status, but it was not obvious, in 1925, that they still had the upper hand. The *Rima* controversy certainly typifies the kinds of battles between academic art and the insurgent avant-gardes that had been raging for some decades. The Royal Academy saw itself bound to uphold traditional styles of representation and, in particular, to safeguard English artistic styles and values. Frank Dicksee, the President of the Royal Academy, called for a return to conventional beauty in the press and insisted that "clean and healthy art" should replace Epstein's *Rima*.[21] On the other side, Epstein's supporters condemned academic art as " 'safe,' dull, entirely undistinguished."[22] They praised *Rima* for defying convention and mocked its critics as timorous and short-sighted: "Are we really to choose for public memorials sculpture which displeases nobody but instructs nobody, or are we to have enough courage to challenge the future?"[23] *The Nation* accused Epstein's detractors of being fuddy-duddies – "elderly gentlemen" keen to ban anything that challenged their old-fashioned tastes.[24] And Epstein himself told the *Daily News* that he was not after either popular or official success: "I do not work for the approval of others."[25]

On one crucial issue, then, everyone seemed to agree. From the tabloids to the House of Commons and from the Royal Academy to the marginal avant-garde, all concurred that Epstein was deliberately defying conventional English tastes. The only question was whether this was a valuable act for a public space. Many argued at the time – and would still argue now – that it does not make any sense to produce elitist, unpopular art for public sites. They would make the case that in a democracy, the "people" should have a say over the art they see and pay for in their public spaces, and they should not have to look at art that offends their sensibilities or outrages their beliefs. But the Epstein example might prompt us to think again about this majoritarian view.

Epstein's avant-garde experimentation was consistently coupled with his Jewishness in the press, and perceived as undermining England and Englishness. Numerous populist voices argued that the foreign artist was deliberately trying to unsettle venerable English traditions by imposing his alien "cult of ugliness" on an English public space. And a few turned violent. Epstein's sculpture was vandalized four times between 1925 and 1935.[26] Epstein's artistic experimentation seemed to nationalist voices to refuse all patriotic affiliation, all commitment to national tradition. *The Hidden Hand, or the Jewish Peril*, a fascist magazine that circulated in the 1920s, argued that "the Jew Epstein [is making] a deliberate attempt . . . to influence our English public into admiration of something very different from what it has . . . admired in the past and so degrading it."[27] The Independent Fascist League scrawled on the memorial in green paint: "God Save Our King and Britain from the Cancer of Judah."[28] By 1928, even the more mainstream *Saturday Review* was characterizing Epstein's aesthetic as symptomatic of his Jewishness: "nearly all the support for violence rather than beauty in art [comes] from Socialists, foreigners, and Jews. Jacob Epstein's name proclaims his nationality."[29]

While anti-Semitism was a violent force at work in the mid-1920s, nationalism got expressed in a range of ways in the *Rima* scandal: newspapers condemned the memorial as "Germanic," "European," "Assyrian," "Oriental," and "Egyptian." One letter to *The Times* complained that *Rima* was "grotesquely out of harmony" with a "typically English public park."[30] The *Morning Post* called the work "hideous, unnatural, un-English, and essentially unhealthy."[31] And these objections went beyond the popular press, too: Eric Underwood, writing a *Short History of English Sculpture* in 1933, refused to discuss *Rima* in the book because Epstein was "with us but not of us."[32] Even those who praised Epstein suggested that his work was forceful because it was "barbaric," "wild," "primitive," and "natural" rather than typically English. In other words, the avant-garde style of *Rima* became something of a symbol of internationalism, and Epstein became an example of the eminently cosmopolitan artist – both detached from provincial and national identity and expressive of a worldly style and sophistication.

Around the same time that Epstein was becoming a subject of intense controversy in the British Isles, German philosopher Carl Schmitt was arguing that there could be no concept of democracy without a sense of homogeneous belonging. While members of a democratic collective might be genuinely different in many ways, "A democracy demonstrates its political power by knowing how to refuse or keep at bay something foreign and unequal that threatens its homogeneity."[33] Schmitt explained that democracies were marked by the basic belief that those who belonged were "friends"; those who did not, "enemies." He rejected the liberal conception of universal rights as implausible for democracy because it imagined a collectivity without an outside, without foreigners to make the group cohere around a sense of shared belonging.[34] He argued, in other words, that democracy and liberalism were mutually exclusive. It may come as no surprise that Schmitt joined the Nazi Party in 1933.

The next two decades would show that powerful nationalist sentiment could all too easily become the tyranny of racial and political majorities eager to extinguish minority "enemies" altogether. But Schmitt raises a more enduring question: does the democratic emphasis on popular sovereignty, with its sense of a coherent "people," always tend toward the literal extinction of minority voices – toward fascism? Contemporary political theorist Chantal Mouffe picks up on Schmitt's arguments about the impossibility of reconciling the liberal insistence on universal human rights with democratic collectives, but she refuses his conclusion. While Schmitt argues that liberalism contradicts the demands of democracy, Mouffe exhorts us to keep democracy and liberalism always in productive tension with one another.[35] She moves beyond Schmitt's friend–enemy distinction to suggest that democratic politics should best be understood as an "agonism" between " 'friendly enemies,' that is, persons who are friends because they share a common symbolic space but also enemies because they want to organize this common symbolic space in a different way."[36]

The Epstein controversy reveals the avant-garde as a "friendly enemy" of democracy itself. Those who despised Epstein were traditionalist in their aesthetics, favoring realism in art; they were also populist, insisting that art should be accessible to the mass of English viewers; and they were nationalist, claiming to speak for England

and the tradition of English art. Voices who wanted to enforce a strong sense of an English "people" typically merged the political unit of the nation with the cultural insistence on familiar styles and traditions. They saw English people, tastes, and traditions as the horizon of "friends." The avant-garde, by contrast, championed artistic innovation; they were elitist, snubbing the ordinary viewer as crude and uneducated; and they were internationalist, claiming to speak for future generations and for global movements and influences. They repudiated the very idea of friendship – seeing their role as one of perpetual challenge and critique. In this context, Epstein seemed like the consummate "enemy" of the English people: a literal outsider – a Jewish-American-cosmopolitan – working in a style that repudiated traditional tastes and symbols.

But the contrast between the two camps is not so deep as it first seems. Both recognized avant-garde disruptions as enemies of "the people." And if the adversaries shared an understanding of the avant-garde as an enemy of Englishness, this – paradoxically – is what made them capable of being friends in Schmitt's sense. Or to be more precise, the two camps were "friendly enemies." They shared the notion that "the people" was a bounded and local category, one that excluded as much as it included, and they agreed that the boundaries around national inclusiveness were being tested and threatened by the avant-garde. What they disagreed about was the value of that inclusiveness.

The basic question raised by the Epstein controversy is therefore perhaps the most fundamental question raised by democratic societies in general. What is the place of outsiders, dissidents, and foreigners in the democratic collective? Some might object to this formulation on the grounds that it does not do justice to the difference between art objects and persons. The avant-garde cannot stand in for democratic outsiders because what societies do to marginalize and oppress living people is much graver than what they do to works of art. But the argument over *Rima* hints at a somewhat different conclusion. The populists who reviled Epstein's work willingly tied politics and culture up together in a single bundle: to them, both the art work and the Jewish artist defied traditional Englishness, the challenges of ethnic otherness and the challenges of stylistic experimentation emerging as equally threatening. Style may not be so frivolous or inconsequential an issue as it sometimes appears.[37] Indeed, around the world, nationalist movements have asserted the importance of shared cultural and artistic traditions in order to justify claims to political legitimacy.[38]

If the avant-garde is defined as that aspect of the cultural field that deliberately challenges dominant assumptions and values, then its social function is to *act as a permanent minority*. In its deliberate repudiation of national traditions and majority tastes, the art work refuses assimilation and consensus and so resists integration into a unified nationalist politics. I am arguing, in other words, that there is a close structural kinship between minority groups – racial, ethnic, religious, or political – and avant-garde experimentation, and that the avant-garde is routinely associated with unsettling outsiders in the rhetoric of those who urge a strongly united "people." Thus although avant-garde artists themselves have spanned the whole political spectrum – some of them fascists themselves – the very configuration of the avant-garde as a challenging outsider repeatedly presents a threat to political projects striving for uncritical homogeneity and solidarity.

It is the role of the avant-garde as threatening minority that explains the fate of artists like Emil Nolde, a fervent German nationalist painter and voluntary Nazi Party member whom Goebbels briefly favored in the 1930s. By 1937 the Nazis were including his work in the infamous "Degenerate Art" show, calling it a symptom of the sickness and impurity they claimed was undermining the strength of the nation. Despite Nolde's own protests of loyalty to the authorities, his willingness to test established conventions of painting with lurid colors and exaggerated forms seemed like a refusal of the kind of heroic and traditional beauty favored by the Nazis, and on the grounds of style alone they cast Nolde as a danger to their purist nationalism. A strikingly similar logic held on the other end of the political spectrum, where avant-garde Russian artists – such as the theater director Vsevolod Meyerhold – committed themselves to the cause of the Bolshevik revolution, imagining that their experimental and forward-looking art would pave the way to a wholly new revolutionary society. Meyerhold eagerly joined the Communist Party and saw his theater as rejecting the illusions offered by realistic, bourgeois modes of theatrical representation. He rose fast in the immediate aftermath of the revolution to become head of the theater division of the People's Commissariat for Education in 1920. But "the fostering of uncritical, regimented belief was the key tenet of Stalinist aesthetics," and Meyerhold's thought-provoking innovations soon came to seem threatening to the consolidation of Stalin's monolithic regime. Decried as an "anti-Soviet formalist," he was executed in prison in 1940.[39]

Putting an emphasis on transforming rather than reflecting approved or traditional tastes, and insisting on artistic experimentation rather than conventionally realistic styles, the avant-garde's deliberate minority status unsettled both extremes in the twentieth century. But it was not only a question for the extremes. *Rima* shows how the avant-garde plays its disconcerting structural role in relation to democratic nation-states as well. This work of art participated in the national collective by occupying an official place in a public park; yet on that site it worked to challenge the boundaries of the collective, to envision alternatives, to drive unfamiliarity into the heart of shared norms and values. As a friend of "the people," the avant-garde shared the common symbolic space of the nation; as an enemy, it sought to question and dislocate this common symbolic space. Bringing the outside inside, *Rima* refused to maintain the boundary between belonging and exclusion – and so threatened the political project of establishing fixed boundaries around "the people."

The peculiar temporality of the avant-garde also had a role to play in its constitution as a friendly enemy to the English people. In the Epstein controversy, a number of contemporary commentators acknowledged that although the mass of viewers might object initially to *Rima*, the work would come to be accepted over time. *The Spectator* advised readers to pause in front of the work before leaping to make a judgment: "to look at Mr. Epstein's panel again and again – to look at it from different angles and a greater distance."[40] Meanwhile, the *Daily Mail* reported an attempt by an art expert to educate viewers in front of *Rima*:

> "You do not understand it," one man shouted to the crowd. "If you would only get a shilling book –"
>
> "Why should we?" chorused the crowd. "If we love beauty why should we pay 1 s. each for something which pretends to teach us to appreciate the ugly?"
>
> "You would learn to understand," said the man.[41]

Here the vision of a public filled with the potential to learn – to become cultivated and sophisticated about art – was offered as the answer to the conflict. Thus a number of voices entreated the press and Parliament to wait for the work to grow on the public. As one critic put it, "The standard of taste will probably be more expansive and more tolerant and will be more remote from that kind of judgment which never encourages a great thing because it is too terribly afraid to sanction a mistake."[42] The Home Office told outraged Conservative MPs that it was only wise "to suspend judgment until the public had a longer opportunity of forming an opinion."[43] And the *Daily Mail* art critic concluded that the paper's own readers would come to see the error of their ways: "The memorial may have failed as an instant popular success," he wrote, "but it will prove itself under the acid test of time."[44]

This insistence on "the acid test of time" accomplishes some useful practical compromises between "the people" and the work of art. The emphasis on the future brings together the notion of an educable public, capable of learning to appreciate the subtleties of the new art, with a daring and authentic avant-garde, bravely testing the boundaries of established conventions. It favors Epstein's faith in the autonomous artist, who refuses to pander to public taste, but it also favors the public, since the object will broaden and develop public taste. Strangely, then, the emphasis on the passage of time offers the artist the unlikely combination of a loving public, on the one hand, and the assurance of his own disinterestedness, on the other: since the world will express its approbation only posthumously, the artist is not compromised by the pursuit of fashionable rewards or popularity.

Characterized as a daring art of the future, challenging entrenched norms and styles, the avant-garde claims to defy the aesthetic inclinations of the past and present but to anticipate the taste of future generations. In this context, the proper public for the avant-garde is the infinitely educable public: that is, *the public of the future*, as yet only dimly foreshadowed. Imagining that the activity of education is the bridge between present and future, between prejudiced populist majorities and knowledgeable sophisticates on the margins, advocates of the avant-garde see art working to transform majorities, to encourage broad-mindedness, new knowledge, tolerance, and good judgment. Understood this way, the avant-garde neither reflects public taste (as friend) nor offends it (as enemy), but challenges it in order to change it (as friendly enemy). And if the avant-garde seeks to transform the public into a more literate, more knowledgeable, more critically capable group, it begins to look something like the project of public education itself, a longstanding democratic project and one that has fierce proponents across the political spectrum.[45] In this light, avant-garde rebellion emerges as far less hostile to traditional democratic ends than we might typically imagine.

Though nationalists and populists tried to rouse enough anger to destroy *Rima* altogether, it turns out, in the end, that they did not succeed. The green paint was cleaned off the sculpture, and when fascist sympathizers lost their hold in Britain during World War II, the public simply lost interest in the fracas over the Jewish-cosmopolitan Epstein and his strange sculptural style. The controversy reflected a moment of particularly intense concern over the question of national identity and pride, one that was more or less resolved with Britain's victory over Germany. Now the sculpture sits in a quiet corner of Hyde Park, largely unnoticed by passers-by. Today it shocks no one, and at the same time it impresses few with its spatial rhythms and wild emotion. Essentially unknown to Londoners, tourists, and art historians alike, *Rima* has been judged by the nation, the world, and the public of the future as entirely unobjectionable and perhaps just a little bit ordinary. Today we may be baffled – and a little surprised – to discover that a quiet bird sanctuary like this one caused such a disturbance in 1925.[46] It seems that we have become the tolerant public of the future.

But taken in the moment of its most intense controversy, the Epstein case offers an enduring warning. It shows that the logic of the avant-garde art evokes exiles and outsiders, the few rather than the many, the margins rather than the center. And it suggests that when we complain that these unfamiliar voices are objectionable or displeasing we are not simply expressing our tastes: we are also, potentially, holding on to deep and dangerous notions about the boundaries of belonging and the eradication of difference. In this context, democracies might do well to encourage a deliberately critical relationship to tradition, chauvinism, even homey familiarity. Since drives toward political homogeneity have brought with them some of the worst violence of the past hundred years, including the terrors of fascism, a public might be prudent to favor not the most popular and familiar styles but the most unconventional and startling public art. Agreeing to foster uncomfortably plural perspectives, a democracy could use the avant-garde to celebrate both its oneness and its plurality.

In this view, avant-garde art is not for the majority, but it is for everyone.

## Majority Rule: Voting Art into Extinction

*Where is "direct democracy" used other than to get rid of art?*
Clara Weyergraff-Serra

The *Rima* controversy might seem far away and long ago, the result of an era that saw particularly ferocious social unrest and disturbance.

50

But a startlingly similar debate over public art erupted in the 1980s, in cosmopolitan New York. Uncanny parallels between the two cases bear out the hypothesis that the conflict between democracy and the avant-garde is a structural one. But there was also a crucial difference: this time, instead of hatchets and green paint, angry citizens destroyed a work of art with a democratic vote.

In 1981, a monolithic, curving steel wall was installed in a plaza in downtown Manhattan. It was 12 feet high and 120 feet long, practically bisecting the space in front of the Federal Building. Reddish in color – looking somewhat rusty – the piece swerved and bowed. Pedestrians complained that they had to go out of their way to walk around it, while art critics praised it as one of the most important sculptural works of the late twentieth century. Puzzling, daunting, massive, and strange, it was Richard Serra's *Tilted Arc* (figure 2.2).

The funds for the piece came from the General Services Administration (GSA), a government office which commissions works of art for new federal buildings, allocating one half of one percent of the costs of construction to a prominent American artist. This Art-in-Architecture program, as it is called, has been responsible for both controversies and successes – including Alexander Calder's *La Grande Vitesse* in Grand Rapids, Claes Oldenberg's *Bat Column* in Chicago, and George Segal's *Restaurant* in Buffalo. In 1979, the GSA asked the National Endowment for the Arts to set up a panel of art experts to nominate an appropriate sculptor for the federal building in New York. Presented with an array of proposals, the committee chose Richard Serra, believing that his work was monumental enough to stand in the shadow of Manhattan's skyscraping monoliths – including what were then the relatively new World Trade Center towers. Serra's project, the committee agreed, would not "be overwhelmed by a city of skyscrapers and such miracles of engineering as the Brooklyn Bridge," while it was exciting enough to "capture the energy, enterprise, and fast movement of the city's inhabitants."[47] Serra was also a perfect candidate for this prominent public arts program since many saw him as "the most important sculptor of his generation."[48]

**Figure 2.2**  Richard Serra, *Tilted Arc* (1981), Jack Manning/New York Times/Redux © 2007 Richard Serra/Artists Rights Society (ARS), New York.

Commissioned by the GSA, Serra set to work on his piece by studying the passage of pedestrians through and across the plaza. He aimed to build a work that would draw attention to the way that people moved through the space. The GSA in New York asked for a detailed study of the impact of *Tilted Arc* on the environment, including safety, pedestrian traffic, lighting, drainage, and law enforcement. Serra altered his proposal to take their concerns into account, and it was approved in 1980.

Even before the work was complete, complaints began to stream in. Initial petitions demanding *Tilted Arc*'s removal boasted 1,300 signatories, many of them workers in the adjacent federal building. Edward D. Re, the Chief Judge of the Court of International Trade, had an office in the federal building, and he was particularly vocal about his dislike of the *Arc*. He circulated petitions and protested vehemently against the "rusted steel barrier" while it was still in the process of construction.[49] The furor later died down, only to be whipped up again three years later, perhaps deliberately by Re, who certainly helped to launch the letter-writing campaign to Washington.[50] In the first four years of *Tilted Arc*'s life, the GSA reported 4,500 letters and appeals urging its removal, lamenting the ugliness, the inconvenience, the incomprehensibility, and the intimidating bulk of Serra's sculpture.

In March of 1985, the GSA's New York Regional Administrator, William Diamond, convened a panel to decide whether or not the *Arc* should be relocated. He held an open public hearing which lasted three days.[51] Those who testified included not only local residents and workers, but art experts, curators, dealers, politicians, arts administrators, sculptors, playwrights, painters, and performance artists. In all, 180 people spoke at the hearing, 122 for preserving *Tilted Arc* in the newly renamed Jacob Javits Plaza, 58 for its removal. By the end of the hearing, the voices raised against the work had persuaded the panel, and *Tilted Arc* was torn down. After all-night work crews torched the work, sawed it up, and carried away the pieces, William Diamond said, "This is a day for the people to rejoice . . . because now the plaza belongs rightfully to the people."[52]

53

Now there are no traces of Serra's monumental work in Jacob Javits Plaza.

If Serra's public sculpture prompted immediate and vociferous outcry, the reasons for the uproar are striking. The work was not obscene, violent, or offensive on grounds of race, religion, sex, or sexuality. It could not be said to cause injury, corrupt the innocent, endanger the community, or threaten the stability of government. It could not be said to be about *harm*.[53] It was not even a threat to national unity or tradition. What was at stake was a matter of style, of aesthetic preference, of taste. Public outcry revolved around what we might simply call dislike.

And dislike had everything to do with the logic of the avant-garde. By the 1980s, artists and critics had long ago announced the death of avant-garde art.[54] And yet, in the *Tilted Arc* hearing, its logic emerged alive and well. Serra's detractors presented familiar complaints about the work's defiance of mainstream taste, its elitism and inaccessibility. "This strip of rust," said one worker, is "an arrogant-nose-thumbing gesture at the government and those who serve the government."[55] Another witness claimed that the tight-knit art world was trying to "intimidate" viewers with "a smoke screen of intellectual mumbo-jumbo about art."[56] Meanwhile, Serra advocates agreed that the object was "confrontational," "bullying," and "aggressive," but this was a good thing: it was precisely the work's tense and critical relations to its surroundings that allowed it to function as a meaningful response to a pitiless urban experience. As one art historian put it: "Before art liberates our vision and develops our judgment, it unleashes our prejudices – acts of violent contempt with which we defend the loss and absence of vision of which art so painfully reminds us."[57] Unsettling the audience was only appropriate, Serra advocates insisted, because "truly creative people in the arts make work that is challenging, demanding that we think of our surroundings, our fellow man, and especially ourselves in a new and unaccustomed way."[58] Some argued that if the country did not encourage such challenges, it would be seriously impoverished, left with only "the conventional, the uninspired and the uncontroversial."[59]

The artist Claes Oldenburg warned that the "effort to . . . please all pressure groups" would result in "mediocrity and decoration instead of integrity."[60] In classic avant-garde fashion, too, Serra himself claimed the integrity of the autonomous artist, telling the press that he had no intention of pleasing the public if that meant pandering to a facile consumerist taste for pretty surfaces.[61]

The logic of the avant-garde presented an awkward challenge to collective decision-making. As long as the artist persisted in valuing the marginal over the mainstream, it was not clear why a public should fund and support the artistic repudiation of *itself*. Some politicians acknowledged the necessity of placating irritated voters, but many also refused to grant majority rule, insisting that it would be absurd to call a referendum on aesthetics. Yet, without a referendum, the debate then ran into the problem of gauging the extent and depth of public dislike: who would speak for the public? Was it the press, the local government, the artistic community, the courts? Even more troubling, which public mattered most? Was it the people who used the space daily – who had to maneuver around the work in order to conduct their ordinary affairs – or was it the whole nation? Was it only the taxpayers who had paid for the work, or did the public include international visitors and future generations? Exposing the difficulties of identifying the proper boundaries around the public in a pluralist democracy, this critical and disruptive work of art uncovered the question mark at the heart of the very definition of democratic public space: namely – which public?

William Diamond, the GSA administrator, decided the case the democratic way. In coming to his decision, he "relied heavily upon the arguments proffered by Manhattan Community Board #1, a legally constituted body which represents more than 250,000 residents in lower Manhattan."[62] Appealing to the most conventional kind of democratic decision-making body, Diamond chose local government as the most representative voice of the public, and saw their unanimous decision as overwhelming: they had voted 22 to zero to remove the sculpture. Diamond also mentioned the 4,500 letters of protest and petitions.

Was this the best way of defining the public? Offering a set of alternative definitions, witnesses had argued for the global impact of *Tilted Arc*, insisting the art was not a local object but an international one. In fact, according to his supporters, Serra had actually single-handedly recast Federal Plaza as a global rather than a local space: now it was on the map as a destination "for informed and sophisticated visitors."[63] Those visitors could not vote in a local referendum, of course, and so – although they were members of the viewing public – they had been disenfranchised. Donald Thalacker, director of the Art-in-Architecture program, managed to skip over the local community altogether when he defended *Tilted Arc*, as "public art for the American people, for visitors from other countries, and [for our] future generations."[64] And in fact, many of the *Arc*'s advocates lobbied not only for an international audience, but for future viewers, since "truly challenging works of art require a period of time before their artistic language can be understood by a broader public."[65]

Dwight Ink, acting administrator of the GSA in Washington, summarized the arguments for and against the *Arc* as follows:

> Most of the people who testified for relocation placed a high value on the wishes of the people who live and work in the area. Those favoring retention focused more on longer-term values of the art work to the public than on the concerns of employees and local residents who are directly affected by the work.[66]

Ink was right: trapped in a struggle between the local and contemporary tastes of the community using the plaza on the one hand, and the more worldly preferences of both an international art community and an unpredictable future on the other, *Tilted Arc* was poised between competing conceptions of the public.[67]

To complicate matters still further, some of the *Arc*'s advocates alleged that Diamond's numbers were not reliable even as a measure of the *local* majority. They countered that the Community Board had not given its usual prior notice before the meeting, failing to publicize its debate on *Tilted Arc*. Only 22 of the 47 members were present, and the others had effectively been silenced. Serra's side also pointed out that the ratio of witnesses in the public hearing was two to one in favor of keeping the sculpture in place, and that the letters defending *Tilted Arc* far outnumbered those against.[68] On the other hand, counting the number of witnesses in the hearing was a troubling gauge of public opinion because the witnesses themselves represented highly variable constituencies. While many who supported *Tilted Arc* represented overlapping pieces of a fairly coherent art world, some of Serra's opponents spoke for discrete and fairly large populations, like Peter Hirsch, who was "authorized" by the Association of Immigration Attorneys to speak out against the art work. ("We feel," he told the panel, "that a good place to put the *Tilted Arc* would be in the Hudson River.")[69] Similarly, one tenant in the federal building claimed to speak for the "thousands upon thousands of people who come to this building each day to work or seek assistance."[70] And this populism was not confined to the *Arc*'s opponents: one art critic described Serra as a representative of the working class, his background and his use of steel speaking for all working people and a long history of American industry and labor.[71]

If it was hard to calculate the many constituencies — vocal and silent, present and future, local and global, elitist and populist — there were some who argued that certain voices simply counted more than others. An administrator in the building urged the panel to reject the voices of those who did not work in Federal Plaza: "They don't have to look at [*Tilted Arc*], and they don't have to negotiate around it to walk across the plaza."[72] Compelled to steer their course around the sculpture every single work day, those who worked in the building should be taken more seriously than occasional visitors, tourists, and distant experts. But on the other side, artists questioned the credentials of non-professionals to judge Serra at all. "With all due respect," said sculptor Tony Rosenthal to the panel, "when Mr. Diamond read your qualifications, I didn't hear anything about knowledge of public art."[73]

The difficulties of measuring and weighing the opinions of diverse constituencies are of course familiar to those who deal with public policy. And we might be tempted to stop here, affirming that the *Tilted Arc* open public hearing represented an attempt to weigh the claims of various local and global communities, along with the art world, in a difficult but deliberative democratic process. In this deliberation, no single group could exert undue power, while all would have the chance to be heard. Writing about the Brooklyn Museum controversy, Peter Levine exhorts all concerned in arts controversies to respect deliberative procedures: "We would ask everyone involved to heed multiple perspectives, respect facts, achieve as much common ground as possible, and examine arguments rather than assault their opponents' characters."[74]

But this kind of exhortation may not get us very far in battles over the arts. Since the dawn of the avant-garde, when both artists and non-artists began to define bona fide art as that which unsettles and challenges the mainstream, the most substantial public revulsion does not necessarily signal that an art work has failed; and the artist does not feel compelled to find "common ground" or to bow to the overwhelming expression of the people's will – as a politician might. On the contrary, public turmoil only bolsters the artist's sense of success. And there are serious reasons for this: the notion of a "common ground" is precisely the object of the avant-garde's deepest skepticism. Since the rise of mass culture in the nineteenth century, artists and theorists have argued that commonality, homogeneity – shared tastes and ideas – are the *products* of a mass mediated culture, rather than emerging, as if spontaneously and authentically, from a preexisting collective. Cultural critic Michael Warner maintains that what has emerged from mass culture has been the "pervasive and troubling" "phenomenon of normalization." Having been shaped by widely disseminated images of "the people" on television and in opinion polls, for example, we have come increasingly to understand and define ourselves by reference to a common cultural standard. Style, Warner argues, following Theodor Adorno, is one of the hallmarks of the dominance of the normal: "Ideas of the good – and . . . the beautiful as well – are distorted in ways that escape nearly everyone's attention, because they have been silently adjusted to conform to an image of the mass. A good style is a normal style. Evaluation depends on distribution: the wider it circulates, the better it must be. . . . The tastes and ideas that become those of the majority do so because people need to believe that their tastes and ideas will be widely shared."[75] It makes sense, from this perspective, that mass culture and the avant-garde should be inextricably intertwined as well as inevitably opposed: to the extent that the mass media seek to reflect and disseminate the most normal, typical, ordinary, and popular tastes and preferences, the avant-garde sets itself up always to unsettle, scrutinize, and disobey this dominance of normalization.

But can we establish that there really is such a thing as a homogeneous mass culture that reinforces an oppressive set of norms? In a study of network television news coverage of the arts from 1976 to 1985 – the year of Serra's hearing – two scholars tracked the way that news anchors repeatedly ridiculed the very idea of contemporary art even before each news story got under way. Rather than dealing with serious issues arising from arts controversies – raising questions about constitutional law or freedom of expression, for example – the news anchors regularly joked about "crazy" "self-styled" artists, and then cut quickly to men-or-women-on-the-street expressing puzzlement or outrage. Thus the anchor "directly communicates to the viewer the message that none of this is to be taken seriously." This is in direct contrast to other news stories:

> The anchorperson . . . is mandated, in order to maintain credibility, not to appear perplexed, ignorant or confused regarding matters deemed to be of national and international importance. Rather, a manner of cool objectivity is the norm. In contrast, the humorous art story seems to offer a chance for the anchorperson to forge a common link with the audience. That is, these stories are often set up as examples of "that loony academic-bureaucratic world out there" and signal a mutual understanding between the anchor and the audience. . . . [T]hese stories serve a boundary-maintaining function. They are an occasion for reaffirming the normative order. . . . Thus the audience is left with the comfortable feeling of being on the inside, at least compared to those eccentrics on the news.[76]

In the structure of this encounter, the avant-garde is recognizable as precisely that which is not "normal," while network television reinforces its own sense of mainstream security by pointing to the cranky oddballs in the arts. Both, it is clear, need one another. The avant-garde takes the mainstream as its target, while the mass media takes advantage of the discomfort offered by the avant-garde, tying the audience to the anchorperson as ordinary and comfortable, in contrast to the "insanity" of those foolish and self-indulgent art-makers. I have suggested that this is a structural encounter, and here we can see why: our sense of the ordinary depends on eccentric outsiders just as much as outcasts are defined by social norms. The mainstream and the counter-mainstream can only be defined by their differences from one another. This is why the battle over "shock art" comes up so often that it has – paradoxically – ceased to shock.[77] The mainstream cannot really do without the avant-garde. Serving as a necessary foil to the ordinariness of ordinary tastes and values, strange and difficult art is part and parcel of a cultural field that constantly invokes and regulates the "normal."[78]

According to proponents of the logic of the avant-garde, the soothing gestures of mainstream normalization come at a serious cost: relinquishing any effort at critical reasoning, independence of thought, or skepticism about what it means to be "normal," we relax into a restful sense of our own belonging. In this process, we do little to exercise our own judgment, succumbing to pre-packaged versions of the good, the beautiful, and the ordinary offered up by a corporate-sponsored media. Any feeling of being normal is thus less a reflection of our preexisting tastes and values than an effect of cozy, chatty news anchors and an array of other media reassurances about our right to feel included in the fold of common sense. It is for this reason that charges of artistic elitism are often wide of the mark: the logic of the avant-garde is less concerned with rejecting popular taste per se than with interrupting the pressures that impel people toward an unthinking acquiescence to standardization.

In keeping with the avant-garde critique of consumer culture, Richard Serra proclaimed that "the governmental decree to remove and therefore destroy *Tilted Arc* is the direct outcome of a cynical Republican cultural policy that supports art only as a commodity."[79] From his position as high-minded outcast, he played up his role as oppressed by the state, democratically elected though it might be. "It is no better than the Soviets bulldozing the work of dissident artists," he said of the *Arc*'s removal.[80] And he was right, at least according the logic of the avant-garde: there is less difference between democratic and authoritarian governments than we might think if the normalizing pressures of the mass media can be as limiting and oppressive as despotic regimes. Contrasting the purity of art to the polluted world of consumerism and power politics, what the artist learned from the controversy was that there was every reason to continue to flout mainstream taste and governmental and legal approval in the interests of the disinterestedness of art.

In short, what distinguishes art from other political problems since the beginning of the avant-garde is that official condemnation and majority outrage are perceived as *strengthening* the art world's sense of its own separation from other social institutions, bolstering the values of artistic isolation, purity, and critical disinterestedness. In this context, avant-garde art and deliberative democracy seem to reach an impossible impasse. A conventional democratic process, with its search for "common ground," will always infuriate and alienate artists concerned about pressures toward normalization, and artists in the tradition of the avant-garde will always use the very grounds of consensus to confront and challenge the will of the public.

But it is not quite a total stalemate. Like Epstein's supporters, Serra clearly imagined pleasing a wider public *later*. As Serra's lawyer explained: "Modern art is, almost by definition, difficult for the public to grasp and accept. . . . But a hundred years from now, such work will elicit praise from posterity for the foresight of officials who made it possible."[81] In keeping with this logic, many in the hearings pleaded for time, like Senator Jacob Javits ("It is only three and a half years since the sculpture was installed, and it has hardly had an opportunity to make its point"), William Rubin ("such a grave decision . . . should not even be contemplated until the work and its public can pass through a period of time required for the artistic language of the work to become familiar"), and Donald Thalacker ("Four years is definitely not sufficient time to evaluate either long term public reaction to or artistic significance of *Tilted Arc*").[82] "New York is beginning to act like a hick town," said painter Steven Davis. "It's a big disappointment."[83] It was time to try to catch up with the future.

As in the *Rima* case, the emphasis on the future helps to produce a remarkably satisfying justification for the avant-garde, brave and autonomous in the moment but beloved and accepted in decades to come. Of course, an attention to the public of the future also leads to some odd conclusions when it comes to policy-making. Those who favor the avant-garde must argue that broad public dislike is both necessary and pointless: mass revulsion is necessary if the avant-garde is to show itself as new, uncomfortable, and unsettling; but it is pointless for any member of the public to hold on to this revulsion, since it will shortly be superseded by the tolerant generations of the future. In effect, this camp argues that the public ought to overcome their own dislike in the moment that they experience it, supporting the art that violates their tastes and preferences in order to fall in line with a future that is inevitably about to come to pass. The history of art speeds up to infinity, here, as the present must disappear into the future in the very moment that present tastes are expressed.

Yet the tension between mass culture and the avant-garde produces a certain productive logic. In a cultural field in which images of the "normal" dominate, the avant-garde is precisely that aspect of culture that is recognizable by its refusal to conform. It therefore depends on mainstream revulsion. But it also tests the boundaries of the normal, offering up alternative images of what could be. It is thus both outside and inside, both friend and enemy. Appealing to the future, new and unsettling art can shift public taste, unsettling the normalizing judgment that it despises, demanding a new public consciousness to rise to the occasion of its insistent challenges. According to this view, it is only by upsetting normalizing tastes that new preferences come into public view, and so art is there to bring the public into the future – and the future into the public. Moving back and forth between the margins and the mainstream, refusing to reflect mass culture while relying on it as both a target and a motive, the avant-garde is not disconnected from the larger public: it emerges from it and strives to feed back into it.

This conclusion allows us to return to the relationship between the democratic referendum and avant-garde art. If the project of democracy and the defiance of the avant-garde have often seemed doomed to a mutual incomprehension, now we can see that their battle actually revolves around a common problem: the public itself. Far from ignoring public taste, the avant-garde stakes its claim on the potential for public transformation.[84] In the process, it hints at the inherent conservatism of the democratic vote. Political democracy relies on procedures that will measure and weigh a range of viewpoints that are already articulated, while the artistic avant-garde asks whether it might be able to bring new perceptions into being. Democracy claims to reflect the will of the people – to bear witness to its current values and desires – while the avant-garde claims to test and transform those values and desires, to urge the public into an embrace of the new and the unfamiliar, of skepticism and radical possibility. Elections, we might say, necessarily look backward, gauging and reflecting what is already in existence, where the avant-garde insistently looks forward, willing to challenge the public into the future. Where democracy aims to represent the people, the avant-garde seeks to provoke and stimulate it.

The final decision about *Tilted Arc*'s fate, then, was made in the name of democracy, but it was a remarkably limited conception of democracy. It represented only the local community and the contemporary majority – that is, the here and the now. It put its emphasis on residents rather than visitors, on the mainstream rather than the margins, and on the present rather than the future. There was no room in this conception of democracy for the possibility of a changing public, one that might grow out of its current tastes and values. The battle over *Tilted Arc* exposes precisely the backward-looking logic of the democratic referendum — which seeks to reflect existing preferences — in contrast to the insistent forward movement demanded by the avant-garde — which invites us to welcome the new. It would of course be naive and unethical to argue that all collective projects and policies ought to provoke and defy public preferences, but I would argue that *art* is one domain where we can afford to project ourselves, imaginatively, into a different and surprising future. The avant-garde offers the public an opportunity to conceive of strange possibilities and unfamiliar ways of seeing. And since history shows us that public taste has been neither static nor monolithic in the past two hundred years, and that art objects have often come into their own only with the passage of time, it certainly seems unnecessarily restrictive to imagine that we will always like what we like at this moment — or that we should bind future generations to the fleeting tastes of the present. We might agree, too, that there is a potential public benefit in being provoked to expand our horizons beyond the immediate present, to welcome the challenges of the unfamiliar. The destruction of *Tilted Arc* foreclosed that possibility.

And so I would like to suggest that something important was lost along with Serra's art work. There was no room in the final decision for the notion that majority rule might itself prove repressive and unreasonable. The *Rima* case offers the most frightening example of how majority rule might misfire, deliberately drowning out minority voices in the name of a racial and national unity. But the Serra case offers a comparable lesson. The public hearing suggested all kinds of difficulties in establishing the populist position persuasively: it revealed the almost insurmountable problem of knowing just what the tastes of the public really were. In the end, the most practical way to make the decision seemed to be the official democratic way, but the results were potentially alarming: the vote of the local representatives spoke for everyone — local residents and global visitors, present tastes and future prospects, mainstream preferences and minority desires. Any policy that insists that art objects must please the local majority must — by necessity — cover over the fact of many publics, some actual and some potential, many in disagreement, voicing conflicting tastes and values. Majority rule narrows the public to a single, local, time-bound perspective.

Any single art work will almost certainly fail to represent more than a narrow notion of the public: one sculpture can only say so much, and it would be impossible, of course, for it to convey the views of all of the different audiences that pass through a busy public space. But with both *Rima* and *Tilted Arc*, avant-garde public art actually offers a better representation of a *plural* public than the art work chosen by majority rule. In contrast to the ethnic and nationalist insistence on homogeneity, on the one hand, and the media-saturated reign of the "normal," on the other, the artistic avant-garde strives to disrupt the totalizing aspirations of political, social, and artistic majorities, and so, inevitably, it generates conflicts. But far from harming the collective, it is by virtue of its very divisiveness that the avant-garde actually exposes the fractured reality of the public, making visible the conflicting tastes, interests, and values that at any moment constitute "the people." And so we might say that if the avant-garde fails to represent the majority, it succeeds in representing plurality, heterogeneity, otherness. Thus while politicians, administrators, and even members of the art world claimed that the most important lesson they had learned from the *Tilted Arc* controversy was to invite more community involvement in public arts projects,[85] this shift in arts policy leads us back to the unsettling questions raised by the debate over *My Name is Rachel Corrie*. Should all prospectively controversial art projects be subject to market research, community consultation, polling? Some would argue that the form of the opinion poll itself has deeply distorted our perceptions of the public, since its simplistic design "has none of the open-endedness, reflexive framing, or accessibility" we associate with genuinely productive public debate.[86] Certainly the format of the opinion survey seems reductive and simplistic compared to art's penchant for subtle ironies and ambiguities. But perhaps more importantly, the danger of relying on community standards from the outset is serious, since it risks quelling dissent before it has even been expressed, and does so in the name of a normalizing democracy. By contrast, the dangers of inviting the avant-garde to do its thing seem slight: the risk not of harm or even of offense in the cases we have seen here, but of popular dislike – of entertaining the strange, the unfamiliar, the critical and utopian otherness that we might even grow to like in times to come.

## The Conflicts Continue

We have seen ferocious fascists defacing a Jewish sculptor's work in the name of the nation, and a voting majority deciding to bulldoze the avant-garde. And I would like to close by suggesting that we are by no means out of the woods: led by the will of the people, democracies can *always* turn tyrannical, can *always* insist on squelching the unpopular voices of rebellious artists. Around the world, in recent years, democratic societies have shown themselves perfectly willing to quell art in the name of the majority. They have typically pitted the will of "the people" against the critical, dissenting view of the artist – and in many cases the artist has lost the battle.

For example, in 2003, in the relatively new democratic state of Poland, artist Dorota Nieznalska was tried and sentenced to six months of supervised community service and forbidden to travel out of the country. Her crime? She had exhibited a work called "Passion," which superimposed a photograph of male genitalia on an image of the cross. This was not the first attack on Nieznalska: she had already been the target of a series of verbal and physical assaults by the League of Polish Families, who have repeatedly struck out against art that affronts conservative Catholic values. They have sued a number of artists, including Nieznalska. They have been known, too, to make physical attacks on artists and art objects. In 2000, two Members of Parliament associated with the League of Catholic Families, Witold Tomczak and Halina Nowina-Konopka, sawed off the legs of a sculpture by Italian artist Maurizio Cattelan that showed the Pope being felled by a meteorite. Tomczak wrote an open letter in which he suggested that the museum director's Jewish heritage was behind the show's offense to Catholics. Neither MP was charged with a crime because both have immunity as long as they serve in Parliament. And, more importantly, none of the news has hurt their popularity: the Catholic Nationalist Party has won increasing support in the past five years.[87]

What may be most disturbing, though, is that the Polish court sided with the League of Polish Families against Nieznalska. Judge Tomasz Zielinski ruled that the artist had offended religious feelings – "abusing a cult object" in the context of a gallery that was open to the public. The judge denied that art had any special legal status, arguing on constitutional grounds that "the fact that a work is within the boundaries of art has no significance for whether it can offend the feelings of other people." Nieznalska's conviction was followed by a flood of reactions, including applause in the courtroom and outrage from a range of sources, including one member of the clergy. Most prominent among the responses was a letter of protest signed by more than 1,500 artists, academics, engineers, businesspeople, and other concerned citizens, who argued that "civic freedoms are not established in order that they may serve one ideology": art, it declared, is "one sphere" for "freedom, incorrectness, difference."[88]

Despite these passionate pleas for pluralism and freedom, the League of Catholic Families prevailed. Poland's democratic constitution does not protect minority expression in the realm of religious values, and so allows majority beliefs to trump artistic critique. It is also a state that protects its elected officials from legal proceedings while allowing the artist they have assaulted to stand trial. And it is a democratic context in which support for majority rule over minority expression is growing.

Poland is by no means the only democratic state, in the past few years, to quash an art object. In January of 2004, the Israeli ambassador to Sweden, Zvi Mazel, ripped out the electrical fixtures lighting an art installation in a Swedish museum and threw them at the art work, causing the whole installation to short-circuit while shouting "shame on you!" at the artists. *Snow White and the Madness of Truth*, by Israeli-born Dror Feiler and his Swedish wife Gunilla Skold Feiler, was indeed meant to shock: sailing in a blood-red pool was a sailboat holding a photograph of Hanadi Jaradat, a Palestinian lawyer who blew herself up in a Haifa suicide bombing that killed 21 Israelis. In the photo, she was smiling. Bach's cantata, "Mein Herze schwimmt im Blut" ("My heart swims in blood"), played in the background. The Israeli ambassador insisted that the work glorified terrorism; others have argued that it did the opposite, emphasizing Jaradat's monstrousness; and still others have claimed that the work was deliberately ambiguous, playing back and forth between the atrocity of terrorism and the tragedy of Palestinian suffering.[89] What is perhaps most important for our purposes is that the ambassador's assault was not a spontaneous outburst of passionate disgust, but an act performed in the name of the people. As the *Jerusalem Post* reported: "The ambassador, previously known as a prudent career diplomat, has admitted his actions were premeditated, discussed beforehand with other Foreign Ministry officials." Mazel earned public praise from Prime Minister Ariel Sharon, who affirmed: "The entire government stands behind him. Our ambassador did the right thing. The phenomenon which we saw there is so grave that it was forbidden not to react to it." Even more to the point, Foreign Minister Silvan Shalom claimed that Mazel had acted in the name of the entire Israeli people: "Ambassador Mazel's actions must be understood as an outcry from all of us."[90] Here, then, is an exemplary case of the logic of the avant-garde at work: while the artists meant to stir up their audiences and clearly succeeded, the ambassador claimed that his attack had been a symbolically collective gesture, an expression of a whole nation's outrage. The artists offered a provocation, and government representatives responded by striking back in the name of the people.[91]

Britain, the US, Poland, Israel: all tell similar stories. And what about India – the world's largest democracy? In September 2000, Indian artist Surendran Nair was about to see his new work, *An Actor Rehearsing the Interior Monologue of Icarus*, unveiled at the National Gallery of Modern Art in New Delhi. Just minutes before the show was scheduled to open, the Secretary in the Central Department of Culture demanded that the painting be removed because it was "unconstitutional." The problem was that Nair's painting included an image of the Ashoka Pillar, the national symbol of India, which shows four lions around a circular abacus on a tall column. On top of the Ashoka Pillar, Nair had depicted a naked image of the Greek mythic figure, Icarus – who flies too close to the sun and so melts his wings and falls to the earth. Invoking this myth about human ambition and failure, Nair seemed to suggest that Indian nationalism had ambitions so grandiose that it was destined for collapse from its own hubris.

According to Mukta Nidhi Sanhotra, Director of the National Gallery of Modern Art, the Ashoka emblem cannot, by law, be shown in a government institution. But she also expressed concern that the painting might prompt a violent reaction from nationalists, and insisted that it was her job to protect the other works in the gallery.[92] In protest, not only Nair but all of the other exhibiting artists withdrew their works from the show. Since freedom of expression is a constitutional right, they argued, the gallery's decision contravened the nation's most deeply held values. As Nair put it in an interview with *Indian Express*: "vigilantism is now part of the political climate where 'cultural propriety' is being decided by the State and its agencies, and interpretations of creative expression get appropriated to suit their cultural agenda."[93]

Two familiar values met and clashed in the Nair controversy: on the one hand, the value of national strength and unity, as shown in official respect for the national symbol – a symbol held to represent the people as a whole; on the other hand, freedom of expression, including the right of skeptics and dissenters to cast doubt on the nature of national unity and the values of the majority. In a democracy, this kind of struggle is all too familiar – we might remember debates over flag-burning and antiwar protests in the US – and if we think about it, it is not too surprising that they clash again and again: all democracies struggle to find a balance between expressing the will of the majority and supporting marginal and dissenting voices. Those who are on the side of the majority worry that nonconformists will undermine beloved traditions and weaken national security. But when the balance falls on the side of the majority, freedom of expression and minority rights are always gravely imperiled.

Let's consider one last example. This is a case that involves art made not by a lone and alienated artist but by a group of people in Santa Clara County, California. In late September, 2003, some citizens of Los Altos Hills started a campaign against the closing of a local charter school. Complaining that they paid taxes and voted for renovations to the school, they protested by encouraging fellow citizens to display "Art Cows" on their property to send the message that the community had been "milked." Members of the community either purchased full-sized wooden cows to display in their front yards or made their own images to show support: cow shrines, cows that glowed, cow-shaped mailboxes (figure 2.3). Rather than casting the

**Figure 2.3** Art Cow (2003), courtesy Scott Vanderlip.

project as political speech, pure and simple, the organizers were clear that the campaign was an artistic one: "Community Art projects are a great way to bring out the best in a community," they argued. "Fun and decorated cows will bring a smile to those passing by as the seasons change. . . . We encourage everyone in LAH to bring out the Matisse and Van Gogh in them by creating their own community cow art."[94] But though the exuberant and folksy "Art Cows" were a hit with many, there were people in Los Altos Hills who strongly disagreed with the political message of the pro-cow contingent. In January of 2004, local newspapers reported a rash of thefts and vandalism. Thirteen of the original 40 cows were defaced or destroyed, and a reward was offered to anyone who could provide information leading to the guilty parties.

Though this is a more whimsical arts controversy than most, there are a few lessons that emerge from this final example. First of all, the Los Altos Hills cows make clear that the artist does not have to be a solitary outcast to provoke public displeasure: even community-based art can raise hackles and provoke the demolition teams. And so we might want to be on our guard against "art attacks" even when the objects are not avant-garde in the strict, historical sense. Secondly, public outrage against the arts is not limited to attacks in the press; numerous art works over the past century have been literally destroyed, the artists assaulted or imprisoned – and this is true not just under authoritarian regimes, but in democracies. In fact, democracy itself licenses those who claim to speak for "the people" – even when an art work is neither offensive nor dangerous, but merely displeasing and unfamiliar. Thirdly, the Los Altos Hills controversy reinforces the idea that fractious art might be a better reflection of the public than mainstream images and traditional emblems that signify harmony and solidarity. Though it is not clear whether the artists or the iconoclasts speak for the majority of the people in Los Altos Hills, what is clear is that a debate is raging, and that this local public is therefore fractured and plural. Democratic forms of government are typically better at tolerating discord and dissension than other political models; but it has become a commonplace to argue that art for democratic public spaces should reflect current majority tastes and values. The controversies described in this chapter point to a different solution: art that is taken as a reflection of "the people" here and now is partial and inadequate, since democratic collectives are always and necessarily self-divided, productive of difference and capable of transformation. The avant-garde is better than any referendum at capturing a changing and dissonant understanding of "the people." And lastly, even if we are solidly with the majority most of the time – perhaps we feel comfortably mainstream when it comes to religion, nation, sexual mores, and aesthetic tastes – there might just be an issue that arises at some point in our lives that marks us as a marginalized minority – our feeling that we have been milked by property taxes, for example – and it is for this reason that all of us need democratic states to commit themselves to the protection of minority expression, and particularly protection for artists in the tradition of the avant-garde who dedicate themselves to resisting the pressure to conform to calls for homogeneity and the rule of conventional taste.

# 3

# *Propaganda for Democracy: The Avant-Garde Goes to War*

May 11, 1942 marked the ninth anniversary of the Nazi book burnings. On that day, the German émigré writer Lion Feuchtwanger wrote to the *New York Times* to say that he had wanted to commemorate this dark event by getting together with two of his friends who had, like him, fled the fascists – the playwright Bertolt Brecht and the novelist Erich Maria Remarque. Ironically, they could not meet to celebrate their freedom because they had all been categorized as "enemy aliens": seen as foreign threats, they were not allowed to travel more than five miles from their homes, to speak publicly, or to go out after 8 p.m. This was particularly regrettable, Feuchtwanger explained, because all three anti-fascist writers would have liked to use the book-burning anniversary to praise America's freedoms in contrast to Nazi repression. "I shall console myself," Feuchtwanger wrote, "with the thought that perhaps on this night, as so often in the past, British pilots will drop leaflets over Germany quoting from my books and praising democracy."[1]

This kind of irony was – and is – not limited to the anniversary of the Nazi book burnings. For the past hundred years, democracies at war against totalitarian and other repressive regimes have wanted to persuade the world that they stand for a better way of life: not only economic well-being, but also that more intangible value – freedom. And this task has not been easy: democracy and freedom, as we have seen, are not actually synonymous. The tyranny of the majority always presents a danger to individual freedoms in democratic

73

contexts, and in wartime the tension between a strong majority and the protection of civil liberties becomes particularly acute: populist leaders often argue that it is essential for a democracy to be united, which means that a nation cannot afford any self-indulgent dissent that will fracture a sense of collective resolve and empower the enemy. On the other side, civil libertarians counter that it is precisely in times of emergency that our liberties most need protection: what use is a right if it is abolished at the first sign of trouble?

During the Cold War, the United States was claiming to oppose the tyranny of totalitarianism with liberal democracy. But it was a daunting task to persuade the world that American-style democracy guaranteed genuine freedom. With the nation under threat, popular enthusiasm grew for restricting civil liberties in the interests of cracking down on the "red menace." Meanwhile, around the world, socialists argued that the US failed to offer economic and social freedoms. They pointed to the plight of African-Americans, whose poverty and second-class status became signs of US hypocrisy. Those with socialist sympathies also made the case that Soviet communism was not the only choice for leftists: a more plural version of socialism, which welcomed dissent and difference, while stressing economic equality, might prove an appealing alternative to capitalist liberal democracy. The crucial challenge for US leaders was to persuade the world that American freedoms were both real and precious.

The end of the Cold War did not put an end to these difficulties. George W. Bush claimed to launch the war in Iraq in the name of US freedom, but he immediately cracked down on civil liberties at home and abroad.[2] Commentators worldwide were quick to point out the hypocrisy of restricting freedoms in the name of a war for freedom, and the results, as many have argued, may prove disastrous.[3] At moments of national insecurity, then, leaders in liberal democracies always run the risk of seeming like hypocrites. And this is not capricious, but rather structural: democracies fighting in the name of freedom must somehow reconcile a disciplined and united collective ready for war with the principle of freedom from state restrictions and majority pressures. Either they limit freedoms in the name

74

of freedom, or they confront the daunting task of persuading citizens to unite around a paradoxical common value – the freedom to dissent from common values.

It is against this backdrop that avant-garde art has emerged as an unlikely instrument of geopolitical warfare. Democracies in the twentieth century repeatedly – and covertly – produced what I call a *propaganda of the avant-garde*, sponsoring shocking, unpopular, even deliberately anti-majoritarian art as part of the struggle to win over hesitant citizens and wavering allies. Why would a democracy support critical or challenging art in wartime? It surely seems counterintuitive to claim that artists reviled by the public and dismissive of the majority could come to prop up democracy. But in their relentless desire to proclaim their freedom from mainstream tastes and values, avant-garde artists offer democratic states a surprising opportunity: the chance to display their hospitality to marginal and dissenting views. As long as the artist stands for liberation – from "normal" values, or the pursuit of money, or the political mainstream – then the state can point to the artist's freedom as an index of the freedom enjoyed by the *whole* society. And so, for the past century, liberal democracies have repeatedly publicized their commitment to freedom by embracing rebellious art works, and they have done so not in spite of art's unpopularity but precisely because of it: the more the art is publicly vilified, the freer the society that puts up with it must be. And so the avant-garde has been put to use to represent the freedom that democracies – supposedly – guarantee.

But the story is far from straightforward. Rebellious artists, committed to their own autonomy and integrity, understandably resist becoming propagandists for the state, even if the state happens to be democratic. Meanwhile, popular sentiment typically finds defiant artists outrageous, and in wartime, that hostility only becomes more acute: citizens coming together to sacrifice for war tend to see the critical perspective of the avant-garde as disloyal and decadent, undermining the need for national strength and unity. So: how can a democracy possibly use the avant-garde to demonstrate its commitment to freedom without alienating both the artist and "the people"?

75

The fate of avant-garde art during the Cold War offers a strange set of answers. I will tell the story here of three curiously interconnected examples: Bertolt Brecht, a communist playwright accused of spreading Soviet sympathies through his writing; Jackson Pollock, an Abstract Expressionist painter secretly supported by the CIA; and Richard M. Nixon, red-baiter turned arts patron, who first thwarted and then eagerly promoted cutting-edge artists and their work. Taken together, these Cold War stories suggest that avant-garde art can serve as remarkably effective propaganda for democracy – but only in the most paradoxical of ways. When publicly elected officials express an open and explicit aversion to the avant-garde, their loathing allows artists to seem like enemies of the electorate, but it also allows them to act as exemplary instances of freedom from majority rule. And so, oddly enough, art does its best as an instrument of democratic freedom when it is both rejected *and* promoted. This account suggests that our usual understanding of artists as either inside or outside the war machine – either enlisted or repressed by the state during times of war – is not quite accurate: the propaganda of the avant-garde involves neither co-optation nor censorship. Instead, a complicated interplay of state powers, both fostering and foiling artists, produces a startlingly effective propaganda – and pushes art into the service of democracy at war.

## Hypocrisy All Round: Bertolt Brecht on Trial

It took a number of years – and quite a few bumps and bruises – for the US to figure out how to use the arts as propaganda. In the early years of the Cold War, US policy toward the arts seemed focused on a fairly straightforward agenda: red-baiters called for the rooting out of all communists and "fellow travelers," fearing that left-wingers were secretly spreading powerful Soviet propaganda. In 1943, Congress shut down the federal arts program, the WPA, in response to accusations that it was supporting communist artists. Participants in the arts who had proudly displayed their socialist sympathies in the 1930s went under cover or lost their livelihoods. And by the late 1940s, the infamous House Committee on Un-American Activities (HUAC) began to investigate subversive influences in Hollywood. Among the first to be called to testify was the world-famous playwright, Bertolt Brecht. The story of Brecht's appearance before HUAC shows us just how difficult it was, in the Cold War context, to make a powerful case for freedom. Both the artist and the state claimed to be fighting for liberty; and both struggled to explain what freedom was and how it worked. But both also got themselves into trouble – appearing most hypocritical where they most sought to protect freedom as a value. What the Brecht hearings make clear is that the democratic state and the artist did not yet know how much they needed one another.

Brecht was an unlikely member of the first group of nineteen witnesses to testify before the US Congress about subversive activity in Hollywood. Although he had been living in Santa Monica for some years, his only foray into film had been an anti-fascist story called *Hangmen Also Die*, made into a film directed by Fritz Lang in 1943. But Brecht was world famous for advocating socialism in his work, and he was known to be consorting with some of Hollywood's biggest celebrities. Tipped off by an anonymous informant, the FBI tailed Brecht for some years, compiling huge files on letters, visitors, reviews of his work, especially in the Soviet Union, and conversations with informants. The FBI's list of Brecht's acquaintances at times reads like a roster of Oscar-winners: Charles Laughton, Fritz Lang, Bud Schulberg, and Charlie Chaplin, among others.[4] What did the FBI make of all of these interactions? Since so many German émigrés had been leftists, and since they were now making movies in Hollywood, it was possible that they were now trying to use the mass medium of film to spread Soviet values.

When Brecht was summoned before HUAC on October 31, 1947, he appeared conspicuously foreign: he spoke with a heavy accent, used a translator whom the committee found difficult to understand, and "puffed at a long cigar" throughout the proceedings.[5] Unlike most of the other Hollywood witnesses, Brecht largely cooperated with

77

the Committee. When asked whether he had ever been a member of the Communist Party, he agreed to answer the question instead of refusing, as the other witnesses had done – and would continue to do – explaining politely that since he was "a guest in this country," he did not want to "enter into any legal arguments."[6] Apparently a model of submission, Brecht testified that he had never been a member of the Communist Party and stated that his work had been dedicated to "the fight against Hitler" rather than direct advocacy of communism. Though he agreed that he had quoted Lenin and mobilized Marxist ideas in his work, he insisted that he had done so mostly for the collective anti-fascist cause. Sometimes he claimed he had included Marxist concepts for aesthetic reasons, merely adapting the works of others. And when asked about the fact that his productions had included workers from the Communist Party, he pointed out that his productions had involved workers of all kinds, including Catholics and Social Democrats. Much of his testimony was given to quibbles over translations, with Brecht arguing that the Committee had the wrong ideas about his work because of misleading connotations in the English texts. On the whole, Brecht appeared to the Committee to be remarkably accommodating, and in the end HUAC thanked him as a model witness. Given the later witnesses who refused to cooperate and were therefore blacklisted, wire-tapped, and sometimes jailed, Brecht could be said to have betrayed his fellow artists by putting on such a show of obedience.[7]

But though he was technically telling the truth, Brecht actually hoodwinked the Committee. For most of his prolific career, his artistic intentions had been steadfastly communist. For the sake of his politics, Brecht had developed a series of radical avant-garde techniques – methods that were intended to prompt theater audiences to think critically about capitalism and its consequences. Rather than consoling audiences with emotional plots and endings, for example, he wrote *Lehrstücke* – or "learning plays" – that contained explicitly didactic messages about class and revolution. And rather than offering them conventionally realistic dramas, he invented a number of practices that were meant to shatter the illusion of reality that most contemporary dramatists were striving for. Famously, Brecht called these techniques "alienation effects." For example, to prevent audiences from getting caught up in the excitement of plot, Brecht typically revealed the end of the story at the beginning. And instead of inviting audiences to identify with characters in his plays, he expected actors to develop an appreciable distance from the characters they played, to express approval and disapproval, to comment on the characters' actions and feelings. Together, these and other alienation effects were supposed to provoke audiences to adopt a critical distance from the events on stage, thinking and questioning rather than enjoying the pleasures of an emotional catharsis.

Having put these strategies into practice with great success, Brecht saw himself at the forefront of a revolution in both art and politics, pushing beyond the boundaries of established theater in the name of a radically different future. It is not really surprising, then, that the story of Brecht's appearance before HUAC is often told as if it were a typical instance of the collision between the brave, experimental avant-garde and the clumsy, ignorant state. The rebellious artist is brought before boorish government authorities, who wield enormous power and the desire to impose tough censorship but have no idea how to assess a work of art. In foolish bewilderment, the state's representatives fail to understand the subtle subversions of art and so let the revolutionary artist go.

And yet the story is much more complex than the standard version of it might suggest. First of all, Brecht seems to have imagined that he could persuade the US government to see the freethinking artist as an ally and recognize its own hypocrisy in clamping down on artists. In a statement he requested to read before HUAC, Brecht made the argument that assaults on freedom in Nazi Germany had begun with the arts:

When Hitler seized power, painters were forbidden to paint, publishing houses and film studios were taken over by the Nazi Party. But even these strokes against the cultural life of the German people were only the beginning. They were designed and executed

79

as a spiritual preparation for total war which is the total enemy of culture. . . . At the beginning, only a very few people were capable of seeing the connection between the reactionary restrictions in the field of culture and the ultimate assaults upon the physical life of a people itself. . . . [L]ooking back at my experiences as a playwright and a poet in the Europe of the last two decades, I wish to say that the great American people would lose much and risk much if they allowed anybody to restrict free competition of ideas in cultural fields, or to interfere with art which must be free in order to be art.[8]

On the one hand, Brecht appealed to quintessentially capitalist values – the "free competition of ideas" – practically pandering to US politicians. On the other hand, he offered a strong warning that HUAC itself was following in the footsteps of the fascists. Either foolish or willfully blind, the Committee judged this statement "not at all pertinent to this inquiry" and restrained Brecht from reading it.[9]

But if Brecht tried to shame HUAC by exposing them as hypocrites, he was himself behaving somewhat hypocritically when he took on the role of champion of artistic freedom. During the hearing, HUAC asked him to defend two specific works of his – a short "learning play" called *Die Massnahme*, or *The Measures Taken* (1930) and his screenplay for Hollywood, *Hangmen Also Die* (1943). Both of these texts clearly advance the message that it is actually proper and valuable to sacrifice individual freedoms for the sake of a larger collective cause. The main character of *The Measures Taken* – called the "young comrade" – explains that he has joined the cause of the socialist revolution because "The sight of unjustice drove me into the ranks of the fighters. I am for freedom." But where does freedom lie? The young comrade disobeys the orders set for him by his fellow revolutionaries. Consumed by his attention to individual distress, he starts to undermine the cause of the revolution as a whole. His fellow agitators persuade him that he has so seriously betrayed the cause that he ought to kill himself. Played out before a tribunal, called the "Control Committee," the play consists of the agitators explaining the events and asking the Committee to pronounce judgment on their actions. The Committee asks them whether the young comrade might have been justified to sympathize with the oppressed: "Is it not right . . . always to combat injustice wherever it may be found?" The agitators respond: "In order to uphold the great injustice, the small injustice was conceded."[10] In the end, the Committee is convinced that the four agitators have done right: comrades must subject themselves to a severe discipline in the interests of the great revolutionary cause.

The second Brecht work that HUAC was interested in was *Hangmen Also Die*, his only Hollywood screenplay. *Hangmen* is, at least on the surface, a wholly different kind of work from the severely disciplinary *Measures Taken*. Not only was it a screenplay made for popular audiences in the US, but it was directed by Fritz Lang, who was not inclined toward communism himself.[11] But like *The Measures Taken*, its plot sets the well-being of the collective against individual freedoms. The story is a fictionalized version of the death of the Nazi leader of Czechoslovakia, Reinhard Heydrich, popularly called the "Hangman." A doctor kills Heydrich, and then flees the scene and seeks sanctuary with Mascha, a young woman merely passing by. In order to catch Heydrich's killer, the Nazis take hundreds of hostages and say that they will kill one group each day until the Czech people give up the assassin. Among the first to be taken is Mascha's father. Torn between loyalty to the cause of Czech freedom and loyalty to her family, Mascha considers betraying the doctor to the authorities (figure 3.1). The doctor himself wonders whether he should turn himself in to prevent the hostage deaths, but a resistance fighter persuades him that his life is crucial for the cause. In the end, deciding to risk the loss of both her father and her fiancé, Mascha helps the Czechs to expel the Nazis and regain the country's freedom. Struck by her countrymen's stoicism and solidarity, she comes to believe that she must subordinate her personal ties to the nation's freedom.[12]

It might seem strange that HUAC knew enough to focus on these two little-known works of Brecht's, both of which seem to showcase the renunciation of individual liberty, but then seemed to misread their messages, happily letting Brecht go, as if he were a great

**Figure 3.1**  Still from *Hangmen Also Die*, Fritz Lang (1943), Wisconsin Center for Film and Theater Research.

friend to American freedom. Why did HUAC go to the trouble to focus on a obscure play like *The Measures Taken* and yet seem to miss its point? And why did the many plays that had made Brecht world famous – *Mother Courage*, *The Threepenny Opera*, *The Life of Galileo*, *The Good Woman of Szechuan* – get no mention at all?

The answer to these questions can be found in a story that was well known at the time but has since been largely forgotten. Brecht was turned in to the authorities by a woman named Ruth Fischer, the sister of his close friend and musical collaborator, Hanns Eisler. Eisler had begun his career as the favorite student of the leading avant-garde composer in Europe, Arnold Schönberg. Eisler soon repudiated Schönberg's esoteric twelve-tone method, however, dismissing it as anti-democratic, and in the 1920s he began writing accessible songs for the communist movement – *Kampfmusik* – including the hugely popular "Solidarity Song," which became a kind of anthem for communist youth. Later, he fled the Nazi regime and settled in the United States. Thanks to a supportive network of friends in California, Eisler paid the bills by writing scores for Hollywood movies. He was able to help Brecht to settle near him in Pacific Palisades (which Brecht would come to call "the mortuary of easy going"),[13] and the two took up their old collaboration again, working together with director Fritz Lang on *Hangmen Also Die*. But like Brecht, Eisler never abandoned his commitments to communism. He eventually returned to Germany, settling in the communist East and composing the East German national anthem.

Hanns's sister, Ruth Fischer, and his brother Gerhart had also left Europe and taken up their work in the US in the 1940s. But not together: the sister was estranged from both brothers on political grounds. All three had, at one point or another, been prominent figures in European communism. While Hanns wrote popular songs for communist youth that were sung across the Soviet bloc, Ruth had been named the head of the Communist Party in Berlin from 1921 to 1924, a remarkably powerful and influential position for a young woman.[14] And Gerhart worked his way up to become a "top red": he was in Stalin's inner circle and was a leading Comintern agent, with stints in China, the US, and East Germany, changing names and identities as he traveled the globe. But the siblings fell out when Ruth Fischer and her lover, Arkadi Maslow, were expelled from the Communist Party in 1926. Fischer claims that she had wanted to lead Germany to a plural, internationalist, and democratic version of socialism, complete with freedom to debate and dissent. Favoring local parties over a centralized Soviet leadership, she actually succeeded in getting elected to the German Reichstag and saw herself as an active part of a parliamentary process. She viewed Stalin as a totalitarian dictator with imperialist aims, not only on a par with Hitler but actually an important accessory to Hitler's rise to power.[15] Moscow, not surprisingly, found her hostile and cast her out of the Party, though not before Stalin had held her captive for ten months in a Moscow hotel. Her expulsion brought about her estrangement

83

from her brother Gerhart, whose commitment to Stalin was stronger than his family ties. She then fell out with Hanns, too, because he was in contact with Gerhart.[16] In the late 1930s, Ruth Fischer left Europe for the States, where she spoke out against Stalin, worked for the CIA's Congress for Cultural Freedom, and wrote a book called *Stalin and German Communism*, which explained how German communists had become the puppets of Moscow. In the 1940s, to her alarm, she discovered that both of her brothers were living in the States, and she feared for her life, believing that either one might assassinate her for the good of the Soviet Union. Intent on encouraging the US government to quell her brothers' Stalinist activities, Fischer immediately notified the authorities. Gerhart, she testified to HUAC, was "a most dangerous terrorist, both to the people of America and to the people of Germany"; and, she said, he had been "directly dispatched from Moscow to take over Communist affairs in this country." Hanns was "close to Gerhart" and thus surely favored Stalin too.[17]

Charlie Chaplin, startled by the global plotting and counterplotting among the Eislers, remarked to Hanns: "In your family, things happen as in Shakespeare."[18] But it was not only family connections that worried Ruth Fischer. She argued that the most significant proof of Hanns's threat to democratic ideals was none other than his collaboration with Bertolt Brecht on *The Measures Taken*. In *Stalin and German Communism*, Fischer singled out *The Measures Taken* as a play that favored precisely the Stalinist ideology she found most repugnant: it made a case for the supremacy of party discipline and for the suppression of any dissent or dialogue.[19] Fischer saw many of Brecht's plays as preaching totalitarian values, "the sacrifice of the individual to the collective, the substitutability of any individual for another, the non-validity of individual morality with respect to the collective, the necessity and inflexibility of the hierarchical order, the inevitability and strange beauty of terror." For her, *The Measures Taken* was the play that "best digests all the terroristic features into the mirror of the totalitarian party."[20] And so, despite the fact that *The Measures Taken* was neither Eisler's most famous musical work nor

Brecht's best known play, it was the work that most unnerved Ruth Fischer, with her commitment to a liberal, pluralist socialism, and it was the play that ended up in Hanns Eisler's FBI file. Presumably, then, it was largely thanks to Ruth Fischer that Brecht, when he testified before HUAC in 1947, was asked to talk about two of his least known works: *The Measures Taken*, which was Ruth Fischer's *bête noir*, and the screenplay for *Hangmen Also Die*, which implicated Hollywood as a whole.

Ironically, although Fischer argued that Brecht's plays perfectly served Stalin's interests, the Soviet government felt that Brecht had blithely disregarded them. The International Association of Revolutionary Writers in Moscow called *The Measures Taken* "a typically petty-bourgeois, intellectualist piece of work" and condemned Brecht for knowing too little about the actual day-to-day work of engaging in a revolution.[21] And the Stalinists were not the only ones to loathe the anti-conventional avant-garde. Influential voices in the United States were busy making the case that the European avant-garde was dangerously un-American. Congressman George Dondero, a Republican from Michigan, named each of the European avant-garde movements and explained how all were "vehicles of destruction," undermining the values the United States stood for.[22] Even the liberal American art world resisted the intrusion of the avant-garde. The Vice-President of the American Artists' Professional League wrote to "question the cultural value of any exhibition which is . . . marked with the radicalism of the new trends of European art."[23] Meanwhile, for Ruth Fischer, with her abhorrence of both Hitler and Stalin, it was precisely Brecht's avant-garde techniques that seemed brilliantly to serve Stalin's Comintern: "In avant-garde abstractions, Brecht achieves the transfiguration and beatification of the Stalinist party."[24] In good minoritarian fashion, the avant-garde techniques of Brecht and Eisler managed to repel all sides.

All sides – HUAC, Brecht, Fischer, the Soviets – claimed to stand for freedom. But it is not easy to decide which one actually claimed the high ground. Ruth Fischer's logic helps us to see how complicated the question of freedom really was. From Fischer's perspective, the severe disciplining of sympathy and dissent and the demand for total obedience which Brecht dramatized in *The Measures Taken* revealed the worst of Stalinist control. But if *Hangmen Also Die* is anything to go by, a remarkably similar moral about discipline and heroism, written by the same author, seemed to serve a wholly different, and for Fischer, far more sympathetic, cause: the struggle of Czech nationalists banding together against the Nazi enemy. And it is far from clear that such a "totalitarian" lesson was so out of place in the US: if the moral of *Hangmen Also Die* was all about self-sacrifice and discipline for a cause, it might include praising soldiers for risking their lives for US freedom and requesting the surrender of certain individual freedoms in the interests of defeating the enemy. These values were certainly not alien − or even particularly disagreeable − to American audiences.

Ironically, then, Ruth Fischer informed on Brecht as an enemy of freedom, but he shared the very values she admired in her democratic allies. Even more ironically, it was in the name of freedom that Fischer turned Brecht in to HUAC, a body determined to curb precisely the freedoms of speech and assembly she was eager to see preserved. And in the end, the very group Fischer thought Brecht was serving − the Soviets − hated the play. Meanwhile, Brecht himself clearly needed the kinds of individual civil liberties Fischer was devoted to if he was going to write and show his work, though the work he wanted to create was all about the repression of individual freedom.

All of these ironies can be traced to a familiar split between the desire for a strongly united collective, on the one hand, and the desire for the freedom of expression, on the other. In the interests of strength, security, and unity, all sides were worried that dissenting voices would undermine their cause; and in the interests of advancing their own positions, all sides craved and protected a freedom of expression that would extend only as far as their own points of view. Ruth Fischer's commitment to freedom got her expelled from the Communist Party, and in retaliation and fear, she collaborated with the US authorities, who were busy clamping down on the very freedoms she had fought for. Brecht and Eisler pleaded with HUAC to recognize the importance of art to freedom, though what they wanted to be free to write was drama that urged rigid obedience to the communist leadership. The Soviets demanded an art that would complement their revolutionary politics, but rather than freeing artists to create radically new work, they insisted on a single style. And Congress was insisting that it was crucial to limit freedom of speech in film and the other arts because otherwise the communists would infiltrate, take over, and limit precisely the freedoms they were already busy restricting.

Just about everyone was looking hypocritical. And what no one realized, yet, was that the freedom of the artist and the strength of the state could join forces, in a subtle and delicate balance that had more power than either one, alone, could ever hope for.

## Freedom as Jackson Pollock

Restrictions on artistic freedom might not seem like too bitter a pill to swallow at home in the US, where people were frightened into giving up their civil liberties, but they were a serious matter when it came to the image of the US in other parts of the world. Both sides of the Cold War, fighting for the allegiance of the unaligned in Europe, Latin America, Asia, and Africa, worked tirelessly to promote their respective systems, and in the shadow of the military build-up they waged a grim battle for the minds of the uncommitted. The Soviet Union charged that the US was a shallow and materialist culture, feeding the people glitzy matinee idols while the poorest starved, and obsessed only with wealth and military might. In 1947, the Assistant Secretary of State, William Benton, argued that the State Department needed to answer the Soviets on cultural grounds, since the "heroes of the Russians are not the generals but the propagandists." He called for an inquiry into "cultural diplomacy." The cornerstone of any diplomatic mission would include the argument that the West supported essential freedoms, including unparalleled liberty for artists, writers, and intellectuals.[25]

87

In the late 1940s, when Brecht testified before HUAC, it was becoming clear that the US was failing quite miserably at the task of broadcasting its commitment to freedom. In 1947, Congressman Fred Busbey of Illinois made a public stink about *Advancing American Art*, a daring new exhibition of modern American painters – including Romare Bearden, Arshile Gorky, Jacob Lawrence, Robert Motherwell, and Georgia O'Keefe – that had been touring Europe and Latin America, funded by the State Department.[26] Since the Armory Show had come to America in 1913, new trends in modern art had seemed to many conservatives to reek of left-wing subversion and alien influence. Tying the avant-garde aesthetics of the show to Soviet politics, the *New York Journal-American* called the paintings "definitely leftish" and publicized links between eight of the artists and the Communist Party.[27] Other newspapers went along with the offensive, and the result was a fierce letter-writing campaign in which outraged citizens demanded that Congress cancel the show.[28] To most committed anti-communists, the suppression of any work that might incorporate subtle Soviet propaganda was justified, and certainly it seemed scandalous for the State Department to sponsor subversive art. On May 5, 1947, the House Appropriations Committee cut off funds for the show, and new Secretary of State George Marshall summarily ordered it dismantled. The individual works were quickly sold off, and lucky buyers found that they could purchase some of the best new American art at a 95 percent discount. Jacob Lawrence's *Harlem* (1946) was snapped up for $13.93.[29]

The withdrawal of the show came as a blow to the State Department, which had been eager for opportunities to showcase US artistic freedom and innovation abroad in order to outshine Soviet art, with its formulaic styles and messages. In this respect, *Advancing American Art* had been a rousing success. Innovative, bold, and unexpected, the paintings had actually begun to persuade audiences in Eastern Europe and Latin America that the US was "not all military might and Hollywood movies, but a country capable of culture."[30] In the Cold War context, the uncomfortable strangeness of the avant-garde was becoming precisely its virtue, where anything experimental, original, or even simply eccentric could be taken as evidence of democracy's capacity to accommodate free spirits. Thus, in answer to the popular question, "Is modern art communistic?" Alfred Barr, Director of the Museum of Modern Art, answered confidently: "The modern artist's non-conformity and love of freedom cannot be tolerated within a monolithic tyranny."[31] But with US opinion at home so thoroughly hostile to contemporary trends in art, the campaign was not going to be easy. Benton, the champion of "cultural diplomacy," was forced to resign from the State Department in disgrace because of his part in *Advancing American Art*, and Joseph McCarthy was about to begin his ferocious witch hunts, including an all-out attack on Benton for his willingness to show "lewd" art works by artists with communist sympathies.

Caught between Soviet attacks on American popular culture and domestic assaults on avant-garde art, US leaders began to craft a complex diplomatic strategy – one that was deliberately paradoxical. Tom Braden, one of Allen Dulles's right-hand men in the newly formed CIA, realized that the greatest obstacle to the making of an art that could glorify democracy was democracy itself:

> I've forgotten which pope it was who commissioned the Sistine Chapel
> . . . but I suppose that if it had been submitted to a vote of the Italian
> people there would have been many, many negative responses. "It's
> naked," or "It isn't the way I imagined God," or whatever. I don't
> think it would have gotten through the Italian parliament, if there
> had been a parliament at the time. . . . You always have to battle your
> own ignoramuses, or, to put it more politely, people who just don't
> understand.[32]

If the US was going to persuade the world into pursuing a splendidly democratic future, it was going to be necessary to bypass democratic processes. "In order to encourage openness," Braden explained, "we had to be secret."[33]

The CIA's role in cultural life in the 1940s and 1950s is now widely known, but at the time they kept their operations successfully covert. They set up false foundations to fund modern art so that neither the artists nor the public would know that the government was supporting radical and unpopular work. They had contacts within the major charitable foundations – Carnegie, Rockefeller, and Ford – whom they persuaded to sponsor exhibitions and performances worldwide to serve US foreign policy aims. In fact, the boards of directors of a vast array of cultural organizations, from the Museum of Modern Art and the Rockefeller Foundation to *Time-Life* and the Boston Symphony Orchestra, included names of men and women who worked for the State Department or had close ties to the CIA.[34] A covert cultural policy specifically targeted the so-called "Non-Communist Left" both at home and overseas, secretly founding and supporting left-leaning journals and intellectual and political organizations, from the *Partisan Review* to the British Labour Party, in order to persuade those whose allegiances might incline toward Soviet Communism – or just as harmfully, toward neutrality – that alliance with the US was appealing because of its hospitality to experimentation, innovation, and freedom of thought. The Congress for Cultural Freedom, a CIA front organization, funded major avant-garde concerts, performances, and art exhibitions worldwide to glorify the US. And they did it all without the knowledge of Congress, which was caught in the grip of McCarthyist panic, sensing Soviet sympathizers around every corner and preoccupied with the task of tearing every trace of communism out of American life.[35] Later, the Congressional "red scare" would seem dramatically overblown, since there were so few card-carrying communists in the United States in the 1950s that it was said that most of the members of the party were actually FBI agents, whose dues payments kept the organization from dying out altogether.[36] But at the time, few were willing to stand up to McCarthy, and most leaders seemed willing to agree, at least publicly, that whatever it took to defeat communism was well worth a few sacrifices.

If HUAC restricted freedom in the name of freedom, the CIA bypassed democratic processes in the name of democracy. But maybe these contradictions should not come as a surprise. Because the majority can turn tyrannical, intent on drowning out marginal and rebellious voices, democracy always runs the risk of limiting freedom. And because a perfect example of freedom is the right of minority and oppositional voices to speak out against the mainstream, freedom always runs the risk of weakening democracy. Both Congress and the CIA would have claimed that the US, unlike the Soviet Union, could be held up as a pillar of *both* freedom and democracy. But the Cold War makes it clear how agonizingly hard it was to serve both values at once. And so Congress betrayed freedom in the name of strong democracy, while the CIA circumvented democracy in the name of freedom.

It was in this thorny political milieu that the avant-garde painter Jackson Pollock came to function as an ideal vehicle for US Cold War propaganda. Pollock was one of a loosely affiliated group of artists who came to be known as the Abstract Expressionists. Joining the intellectual work of cubist abstraction with the expression of strong emotion found in fauvism and expressionism, they opened up a radically new avenue in painting.[37] Among the painters associated with the movement were Arshile Gorky, Willem de Kooning, Lee Krasner, Robert Motherwell, Barnett Newman, Mark Rothko, Clyfford Still – and, most famously, Jackson Pollock.

Unlike most of his Ab Ex fellows, Pollock was recognizably – even stereotypically – American. Born in Wyoming, he swaggered and drank like a cowboy. He had studied with American regionalist painter Thomas Hart Benton and began his career painting figurative scenes. Later he worked with the radical Mexican muralist David Alfaro Siqueiros, making Marxist-inspired "art for the people," including a float for a Communist Party rally which showed the destruction of Wall Street financiers by angry workers.[38] But in the late 1940s, Pollock began turning away from figurative painting in favor of abstraction, numbering rather than naming many of his works. He introduced a shocking new signature method – "drip painting" – which did not involve conventional brushwork at all. Instead, different actions of the artist's wrists and arms – throwing, flicking, dribbling, and pouring – produced a range of expressive patterns on the canvas. Tough and athletic, Pollock offered a usefully masculine

**Figure 3.2** Jackson Pollock in his East Hampton studio, ca. 1947. Image originally photographed by Wilfrid Zogbaum, and is courtesy of the Jackson Pollock and Less Krasner papers, ca. 1905–1984, in the Archives of American Art, Smithsonian Institution. © 2007 Estate of Wilfrid Zogbaum/Artists Rights Society (ARS), New York, © 2007 Pollock-Krasner Foundation/Artists Rights Society (ARS), New York.

understanding of the art of painting, drawing attention to its potential for vigorous physicality. His works were often enormous in size, and they could appear violently emotional – rebellious, enraged, sorrowful, and joyous (figure 3.2). Casting off a whole assortment of painterly conventions, Pollock boasted of liberating painting with his ground-breaking techniques, and allowed himself to be photographed throwing himself into startlingly dynamic activity.

The CIA saw in Pollock a kind of perfect distillation of Cold War aims. Defiant and challenging, staggeringly original and anti-conventional, he proved that American culture had taken precisely the road the Soviets had refused. But here Pollock's story, like Brecht's, gets complicated. Pollock could not simply make his art and, by doing so, automatically stand for American art as a whole. As far as the CIA was concerned, he first had to become a public figure. So the Agency helped to build up a complex institutional framework that allowed Jackson Pollock to represent the rebellious, freethinking outsider on a global stage, liberating art from its conventional shackles and demonstrating American freedom to the world.

First of all, Ab Ex needed to become famous. Pollock and most of the artists in his circle had been laboring in obscurity for some years, poor and marginal.[39] But a complicated network of arts institutions would come to the rescue – all of them with close ties to the CIA. When the State Department sheepishly withdrew the *Advancing American Art* show in 1947, John Hay Whitney and Allen Dulles of the CIA "agreed that they had to do something about modern art."[40] But they knew they could not fund artists openly, because the artists would probably object to working for the CIA:

> matters of this sort could only be done through the organizations or the operations of the CIA at two or three [steps] removed, so that there wouldn't be any question of having to clear Jackson Pollock, for example, or do anything that would involve these people in the organization. . . . [M]ost of them were people who had very little respect for the government in particular and certainly none for the CIA.[41]

93

This was a new version of the paradox. In order to find and promote artists who stood for the kind of freedom the American government wanted to broadcast to the world, that government had to hide their support from the artists, who saw themselves as outside the system, too radical and anti-conventional to act as agents of government policy. The Ab Ex painters would have felt that they were precisely too free to act as official representatives of freedom.

So the CIA kept one step ahead. Friends and connections at the Museum of Modern Art in New York, for one, offered clandestine help. René d'Harnoncourt, the Museum's director from 1949 to 1967, consulted with the National Security Council's Operations Coordinating Board, and his own rhetoric was in keeping with the state's efforts at cultural diplomacy: modern art, he said, "in its infinite variety and ceaseless exploration, is the 'foremost symbol' of democracy."[42] Sponsoring shows and collecting works of the Ab Ex painters through the 1940s, MoMA helped to boost the artists from obscurity to international renown. The CIA also worked under cover of the Congress for Cultural Freedom to send exhibits abroad; one of the CIA front organizations, the Farfield Foundation, doled out money to artists as though it was a private donor; and trustees of the major museums, with their ties to the CIA and State Department, agreed to establish international recognition for American avant-gardists for the sake of the US image abroad (figure 3.3). MoMA organized the first show dedicated solely to Ab Ex painters in Paris, a show that was actually funded by Nelson Rockefeller, later Eisenhower's special advisor on Cold War strategy, and planned covertly by the American embassy in Paris.[43] At home in the States, influential figures within the art world who had government ties undertook similar efforts to make the Abstract Expressionists famous. Alfred Barr, d'Harnoncourt's predecessor at MoMA, persuaded his friend Henry Luce of *Time-Life* to support Abstract Expressionism because it represented the kind of "artistic free enterprise" that was abhorred by the Soviet Union.[44] One result was a major piece on Jackson Pollock in *Life* in 1949, which lent the artist a notoriety among the general public unprecedented for

**Figure 3.3**  Installation view of the exhibition "Modern Art in the
United States: Selections from the collections of the Museum of
Modern Art," organized by the International Program of the Museum
of Modern Art (July 6–August 6, 1956). Kalemegdan Pavilion, Belgrade,
Yugoslavia. Photo: Museum of Modern Art, New York. Digital Image
© Museum of Modern Art/Licensed by SCALA/Art Resource, NY,
© 2007 Pollock-Krasner Foundation/Artists Rights Society (ARS),
New York.

the American avant-garde.[45] Cast as a complex mixture of Wild West
frontiersman and romantic artistic rebel, Pollock would eventually
become a mythic figure in popular culture: "all-American tough guy,
drunkard, folk hero."[46]

Pollock's fame did not bring him unqualified praise. To the contrary: *Time* magazine nicknamed him "Jack the Dripper," and a host

of other magazines and newspapers mocked his wild technique. But this was all to the good, from the CIA's point of view. After all, an artist like Jackson Pollock could not demonstrate his unsettling and revolutionary shattering of constraints unless he managed to disturb conservative audiences. In this context, it was only an advantage that modern art drew public revulsion and scorn: mocked by the press for their wild daubings and loathed by populists in Congress for their enigmatic innovations, the Ab Ex group were the ideal figures to demonstrate to the world that no matter how distasteful artists might seem to the general public, the United States still allowed them to flourish. One CIA official went so far as to suggest that if an artist found himself "closer to Moscow than to Washington," then "so much the better": his early communist ties would help to hide the government's involvement in the arts and allow the artist to seem the perfect rebel, entirely untrammeled by official recognition or connections.[47] Though it has become a commonplace that Ab Ex painting suited the propaganda needs of the Cold War because it rejected explicit thematic content – and so could seem apolitical rather than "left" – the CIA seems not to have minded the left-leaning associations of Pollock and his cohort. The logic of the CIA's cultural propaganda campaign was in fact consummately avant-garde: its figures had to be vilified and rejected, estranged from the mainstream and intent on casting off the past.

For propaganda purposes, then, it was actually crucial for the avant-garde to operate both outside and inside the democratic state. Though the US government had helped to organize a complex clandestine network of funding sources, museums, galleries, and publications to draw international attention to a group of rebellious artists, the artists needed to feel – and appear – like outsiders. Propaganda for the state worked best when the artists felt brave and daring, derided by the press and rejected by lovers of more traditional art. The government could then tell skeptical foreigners that the US was a safe haven for artists even when – as it could safely claim – it disagreed with their messages. Thus Abstract Expressionist painters became propagandists for the state precisely because they refused to work on behalf of the state, and they became representatives of democracy precisely because they were hated by "the people."

By 1954, President Eisenhower himself was starting to sound a little like Bertolt Brecht, arguing that restrictions on artists signaled constraints on freedom for everyone:

> Freedom of the arts is a basic freedom, one of the pillars of liberty in our land. For our Republic to stay free, those among us with the rare gift of artistry must be able freely to use their talent. . . . As long as artists are at liberty to feel with high personal intensity, as long as our artists are free to create with sincerity and conviction, there will be healthy controversy and progress in art. . . . How different it is in tyranny. When artists are made the slaves and tools of the state; when artists become chief propagandists of a cause, progress is arrested and creation and genius are destroyed.[48]

It is hard to miss the irony. Eisenhower's encomium to artistic freedom was itself part of a canny strategy to make artists into "slaves and tools of the state" and "chief propagandists of a cause."

## Avant-Garde Cold Warrior: Richard Nixon

Only one major figure in the Cold War seems to have stood on both sides of the strange logic of the avant-garde, supporting both majority rule and artistic freedom. Richard Nixon is an unlikely ally of the avant-garde, to be sure, but he – of all people – is one of the few to have taken advantage of its rebellious marginality by both decrying art as an enemy of the people and celebrating it as an emblem of American freedom.

Nixon first made his name as an aggressive young member of HUAC. His maiden speech to Congress warned of the danger posed by a particularly dangerous resident alien, "Gerbert Eisler, alias Berger, alias Brown, alias Gerhart, alias Edwards, alias Liptzin, alias Eisman, a seasoned agent of the Communist International, who had been shuttling back and forth between Moscow and the United States from as early as 1933, to direct and mastermind the political and espionage activities of the Communist Party in the United States." Nixon took advantage of the dangers posed by Gerhart Eisler to suggest that it was sometimes necessary to limit freedom in the name of freedom:

> It is essential as Members of this House that we defend vigilantly the fundamental rights of freedom of speech and freedom of the press. But we must bear in mind that the rights of free speech and free press do not carry with them the right to advocate the destruction of the very government which protects the freedom of an individual to express his views.[49]

Eisler was the first, but he was by no means Nixon's only target. The young politician won his seats in both the House and the Senate by smearing his opponents as communist sympathizers, and he was most famous for his interrogation of Alger Hiss, the case that helped to catapult him to the vice-presidency. He was absent from the HUAC hearings on the day that Brecht testified, but as a member and sometime chair of HUAC, he took an active part in the investigation of suspected communists in Hollywood. In 1949, Nixon took the campaign against leftists in the art world to a new extreme, urging Congress "to make a thorough investigation of . . . art in government buildings with the view of obtaining removal of all that is found to be inconsistent with American 'ideals and principles.' "[50] Thus he began his powerful career by red-baiting not only fellow politicians, but visual artists, writers, composers, and actors whose rebellious defiance was enough, at that time, to get them categorized as a danger to national security.

By December 10, 1969, Richard Nixon had changed his tune. Now President of the United States, he sent a special message to Congress arguing for the importance of federal support for the arts:

> The arts have attained a prominence in our life as a nation and in our consciousness as individuals, that renders their health and growth vital to our national well-being. America has moved to the forefront

as a place of creative expression. The excellence of the American product in the arts has won worldwide recognition. . . . Our creative and performing artists give free and full expression to the American spirit as they illuminate, criticize and celebrate our civilization.[51]

Nixon was right. Thanks in no small part to the efforts of the CIA, American artists had indeed gained international renown, not only by illuminating and celebrating US values and traditions, but also, as Nixon claimed here, by criticizing them.

Gesturing to the international value of the free and critical artist, Nixon asked Congress to approve a significant increase in support for the arts. In so doing, he startled not only his opponents but his own Republican base.[52] Even the original tiny amount of $5 million allocated to federal arts support had been bitterly opposed by Republicans and conservative Democrats in the House. And in the late 1960s, under pressure from conservatives concerned about leftist art works, Congress cut individual grants to artists.[53] But Nixon's first year in office marked a dramatic rise in federal arts funding. From 1969 onward, his commitment to the arts was ever more extravagant. He proposed to double the NEA budget initially, and Congress agreed, providing $20 million for 1971, $30 million for 1972, and $40 million for 1973. When the NEA was reauthorized again in 1973, Nixon requested yet more money, climbing to an all-time high of $126 million.[54] As late as 1974, he was praising the NEA for "encouraging original fresh expression" and conveying "most fully the ideals of this Nation."[55] The "improbable patron" also invited Duke Ellington to the White House and sent the rock group Blood, Sweat and Tears on a tour of Eastern Europe, publicizing both events internationally so that young people around the world would be impressed by White House inclusiveness.[56]

Given Nixon's long-term dedication to routing out subversive elements in American culture, what was it that prompted his about-face concerning artists? His decision to pour unprecedented sums of money into the arts was particularly surprising given his own disdain for modern art and the fact that it came at a moment

99

when artists were raging against the state, the Vietnam War, and US imperialism. Historian Richard Jensen offers one hypothesis:

> Richard Nixon's main political rival in the 1960s was Nelson Rockefeller, and as president, Nixon used the NEA in competitive fashion. To run NEA, Nixon chose Nancy Hanks, a former close aide to Rockefeller who had played a central role in promoting local arts councils. When Rockefeller boosted the New York State Arts budget from $2 million in 1970 to $20 million in 1971, Nixon stunned the arts world by asking for and getting comparable increases from Congress.[57]

Rockefeller was one of the powerful figures in the network of Cold Warriors who linked the art world to the CIA.[58] By funneling money into the arts, Nixon was not only competing with Rockefeller, he was also making use of his rival's savvy about cultural diplomacy.[59]

Just as Nixon was the only President who could go to China and escape being labeled soft on communism, he was perhaps the only one who could openly insist on doling out record sums of money to the arts without becoming known as an effete, left-leaning intellectual out of touch with popular taste.[60] On the one hand, as a leading voice in HUAC, he had helped to channel and encourage the feelings of a frightened mainstream, scared by communism and unsettled by modern art. Fighting for a united and strong democracy in a time of apparent crisis, he had made an impassioned case for limits on freedom. On the other hand, as President, Nixon used modern art to play to the elite and the left-leaning intelligentsia, the minority interests who hated him precisely for his HUAC populism. Fighting for the arts as exemplars of American freedom, he ditched his populist base and defended the voices on the margins. Thus in his dual persona – first as fanatical censor of the arts and then as generous patron – Nixon lived out the complex logic of the avant-garde. Standing for both populist outrage and minority expression, for both a strong democracy and the challenging voices of dissident freedom, he was the improbable embodiment of a self-contradictory US policy toward the arts in the Cold War.

## Conclusion

The story of avant-garde propaganda suggests a complex and clandestine support for the arts, a set of sinister machinations on the part of the state. But what this Machiavellian complexity obscures is the fact that the government did not simply censor artists; nor did it force them to sell out. Rather, two arms of the government worked together, albeit unwittingly, to *produce* the logic of the avant-garde. During the Cold War, the CIA and the Congress might have seemed at odds, but together these governmental institutions created the structure that allowed the crucial tension to materialize: while Congress spoke for the majority, the CIA reclaimed the beleaguered margins; while domestic policy produced a sense of a strong mainstream, foreign policy showcased the startling innovations of some remarkably rebellious talents. The same government that had Brecht tailed and confined as an "enemy alien" allowed Pollock to stand as an emblem of American freedom.

If liberal democracies seem strangely self-divided – even hypocritical – when it comes to wartime propaganda, these contradictions are a logical outcome of the form of liberal democracy itself. The liberal democratic state typically prides itself on internal checks and balances, on resisting tyranny precisely by refusing the model of the single, streamlined government in favor of complex networks of conflicting institutional bodies, some elected and some appointed, some answerable to popular sovereignty and others to executives, bureaucratic hierarchies, or legal precedents. Liberal democracies typically include bodies that unsettle both mob rule and special interest groups within the state apparatus. They are always internally split. It is therefore only if we think of the state as a single monolithic entity that its divisions seem bizarrely self-contradictory. To be sure, there is no question that restraining freedom in the name of freedom is hypocritical – even dangerously so. But restraining democracy in the name of freedom and restraining freedom in the name of democracy are less acts of hypocrisy than structural facts of the internally divided and necessarily contradictory liberal democratic state. In this context, the divisive and rebellious avant-garde plays a counter-majoritarian role that is part and parcel of the careful balance struck by liberal democratic governance: the artist takes the position of freedom in the longstanding, tense standoff between the strong, united collective and the principle of counter-majoritarian dissent.

So it would be a mistake to say that renegade artists are victims of state repression, just as it would be inaccurate to say that these artists are entirely free from political interests or institutions – even when they think they are. Nor is unpopular art an enemy of democracy, as its detractors sometimes claim. During the Cold War, thanks to Congress and the CIA together, the most experimental artists refused to serve the state – and so ended up serving the state.

Perverse though it is, this is the logic of the avant-garde at war.

# 4

# *Obscenity and the Democratization of Culture*

> Two little girlies
> Went to court for fun.
> The lawyers read Ulysses –
> Then there was one.
> *New York Daily News* (May 18, 1934)

From Gustave Flaubert to Allen Ginsberg, the art world has entered the courtroom in a blaze of contempt and derision. How dare the courts repress art's radical expression, its libidinal play, its emancipatory openness? In artists' accounts, obscenity trials emerge as particularly loathsome. D. H. Lawrence could hardly contain his scorn for the "censor-moron," and when Robert Mapplethorpe's art went to trial in Cincinnati, the *Village Voice* groaned, "Your Patriarchy at Work."[1]

As we have seen, artists since the dawn of the avant-garde have been inclined to take on the role of rebellious outsiders, rejecting social norms, commercial pressures, public approval, and official sanction. It seems logical, in this context, for resistant artists to find themselves locked in a hostile struggle with the disciplinary agents of the law. Voices on opposing sides of legal battles over the arts tend to confirm this view, claiming either that artists are subversive outsiders hunted down by a narrow-minded judiciary, or that they are no better than criminals who need to be brought into line by the responsible force of law. But this chapter will show that both

103

sides miss the mark: the history of obscenity law is closely inter-twined with the story of the avant-garde, and the two are far more harmonious than we have come to expect.

Intriguingly, obscenity law and avant-garde art emerged and matured at about the same time, the first significant spate of ob-scenity prosecutions happening around the same time as the first avant-garde artists were distancing themselves from their societies.[2] Historians typically link the upsurge in obscenity prosecutions to the sudden flood of popular culture in the nineteenth century: faster and cheaper technologies of print and paper production, dramatic increases in literacy rates, and inexpensive photographic reproduc-tions brought a flood of accessible cultural objects into a newly vast marketplace. And with the rise of cheaply made and widely distributed "mass culture" – "when it began to seem possible that anything at all might be shown to anybody" – anxieties about moral instability began to escalate, and new barriers were imposed on expression.[3] "In other words," writes historian Lynn Hunt, "pornography as a regulatory category was invented in response to the perceived menace of the democratization of culture."[4] Just as in our own time, when the internet has provoked new apprehensions about the dramatic democratization of media, in the nineteenth century it was the explosion in print and photography that threatened a sense of stable culture.[5]

Surprisingly, then, obscenity law – like the debates over public art and propaganda – turns on the question of democracy. In the first spate of obscenity prosecutions, the most contentious debates about the relationship between art and democracy concerned the regula-tion of high culture. Some courts argued that classic works of art, though safe for refined elites, were corrupting if they reached the masses. In one infamous instance, the tireless warrior against smut, Anthony Comstock, set up a trap to catch Herman Knoedler, an eminent Fifth Avenue art dealer, who was selling photographic reproductions of paintings – including nudes – from Paris. The press was outraged that such a respected and exclusive gallery should come under fire, and Knoedler and his supporters stated that "his customers were among the most refined and intelligent people in the country."[6] But Comstock himself protested that he was carefully distinguishing between genuine art and cheap copies:

> These photographs I have seized, sir, are not works of art. They are sold wholesale at fifty cents a piece to small dealers. . . . A grand oil painting, with its massive coloring, its artistic surroundings, its grand shadings and streaks of light, all of which create a work of art, ceases to be such when presented in a photograph, which gives mere outlines of form, and that is all. Again, let me add, if you please, that the very cost of art precludes it from being gaped at – stared at by the masses, who have no conception of the grandeur of the merits of such a work – and would, if they had a chance, merely admire . . . the bare nudity if you so call it, without letting their minds or their eyes, even if they could, rest upon the grand surroundings.[7]

As usual in arts controversies, the opposing sides actually held a surprisingly deep set of assumptions in common: Knoedler's supporters defended him on the grounds that his clients were too refined to be accused of indecency, but Comstock too distinguished between elite, "safe" audiences for high art and the unthinking masses who could neither afford nor appreciate great canvases. The real difference hinged on the social value of high art when it *crossed over* into mass culture. Comstock argued that photographs widened the works' distribution so far beyond the gallery's sophisticated milieu that they allowed art to travel where it would no longer seem grand and dignified. Knoedler's side responded with the assertion that "the popularization of such works of art by photography [is] of the greatest educational benefit to society."[8] The democratization of art itself was at stake. In the end, the judge ruled cautiously, finding two of the 37 photographs obscene and dismissing the charges against the rest.[9]

The courts would go back and forth, over the next few decades, about the dangers and values of high art in a world of cheap mass production. A few judges would rule in favor of classic or highly respected art works, struggling to protect works of high culture that might be mistakenly lumped in with obscenity. These decisions typically drew on elitist arguments. In the words of one New York judge: "There is no . . . evil to be feared from the sale of these rare and costly books . . . [which] would not be bought nor appreciated by the class of people from whom unclean publications ought to be withheld."[10] And although the courts came to different decisions, they tended to agree on their picture of the cultural field as a whole: there were two audiences out there, one high and one low, one sophisticated and one uneducated, one susceptible to corruption and the other unassailable. There were also two kinds of culture: the "rare and costly" as opposed to the inexpensive and mass produced. And whichever way the courts went, the law typically emerged as a force against the democratization of culture: either it protected an art that was too elevated for the people to appreciate, or it protected the people from corruption by an art they might choose to consume.

While the law was busily responding to the sudden power of mass production by holding on to the distinction between "high" and "low" culture, the artists associated with the newly emergent avant-garde were reacting to the same divisions in the cultural field. But unlike the courts, the artists began to set themselves against *both* traditional "high" art and the sudden and overwhelming tide of "low" culture, struggling to carve out a sphere that would be free of both traditional elites and the masses. Their insistence on an autonomous art – unconstrained by the pressures of tradition, the market, academic standards, the state, and popular taste – gradually took hold as a defining aspect of art itself. And as the challenges of the avant-garde grew more visible and more inescapable, the courts gradually adopted a new way of reasoning about art. Rather than worrying about art's power to corrupt and deprave mass audiences, obscenity law began to define art's value as distinct from its effects on "the people." What gradually emerged in legal judgments was an art that was neither elite and refined nor dangerous and destructive: it was, instead, autonomous, innovative, often difficult, and valiantly anti-conventional. Obscenity law, as we will see, began to adopt the logic of the avant-garde.

106

I suggested in the first chapter that the judiciary in liberal states is often understood as a *counter-majoritarian* institution – a check on the whims and swings of a volatile majority. This is not a simple claim, of course, since the courts are themselves checked by the other branches of government.[11] They are also famous for following election returns – reflecting the nitty-gritty of democratic politics rather than rising above it.[12] And in fact many legal theorists have argued that the image of the court as "counter-majoritarian hero" is overblown.[13] But if the judiciary is not wholly independent of popular sovereignty, its limited autonomy is nonetheless often understood to provide a curb on majority tyranny. A famous footnote in the 1938 case of *United States v. Carolene Products Co.* calls for "judicial inquiry" in cases where legislation grows out of "prejudice against discrete and insular minorities."[14] In his classic work on Constitutional law, *Democracy and Distrust*, John Hart Ely argues that the *Carolene* footnote is no anomaly: the framers of the US Constitution assumed that the majority could always be trusted to protect its own interests, but that a fair democratic political process must ensure procedural protections for the few who might be unjustly burdened for the sake of the many. Elected representatives cannot be trusted to provide for minority groups because they are beholden to majorities, and so appointed judges, "comparative outsiders in our governmental system," are the proper figures to assess whether the laws are "acting as accessories to majority tyranny."[15] Democracies depend on an "outsider" judiciary to protect social outsiders. The courts have certainly been inclined to cast themselves this way – as "havens of refuge for those who might otherwise suffer because they are helpless, weak, outnumbered, or because they are nonconforming victims of prejudice and public excitement."[16]

Who more likely to emerge as "nonconforming victims of public excitement" than the avant-garde? The rebellious artist, deliberately resisting the tyranny of the majority, and alienated from both high and low culture, would appear to be the perfect candidate for such legal protection. Indeed, given the judiciary's sense of *itself* as a "counter-majoritarian hero," we might expect the courts to go to some trouble to protect radical, eccentric, anti-establishment art. And yet, artists and arts advocates have complained bitterly about the intrusion of the law into the domain of art for the past hundred years. Are they simply wrong? This chapter argues that they have certainly missed the fact that the courts act as a crucial democratic ally. A specific affinity between the art world and the law has grown increasingly powerful in the past century. Artists and the courts have gradually come to share an understanding of themselves as counter-majoritarian forces, constructing an autonomous sphere that is not answerable to popular tastes. And the courtroom itself has emerged as a bridge between "the people" and the avant-garde, a place where the "average person" has a chance to be challenged and transformed by anti-conventional art.

This chapter focuses on the American trial of James Joyce's *Ulysses* in 1933, the case against D. H. Lawrence's *Lady Chatterley's Lover* in England in 1960, and the trial of rap group 2 Live Crew in the US in 1990. British and US law differ in significant respects, the most significant of which is the United States' reliance on a written constitution. Obscenity statutes in the US are usually construed as distinctive exceptions to First Amendment protections for speech and interpreted against a constitutional backdrop, and scholars often argue that US law therefore provides a stronger set of safeguards for expression than British law.[17] And yet, obscenity law also reveals an important set of transatlantic continuities. Historically, the first legal definition of obscenity emerged in the British case of *Regina v. Hicklin* (1868). The so-called "Hicklin test" defined material as obscene if it had "the tendency . . . to deprave and corrupt those whose minds are open to such immoral influences, and into whose hands a publication of this sort may fall."[18] Concerned with the most vulnerable audiences, *Hicklin* implied that if a work might reach and harm the most innocent of schoolchildren, it was the law's duty to restrict it. Most US states readily adopted the *Hicklin* definition in the late nineteenth century, and both British and US courts continued to rely on it for decades.[19] Gradually, however, courts in both nations began to dispute and undermine it. Thus all three obscenity trials

108

we shall investigate here share a skeptical relationship to the *Hicklin* definition of obscenity. All three stage a tense and dynamic interaction between democratic majorities and artistic outsiders. And all three suggest that Anglo–American law has come to reserve a special place for the logic of the avant-garde.

## *Ulysses*, the Experts, and the People

As the courts argued about the relative importance of high art and mass culture in the late nineteenth and early twentieth centuries, those who wanted the law to protect art from censorship typically tried to introduce the opinions of respected artists and art critics as proof of the work's seriousness. But this was no easy task. Expert testimony is admissible in court only if it can aid the jury by providing opinions outside of the field of ordinary knowledge and experience. In cases where complex scientific conclusions lie well beyond the scope of an ordinary person's knowledge, expertise is widely understood as indispensable.[20] But does the ordinary person need the help of experts when it comes to the arts?[21] This was implicitly a question about the democratization of culture: does art belong to ordinary people to judge and appreciate, or is it a sphere that requires special skills or insight?

Fifty years of wrangling over the role of the expert witness culminated in the *Ulysses* decision. In the first major phase of obscenity prosecutions, the courts repeatedly fought off attempts to introduce expert witnesses. According to the logic of *Hicklin*, obscenity was a problem that could be settled by ordinary experience, and so any claim to special artistic expertise was immaterial. In 1870, a Pennsylvania court ruled that "Obscenity is determined by the common sense and feelings of mankind, and not by the skill of the learned."[22] In the case where Anthony Comstock had trapped Knoedler, the art dealer, the judge stated that "the jury, and not so-called experts, were the proper persons to determine the morality or immorality of the pictures."[23] And as late as 1928, in the famous trial of Radclyffe Hall's lesbian novel, *The Well of Loneliness*, a British court ruled against expert testimony on the grounds that the question of artistic quality was simply irrelevant to decisions about obscenity: "A book may be a fine piece of literature and yet obscene. Art and obscenity are not dissociated at all."[24]

But the law would soon begin to dissociate them. In the early decades of the twentieth century, as anti-conventional and opaque art works grew more visible and more culturally significant, it became increasingly common to argue that judges and juries could not make sound judgments about art purely on the grounds of their own knowledge and experience. As Oliver Wendell Holmes wrote in 1903:

> It would be a dangerous undertaking for persons trained only in the law to constitute themselves final judges of the worth of [a work of genius], outside of the narrowest and most obvious limits. At the one extreme, some works of genius would be sure to miss appreciation. Their very novelty would make them repulsive until the public had learned the new language in which their author spoke. It may be more than doubted, for instance, whether the etchings of Goya or the paintings of Manet would have been sure of protection when seen for the first time.[25]

The case for expertise here rests on the clearest avant-garde narrative: Holmes cites anti-conventional art works that were once so innovative that they left mainstream tastes and values far behind, but once the public had learned their "new language," they were widely recognized as works of genius. This story, for Holmes, has clear legal consequences: if an appreciation of the art of the future requires special skills or insights, jurists should recognize the limits of their own judgments and defer to the experts.

Joyce's *Ulysses* was famous for defying ordinary skills and knowledge. Widely hailed by critics as the most important literary work of its time, it was also said to be "far too tedious and labyrinthine and bewildering for the untutored and the impressionable who might conceivably be affected by it."[26] The novel was so notoriously incomprehensible, in fact, that – as Barbara Leckie argues – it offered a kind of paradox for obscenity law: "A work is censored, after all, because of its perceived threat to a wide segment of the population . . . Censorship, then, presupposes popularity."[27] Despite its inaccessibility, however, it was also shocking to conventional morals, filled with four-letter words and detailed explorations of sexual desire. During the trial, one woman reportedly fled the courtroom as a blushing lawyer read salacious passages from the novel aloud. The US Attorney asserted that *Ulysses* "begins with blasphemy, runs the whole gamut of sexual perversion, and ends in inexpressible filth and obscenity."[28]

How should the courts deal with a text that promoted lustful thoughts on the one hand, and yet remained radically inaccessible to the ordinary reader on the other? Both parties in the *Ulysses* case waived their right to a trial by jury. Judge Woolsey applauded this decision: "on account of the length of 'Ulysses' and the difficulty of reading it, a jury trial would have been an extremely unsatisfactory, if not an almost impossible method of dealing with it." But the judge did not himself claim special insight or expertise. In fact, he offered a creative new solution to the problem of art experts and democracy. He himself tacked back and forth between "the people" and the experts: on the one hand, he claimed to represent the "normal man," as an ordinary jury would; and yet, he also devoted many weeks not only to reading the text but also to scholarly articles and books about it. And ultimately, the judge made clear that although he had taken the experts seriously, he had not deferred to them altogether: after extensive reading, he produced his own interpretation of the novel and then checked it with two other "normal men," who, he said, agreed with him wholeheartedly.[29]

Woolsey's "epoch-making" final decision marks two clear breaks from precedent.[30] First of all, he abandoned *Hicklin*'s concern for the most vulnerable readers in favor of a new standard: the adult male.[31] Second, his decision welcomed literary expertise: the "normal man" was happy to follow the lead of literary experts both for their interpretative help and for their critical judgment of the text, though he then trusted to himself to decide whether or not their assessments were just. "The reputation of 'Ulysses' in the literary world," he explained, "warranted my taking such time as was necessary to enable me to satisfy myself."[32] With the *Ulysses* decision, then, the "normal man" no longer seemed to be the untutored and susceptible victim of mass circulation. The ordinary person was one who could learn – with the help of experts – to appreciate the most challenging of art works.

Judge Woolsey's *Ulysses* opinion is famous, but on appeal the logic of the avant-garde emerged with even more striking clarity. "Art certainly cannot advance under compulsion to the traditional forms," wrote Augustus Hand for the Second District Court of Appeals, "and nothing in such a field is more stifling to progress than limitation of the right to experiment with a new technique." Against this plea for experimentation and innovation in the arts, a dissenting judge affirmed the demands of majority rule: "the effect on the community can and must be the sole determining factor . . . [W]hile there may be individuals and societies of men and women of peculiar notions or idiosyncrasies . . . the exceptional sensibility, or want of sensibility, of such cannot be allowed as a standard." Minority tastes were to be disregarded, and art understood as serving the community as a whole: "literature exists for the sake of the people, to refresh the weary, to console the sad, to hearten the dull and downcast, to increase man's interest in the world, his joy of living, and his sympathy in all sorts and conditions of men. . . . [A]rt for the people's service is a noble, vital, and permanent element of human life."[33] On the one hand, the rejection of tradition, the promise of the future, and the value of experimentation; on the other, perpetual service to "the people."

Why does this contest between majority tastes and aesthetic innovation matter? I want to suggest that there are three reasons that are important here. First of all, while it is well known that the *Ulysses* trial helped to shift the logic of obscenity law,[34] I want to make a specific case for its legitimation of the logic of the avant-garde. What had first emerged in obscenity trials as a battle between high and

112

low culture was transformed with *Ulysses* into a battle between major-ity values and innovative, difficult, experimental art works. As legal scholar Frederick Schauer argues, the courts became less willing after *Ulysses* "to 'level' the available reading matter to the majority" and more inclined to find in favor of "works which clearly have an intellectual appeal to only a minority of the population."[35] And cru-cially, that minority had ceased to be the wealthy, refined elite of Knoedler's clientele; it had instead become the art world, composed for the most part of vehemently anti-bourgeois outsiders. Many of the experts whose opinions were consulted in the *Ulysses* trial, for example – such as Theodore Dreiser, Archibald MacLeish, John Dos Passos, and Malcolm Cowley – had ties to the radical left and the historical avant-gardes. The masses too had changed their charac-terization in obscenity law with the *Ulysses* decision: emerging less often as susceptible, vulgar, and untutored, they were now more likely to be cast as the bearers of "community standards," the dependable middle-of-the-road. Thus the obscenity battleground increasingly took shape as a struggle between mainstream values and the challenges of strange and unsettling outsiders.

Secondly, the *Ulysses* trial secured the role of expert witnesses in defending the logic of the avant-garde. While everyone agreed that the experimental *Ulysses* was difficult and inscrutable – beyond the comprehension of ordinary readers – both Woolsey and Hand affirmed the value of expertise in helping the nonspecialist to come to a proper assessment of the book.[36] Members of the historical avant-garde themselves routinely scorned experts, suggesting that their own work needed to be unfettered by institutional approval,[37] but when the logic of the avant-garde met the logic of the law, it made sense for expertise to play an essential role. Precisely because the juror rep-resented the "average" or "normal" person, and art deliberately defied the average and the normal, the jury began to seem inadequate to questions of art. And since the law's only significant exception to the rule of ordinary judgment was expertise, art experts – includ-ing rebellious artists themselves – became the proper spokespeople for art's exceptional status.[38]

113

Thirdly, the *Ulysses* trial reveals the complex relationship between insiders and outsiders in the context of obscenity law. By allowing art experts to testify in obscenity cases, the court implicitly empowered three distinct minorities to work against the pressure of majority rule: the counter-majoritarian institution of the judiciary itself; art experts, defined by the special knowledge that transcends ordinary experience; and anti-conventional artists, deliberately repudiating the tastes and values of "the people." And yet, none of these groups are outsiders in any simple way. The courts are part of the larger institution of the liberal state: they assert their independence from executives and legislatures, but they are subject to checks by elected officials in turn. Even more importantly, unless both sides agree to dispense with a jury trial, the courts are obliged to incorporate a little microcosm of "the people" into their own proceedings. Traditionally, the jury is understood to be a crucial institution of democratic freedom: as an impartial group of ordinary citizens who can consult their own consciences and experience, they provide a "common-sense" safeguard against retaliation or corruption by judges or other government officials. They are thus a kind of independent check on the state – including the judiciary – within the judiciary itself.[39] Turning democracy outside-in, juries are representatives of the majority inside the counter-majoritarian realm of the courts. Experts in the courtroom complicate this picture still further, since they are outsiders when it comes to "common sense," but, as sociologists have argued, can themselves often be consummate insiders in their own contexts: licensed and credentialed by tight professional networks that encourage conformity and suppress dissent.[40] By law, in fact, the courts require that experts establish their qualifications on the stand, and so typically they recognize formal degrees or certificates, notices in recognized publications, official positions in arts institutions, or evidence of significant practical experience.[41] The court's experts must therefore prove that they are institutional insiders. The issue of insiders and outsiders becomes even more complex when we consider the relationship between ordinary readers and experts in the courtroom: expert witnesses are capable

114

of educating the "average man," as Judge Woolsey made clear, and indeed, given the frequency with which juries have found in favor of art since experts have been part of obscenity trials, it would seem that expertise can help to convert potentially skeptical "average" audiences into supporters of art. With clear and careful explanations by expert witnesses to bridge the gulf between the ordinary layperson and the knowledgeable insider, the obscenity courtroom can sometimes seem strikingly like a classroom.[42] But if juries, judges, and experts are all *both* insiders and outsiders, what about rebellious artists themselves, with their long tradition as proud exiles from the mainstream? In the obscenity courtroom they can hardly claim to be the radical outliers they might like to seem, since from *Ulysses* onward, they have won special legal protection, and they have done so by relying on the most normative of institutions. Experts, authorized and certified by arts institutions, join with the state to safeguard the shocking challenges of the avant-garde.

## The Whole-Book Rule

There was a second legal question that concerned the special role of art in democracy, and also came to a fruition with *Ulysses*. This was the question of the whole work of art. The broad standard set by *Hicklin* in 1868 allowed prosecutors to argue for obscenity on the basis of selected excerpts from a book, considered in isolation from the rest of the text. A few lawyers and judges found this troubling.[43] Most courts, however, stuck to the *Hicklin* model until 1922, when the New York Court of Appeals asserted that "No work may be judged from a selection of such paragraphs alone." To focus on passages taken out of context would allow such a broad interpretation of the law that it would embrace not only pornography but the most respected literary classics: "Aristophanes or Chaucer or Boccaccio or even . . . the Bible."[44] There remained opposition, however: some courts continued to argue that if a few passages could "corrupt and deprave" susceptible readers, the work was clearly harmful, and the fact that the book contained other elements would not make it safe.[45] The difference between relying on selected passages and taking the text as a whole was effectively a difference between incommensurable criteria: aesthetic value, on the one hand, and moral corruption, on the other. And there was no convincing way to separate the value of literature from the dangers of depravity because they too often overlapped and did not cancel one another out.[46]

As the twentieth century wore on, the courts increasingly used the whole-book rule to side with the explicit protection of artistic value over moral standards. In 1933, for example, a lower New York Court found in favor of Erskine Caldwell's novel, *God's Little Acre*. After reading letters of support from literary critics, editors, and writers – including recent Nobel laureate Sinclair Lewis – the judge approved the book's strong and successful attempt at a realistic portrayal of life on a Southern farm. The art work was not reducible to its most shocking passages, but must be understood as a *totality*: "Those who see the ugliness and not the beauty in a piece of work are unable to see the forest for the trees," affirmed the court.[47] Later that same year Judge Woolsey clinched the importance of the whole when he justified the "dirty words" used in *Ulysses*: "Each word of the book contributes like a bit of mosaic to the detail of the picture which Joyce is seeking to construct for his readers."[48]

I want to suggest that the whole-book rule, like the use of expert witnesses, reveals the courts' counter-majoritarian inclinations when it comes to protecting works of art. After all, to stipulate an attention to the whole book is to prescribe a way of reading that is not necessarily representative of the ways that most people actually read books. Reading from cover to cover seems an especially unlikely way of reading in the case of difficult and experimental works, where the vast majority of readers might well give up after a few pages. Many commentators at the time expressed skepticism that "anybody who was going to be corrupted or depraved would ever succeed in getting through [*Ulysses*]."[49] It is questionable, too, whether books that are especially famous for their scandalous representations of sex will be read carefully, from beginning to end: the bulk of readers may be more likely to skip to the most sensational passages. And so, the whole-book rule implicitly leaves behind *actual* readers in favor of a single, *normative* way of reading. Judge Hand implied in his *Ulysses* decision that reading for the whole was in fact a way of granting "immunity" to genuine works of art.[50] Intriguingly, then, by insisting on a particular model of reading that involved taking the work as a whole, the courts evinced their respect for the autonomy of the art object, its parts interrelating to make up a self-sufficient totality. When those parts worked together as part of an intricate aesthetic design, as they seemed to do in *Ulysses*, the ordinary mass of readers began to seem irrelevant, overpowered in the courtroom by the art object's own integrity.

## *Lady Chatterley's Lover*: Ordinary and Extraordinary Readers

If *Ulysses* secured the importance of experts and the whole-book rule in the United States, *Lady Chatterley's Lover* set the precedent in Britain. D. H. Lawrence's novel may be the most famous dirty book in the English-speaking world. Banned for over thirty years after its author's death, it became well known through an expurgated version and through countless pirated editions, printed on cheap paper and smuggled into the United States and Britain from little presses in Italy and France. Long before it was legal to publish unabridged copies of the novel, the story had become common knowledge: all kinds of readers, from schoolboys to scholars, could recount the tale of the melancholy woman, married to an English aristocrat, who has a torrid affair with the gamekeeper on her husband's estate and eventually runs off with him. Even after the laws on both sides of the Atlantic had legitimated the novel, it kept its reputation as sordid, steamy, and shockingly explicit. But unlike many other notoriously sordid books, this one was as widely praised for its high literary quality as it was condemned for its wicked depravity. In the 1940s and 1950s, D. H. Lawrence was hailed by many literary critics as one of the most important writers of the twentieth century.[51]

Late in 1959, the British Parliament passed a new and more liberal obscenity law, called the Obscene Publications Act. Lawmakers had gone to some trouble to make a special exception for artistic value in the new law, including three new provisions: expert witnesses could testify to the "literary and other merits" of the book for the first time; the text should be taken "as a whole" rather than reduced to its most shocking fragments; and jurors could now decide that a text's literary merit outweighed its potential for corruption.[52] Encouraged by this loosening of the law and by the recent legalization of *Lady Chatterley's Lover* in the US,[53] the highly respectable Penguin Books decided to publish a new, unexpurgated paperback edition of D. H. Lawrence's novel. The press printed 200,000 copies of the text and announced to the courts that they were about to send these out to distributors. The result was the famous case of *Regina v. Penguin Books*, known not least for its parade of prominent witnesses, including Rebecca West, E. M. Forster, Raymond Williams, and Cecil Day-Lewis.

The *Lady Chatterley* trial is important here because it brings together the tensions at work in obscenity law that we have been following so far: tensions between a mass readership and an unconventional art that appeals to a select few, between ordinary audiences and knowledgeable experts, and between selected passages and the whole text. One might object, of course, that *Lady Chatterley's Lover* and even *Ulysses* should not be too easily lumped in with the avant-garde. Literary critics usually categorize both as "modernist" rather than avant-garde: both texts, instead of struggling to break the world apart to usher in a revolutionary new way of being, make the aesthetic realm seem like a separate, autonomous sphere that maintains a coherent, even mythical wholeness.[54] The two works also differ markedly from one another: *Ulysses* constantly frustrates ordinary reading practices with its experiments in technique, while *Lady Chatterley* reads easily and accessibly, relying largely on conventional realist representational strategies to introduce its shockingly explicit content. Even more to the point, by the time of the trial in 1960, *Lady Chatterley's Lover* seemed more of its time than ahead of it. But if the works themselves do not belong to the historical avant-garde, their trials help us to see how the logic of the avant-garde came to work itself into the law. In both cases, the courts recognized that art was no longer best appreciated by refined elites; nor did it express or serve the spirit of "the people." Art's shocks and innovations might well refuse mainstream tastes and conventional aesthetic standards and yet retain a social value – a value that could not be measured in terms of popularity or tradition. Indeed, despite the fact that only a minority might ever appreciate the work of art, its value to the society as a whole was taken, by law, to trump its capacity to out-rage or corrupt the majority of its readers. And yet, importantly, the art object was not out of the reach of the people: though it might startle the mainstream out of their most familiar habits and tastes, the "average person" could learn to appreciate its experimental effects and shocking, eccentric content. Thus the rigorously minoritarian reasoning of transatlantic obscenity law underwrote a specific under-standing of democratic culture: rather than taking the public on its own terms, the law – in classic avant-garde fashion – presumed that "the people" were capable of transformation in the face of the chal-lenge of art.

The democratization of culture became a focal issue in the trial. Those who wanted to see *Lady Chatterley's Lover* legalized saw it as a valuable art work that was crossing over into popular culture. Mass accessibility was absolutely central to Penguin's social mission. Sir Allen Lane, Penguin's founder, testified during the trial that he had started the company in order to sell a high-quality kind of book "which would sell at the price of ten cigarettes, which would give no excuse for anybody not being able to buy it, and would be the type of book which they would get if they had gone on to further education."[55] Yet Penguin's democratizing impulse, noble though it might seem, was not necessarily an advantage in the courtroom. The new Obscene Publications Act, intending to liberalize the *Hicklin* stand-ard, asked the courts to consider the most *likely* readers of a book rather than the most susceptible ones. But that meant that the broader Penguin's readership, the more probable it was that Penguin's books would reach the very vulnerable members of Britain's literate population that *Hicklin* had worried over. As the prosecution put it, "there is no limit, is there, to the number and kind of people who may read this book which would be on sale at every book-stall, paper stall and bookshop, all for the price of three shillings and sixpence?" (282).

Haunting the *Lady Chatterley* trial was the specter of a vast and wide-ranging reading public. And what emerged in the proceedings was a familiar split between two understandings of democratic culture: on the one hand, the defense painted a portrait of a virtuous, aspirational audience, a working class eager to improve themselves but unable to afford a university degree; on the other, the prosecution treated the jury to a gloomy picture of a tasteless mass culture, one where the lowest and most vulgar preferences perverted public life as a whole. In one example, after hearing the testimony of Elizabeth Russell, a writer who claimed that the novel represented sex as "holy," the prosecutor asked: "Can that be a realistic view? Is that the kind of way in which the young boys and men leaving school, thousands of them, tens of thousands every year, I suppose, leaving school at the age of fifteen, going to their first jobs this last September, is that how they are going to read this book – as a treatment of sex on a holy basis – or is [that] wholly unrealistic?" (285–86). These are potent scare tactics: glossing over the middle-class woman writer who could recognize Lawrence's spiritualizing of sex, the lawyer called up the image of thousands of young workingmen, a rough, crude readership collecting in hordes.

So which was it? Was the working class eager to gobble up the novel for its immoral sexuality or eager, instead, to gain access to one of the great writers of the twentieth century? Though this question seemed absolutely central to the trial's proceedings, the Obscene Publications Act did not actually allow the court to call ordinary readers to the stand to hear evidence about how they read the novel. The only witnesses allowed to testify were experts who could establish their credentials in ways acceptable to the court.[56] Though on the face of it this might seem illogical or even unfair, the courts' reasoning is that the jury represents the "average" person.[57] There is no need to hear from ordinary readers, since they are embodied by the jurors themselves.

As the trial went on, the value of expertise was hotly contested. The prosecution did not invite a single expert to testify against *Lady Chatterley* and instead complained about the new provision for expert witnesses in obscenity trials.[58] Knowing that the defense had some of the best known literary critics and writers on their side, the prosecution apparently felt it would be wiser to condemn the idea of expertise itself than to try to line up an array of equally credible experts on the other side. And so, the chief counsel on the Queen's side sought to undercut the experts by making their interpretations seem bombastic and pretentious, a far cry from the ordinary reader's experience. At one point, he interrupted Richard Hoggart, a Lawrence scholar who was explaining why the novel was puritanical: "the question is quite a simple one to answer without another lecture. You are not addressing the university at the moment" (149). Professors repeatedly revealed themselves as eccentric and arcane readers in the prosecution's hands, and the working class emerged, by contrast, as reading bluntly for dirt, sex, and the simple events of the plot. But legal battles make strange bedfellows. In order to dismiss the experts as pompous and out of touch, the prosecution ended up arguing that the working class, crude though they might be, had their "feet . . . firmly planted upon the ground" (284) – and were actually *better readers* of the novel than the professors. Their lascivious reading fit the obscenity of the text. This meant, oddly enough, that the working classes needed to be protected from a text which they read better than the experts. The academic reading, by contrast, was innocuous – but only because it was absurdly overblown.

The prosecution repeatedly maintained that there was a difference between reading a text and *reading into* it. When Rebecca West made the case that "the baronet and his impotence are a symbol of the impotent culture of his time, and the love affair with the gamekeeper [is] a return of the soul to the more intense life," the lawyer responded: "I have no doubt that with the learning and reading that lies behind Miss Rebecca West she is capable of reading all that into the book, but I ask you, is that typical of the effect that this book will have upon the average reader?" (288). Reading into, in the prosecution's context, meant superimposing an artificial and arbitrary structure of learning onto the substance of the text.

While the prosecution attempted to make the experts seem pretentious and out of touch with the mass of readers, the defense cannily called expert witnesses who happened to be members of the working class themselves, or taught in workers' colleges. They asked one witness to testify because though he was an expert, he was also "a teacher in ordinary schools, he had worked as an agricultural worker . . . and was parachuted into France and received several medals" (250–51). Similarly, Raymond Williams was a famous critic who came from a poor mining town in Wales, and Richard Hoggart had written a well known study of contemporary working-class readers. Using experts on literature who could also speak for the working class, the defense tried to bring these two groups so close together that the erudite scholars and the mass public began to seem one and the same.

Both sides were making an unstated appeal to populist sympathies: the prosecution tried to belittle expertise, while the defense sought to cast the experts as people who were fully in touch with common readers. And so, both argued that their side was simply reading like ordinary people. The defense, for example, put the following question to Richard Hoggart: "It has been said that . . . descriptions [of sex] have no variation and no difference except in the place that they take place. What would you say about that?" Hoggart responded:

> I would deny that absolutely. . . . it is a gross misreading of the whole book. I don't know how many times sexual intercourse takes place in the book, perhaps eight or ten times, and any good reading of the book, *I don't mean a highbrow's reading, a good decent person's reading*

*of the book*, shows there is no one the same as the next, each one is a progression of greater honesty and a greater understanding. If one reads them as being a series of sexual intercourse, one is . . . not reading *what is in the text*. (143, my emphasis)

Hoggart was suggesting, here, that anyone who read well, anyone who did not willfully misread, would come to his, the expert's, conclusion. Of course, Hoggart begged the question: how do we know how a good, decent person reads? But he also posed a more important question: what makes a good reading of a text, a reading that is not patently a misreading? What does it mean to read *"what is in the text"*?

For Hoggart, to read the text improperly and unjustly meant selecting out certain scenes and reading them in isolation, ignoring the rest. The reading he favored would instead make sense of the whole design of the narrative – interpreting the sex scenes as developing with the arc of the story. In Hoggart's view, this was both the reading that fit what was actually in the text and also the one that reflected what "decent," ordinary people actually did with books. There are two potent claims here: one is that Hoggart's reading is *right*, and the other that it is *representative*. Both claims rest on shaky grounds: a number of critics have disagreed with Hoggart's reading of the progression of sex scenes;[59] and the prosecution hinted that the expert's reading was far from typical, since it was just as likely that the ordinary reader would scan through the text looking only for the lewdest parts.

But in the end, it did not matter whether Hoggart was wrong or right, representative or unique. The new obscenity law, it turned out, had *legislated* his way of reading as the proper method of assessing a text. That is, having written into law that the book should be taken "as a whole," the Obscene Publications Act stipulated that it was actually illegal to take the lewd reader as the standard. It might be true that schoolboys were "skimming through looking for the dirty bits" and ignoring the rest, but the way that ordinary readers *really* read the novel was, by law, irrelevant.[60]

If ordinary readers were sidelined by the new Obscene Publications Act, they were present in the trial in the form of the jury. But although the "average person" who made up the jury might be a reasonable cross-section of the general public *before* the trial, once they were gathered in the courtroom, they were not actually encouraged to act like ordinary people who might pick up the novel and read it on their own. Instead, the court insisted on three highly specific and artificial procedures for reading the text. Firstly, in order to ensure that they did indeed take the novel in its entirety, the judge ordered jurors to sit in the jury room and read the whole novel before the trial could begin. And he made it clear that though this was an unrepresentative setting, it was necessary to enforcing the law:

> I am very sorry, members of the jury. I don't want to condemn you to any kind of discomfort, but if you were to take it home you might have distractions. One knows perfectly well in one's home things do happen unexpectedly. There are distractions. You are trying and carrying out a very onerous duty, and I think it would be much better if you were to read the book in your room. (86)

Reading at home, in the ordinary comfortable way, suddenly emerges as reading *inattentively*, a clear obstacle to taking the text as a whole.[61] An uncomfortable chair in a jury room is a controlled environment that compels a proper reading of the text.

The second difference between the jurors and ordinary readers came next. Once they had read the novel attentively and in its entirety, they heard several days of testimony by experts who offered interpretations and assessments of the novel and who were examined and cross-examined on the stand. In keeping with the law's emphasis on the "whole" book, the witnesses repeatedly offered interpretations that took account of the large arc of the text, accounting for its details as part of a larger design. When the prosecution claimed that the novel was only an excuse for writing about sex at every "conceivable opportunity," (93) for example, the defense countered that if that were true, then some of the novel's details did not make sense.

If Lawrence was simply writing about a promiscuous woman, the defense asked, why would she take only two lovers? Why wouldn't Lawrence have had her sleep with men "in every hedge and ditch around Wragby" (149)?[62] The prosecution's reading of the novel failed to account for all the details of the novel that had to do with things other than sex. Thus a long procession of witnesses put forward readings of the novel that interpreted the sex scenes as part of an overarching narrative plan: one claimed that they were part of a larger "condemnation of the mechanisation of humanity in an industrial society,"[63] another that the explicit sex contributed to "an exposition of the beauty and goodness of physical love at its best . . . the redeeming power of sex and the importance of tenderness,"[64] and yet a third that the novel as a whole was about "the slavery of all classes . . . to 'the Bitch Goddess, Success,' so men have become remote from each other and remote from the true sources of life and happiness."[65]

Thirdly, the jury differed from ordinary readers in that they had to make a decision about the book's social value. And here the relationship between ordinary and extraordinary readers grew especially complicated. The judge's final advice to jurors involved trying to return them to their status as representatives of "the people." He urged them to trust to their own judgments, and to maintain a skepticism about the interpretations they had heard from the university-educated scholars and writers on the witness stand:

> You must, of course, consider the public – not so much the student of literature who reads or may read the book under the guidance of a tutor at a university, but the person who perhaps knows nothing at all about literature, and knowing nothing at all about the author Lawrence, but who buys this book for three shillings and sixpence or borrows it from a library and reads it, shall we say, during the lunch time break at the factory and takes it home in the evening to finish. . . . If a person is an authority on English literature . . . then this book you may think might present a very different picture . . . than it would to a person with no literary background, no learning or little learning, and no knowledge or little knowledge of Lawrence. (312)

On the one hand, the judge expected the jury to read the whole book attentively, from beginning to end, but on the other, he warned them to remember that the world was not made up of literary scholars. The judge's logic thus presumed a remarkably specific reader: an uneducated person who would take the text as a unified whole but did not depend on a store of specialized learning to make sense of that whole. This interpretive practice might be thoroughly atypical when it comes to the mass of readers, but it will no doubt sound familiar to any student of literary criticism, since it was actually the academic way of reading most in vogue at the time of the trial – called "Practical Criticism" in England and "New Criticism" in the United States. This kind of reading became popular and widely known in the 1940s and 1950s. Advocates of the New Criticism typically insisted that works of literature were formally organized unities, constructed according to intricate overarching designs. It was important, they argued, to learn to concentrate the reader's attention on the aesthetic arc of the text – the way its details fit together into a large and complex unity. They were emphatic, however, that reading the New Critical way required no particular scholarly expertise. Indeed, New Critics generally argued that the author's intentions and historical contexts were irrelevant to an appreciation of a work's formal design.[66] Thus readers should read the "whole" text, but they needed no special background to do so.

Two facts about the New Criticism are particularly salient for our purposes. The first is that it developed as a specifically *democratic* way of reading. The New Critics advocated a practice that allowed ordinary readers to construct interpretations of literary texts without recourse to an apparatus of historical scholarship. To read well, there was no need to do extensive research, and no need to become professional scholars. It was therefore a technique "ideally suited" to the new conditions of higher education after World War II, when higher education expanded dramatically, and suddenly universities faced an unprecedented number and range of students.[67] In keeping with this democratic mission, the New Critics were deliberate about transforming the way that literature was taught in the undergraduate

126

classroom, and produced influential textbooks that thoroughly reshaped literary pedagogy for a new population. Revolutionizing the teaching of literature, they made it clear that ordinary students from different backgrounds could produce strong interpretations of literary texts without specialized knowledge.[68]

The second noteworthy fact is that reading for "the whole" emerged as an antidote to the passive reading habits encouraged by mass culture. The New Critics wanted to find a method of approaching art that would replace the inattentive, sloppy, and selective reading they feared was the first and laziest inclination of the masses. British critic I. A. Richards, for example, first launched his argument for a new method by showing how Cambridge University students, when left to their own devices, "read and judged poems with a spectacular incompetence."[69] Richards maintained that for the good of democracy, it was essential to develop rigorous reading practices to unsettle "stock responses," unthinking habits of assuming meaning rather than actively investigating it: "If we wish for a population easy to control by suggestion we shall decide what repertory of suggestions it shall be susceptible to and encourage this tendency except in the few. But if we wish for a high and diffused civilization, with its attendant risks, we shall combat this form of mental inertia."[70] Richards worried specifically about the power of mass culture to deaden and homogenize readers' responses and wanted to make them more "reasonably self-reliant." He argued that "practical criticism" would encourage a skeptical, active reading that could curb settled clichés and unthinking, conventional assumptions. Similarly, US critic Allen Tate warned that a "mass society" was always in danger of turning totalitarian, and he urged a new critical reading practice as a way to prevent readers from passively acquiescing to majority tastes and values instead of thinking for themselves.[71]

Setting themselves against both the elitist assumption that only the most refined readers can grasp great art *and* against the populist claim that the most widespread reading practices of the mass public are the only ones that matter, the New Critics imagined a specifically educable public, one that could learn – by way of new skills – to appreciate works of art. What is important for our purposes here is that the law too favored this same reader. By subjecting the "average" person to the normative model of reading for "the whole," the law showed that it was no longer willing to accept the real reading practices of the average person, who might well read lewdly and lazily, casually and inattentively. And so, although we cannot learn from the trial proceedings how the mass of working-class readers did in fact interpret the novel, we know that both the law and the New Critics imagined that all readers could learn to read the novel "as a whole." And we also know that the law had begun to care less about how people actually read and more about how they *should* read. Works of literature would no longer be assessed by their effects on mass audiences; now the only reader who mattered was the one who learned to understand the text as a carefully constructed whole. It is not surprising, then, that Penguin ultimately prevailed: the defense invited experts to account for all of the details of the novel as part of an inclusive overarching design, while the prosecution returned again and again to the ways that the mass of people actually went about reading books.

Both *Ulysses* in the US and *Lady Chatterley* in Britain suggest that the art world and the law shared a commitment to resisting the real habits of ordinary readers – who might make up the majority of a work's audience, but who might also be willing to skim or to daydream, to read inattentively or indecently. Indeed, these trials reveal that the state offers its protection to unpopular works of art precisely by favoring some austere, highly controlled techniques of reading over others. And this fact has consequences for our understanding of art's social impact. Artists might expect their unconventional works to shock the mainstream out of its complacency, and audiences worried about obscenity might seek to ban works that could corrupt and deprave vulnerable members of the mass public. But the trials of *Ulysses* and *Lady Chatterley's Lover* hint at a more complex infrastructure of social change. The law refused to take the public simply as it was and instead challenged it to become something new. Specifically, both trials relied on the mediating machinery of the courtroom-as-classroom as the real test of art: starting with ordinary readers as they actually behaved in the world, both trials set about retraining the layperson to read in specific, highly normative ways, led by the art world's knowledgeable insiders. The courts thus built a kind of didactic bridge between the people and the work of art. When, after being trained by both the law's norms and the experts' interpretations, the "average person" saw value in the text, then shocking, anti-conventional, unpopular art could transform its audiences and win the day (figure 4.1).

**Figure 4.1** A Sell-Out: *Lady Chatterley's Lover* after publication of the unexpurgated text by Penguin in 1960, courtesy Foyles.

## In the Name of Art: 2 Live Crew in Court

If *Ulysses* and *Lady Chatterley's Lover* are not avant-garde in the strict sense, the rap group 2 Live Crew is even more strikingly remote from any usual definition of avant-garde art. And unlike Joyce and Lawrence, at the time of the trial 2 Live Crew was not widely acclaimed by the art world. And yet, I want to suggest here that the obscenity case against 2 Live Crew proves that the logic of the avant-garde continues to shape the workings of obscenity law into our own time. This trial is intriguing, too, because it suggests a link between political minorities and artistic experimentation. To loop back to Epstein's *Rima*: 2 Live Crew shows us how unconventional art can actually forge an effective counter-majoritarian alliance with oppressed social groups.[72]

But first: a brief background on changes to US law between the trial of *Ulysses* and the case against 2 Live Crew. In the 1950s, obscenity law on both sides of the Atlantic formalized the protections for artistic value that had arisen piecemeal since the late nineteenth century. Like the Obscene Publications Act in Britain, the 1957 Supreme Court case of *Roth v. United States* separated art from morality and insisted that every art work should be taken as a whole. Relying on the strong protections for speech granted by the First Amendment, *Roth* also made an explicit case for the counter-majoritarian role of the courts in matters of free expression. The court articulated its own role as protecting "all ideas having even the slightest redeeming social importance – unorthodox ideas, controversial ideas, even ideas hateful to the prevailing climate of opinion." Obscenity was restricted to that which was "utterly without redeeming social importance."[73] A few years later, the Supreme Court revised *Roth* somewhat: in the landmark case of *Miller v. California* (1973), it ruled that *Roth's* definition of obscenity was overbroad, and that it was impossible to prove such a thoroughgoing negative. *Miller* put forward a new test, which set the legal standard for obscenity in use in the United States today. According to *Miller*, a work must meet all three of the following criteria to be judged obscene:

(a)   whether "the average person, applying contemporary community standards" would find that the work, taken as a whole, appeals to the prurient interest . . .

(b)   whether the work depicts or describes, in a patently offensive way, sexual conduct specifically defined by the applicable state law, and

(c)   whether the work, taken as a whole, lacks serious literary, artistic, political, or scientific value.[74]

"Artistic value" does not get sustained attention in *Miller*, but the absence of defining constraints is itself important when it comes to the question of the relationship between art and democracy.[75] The first two prongs of the obscenity test – prurient interest and patent offensiveness – are defined *locally*. The court assumes that standards can change not only from person to person, but from place to place, and also over time. Like the panel in the Serra controversy and the US Congress during the Cold War, the law appeals to the local majority: "contemporary community standards."[76] Similarly, the court does not determine "offensiveness" by appealing to any abstract definition: state law articulates specific local standards, which the Supreme Court agrees to honor.[77] But "literary, artistic, political, or scientific value" is not constrained by place or time. As the Supreme Court held in *Pope v. Illinois* (1987): "The ideas that a work represents need not obtain majority approval to merit protection, and the value of that work does not vary from community to community based on the degree of local acceptance it has won."[78] In his dissenting opinion in *Pope*, Justice Blackmun made even more explicit the counter-majoritarian argument for why the third prong of the Miller Test should not be judged by local standards: "the First Amendment does not permit a majority to dictate to discrete segments of the population – be they composed of art critics, literary scholars, or scientists – the value that may be found in various pieces of work."[79] Thus *Miller v. California* incorporates *both* understandings of democracy we have encountered in tension throughout this study: the majority, taken as it is in the here and now, as opposed to the special world of art, which challenges the mainstream to accommodate the radically new and unfamiliar. But *Miller* does not give both versions of democracy equal weight: it is the logic of the avant-garde that takes priority. No matter how appalled or corrupted the local community, majority rule cannot override the distinct – potentially tiny – segments of the population who value artistic and scientific works. The Supreme Court's interpretation of obscenity law makes clear that art's social value is not contingent on its effect on the mass public. Ultimately, however, "the people" do matter, since it is judge or jury who make the decision. Art's specialists must be able to convince jurors and judges that a minority of people have good reason to find value in the object.[80] Moving back and forth between experts and "the people," obscenity trials continue the tradition set by *Ulysses*.

In the late 1980s, a Miami-based all-male rap group became famous for their outrageously graphic sexual lyrics. Notorious for songs like "Dick Almighty" and "Bad Ass Bitch," 2 Live Crew's style was sometimes called "booty rap." A fairly typical line from one of their songs reads, "I'll break you down and dick you long, bust your pussy and break the backbone."[81] In May of 1990 their album *As Nasty as They Wanna Be* was hauled into court in Broward County, Florida. The sheriff's office there had declared it obscene.

On aesthetic grounds, 2 Live Crew had both detractors and defenders. Some commentators argued that the rap group was neither talented nor original, and their work had more in common with pornography than with art. In 1988, hip hop critic Nelson George condemned 2 Live Crew as "crude on all levels": "the raps were witless . . . the elocution sloppy, and the recording quality awful." He did praise the group for inventing a new "down home" style of rap that provided a "defiantly country" alternative to the hipper urban music coming out of New York and Los Angeles, but later George concluded that 2 Live Crew's "lyrical violence towards women" only really provided "an ugly compensation for their absence of rhyme skills."[82] Yet the group also had its aesthetic champions: Henry Louis Gates, though he later admitted that he "loathed their lyrics,"[83] argued persuasively at the time that 2 Live Crew's very outrageousness was a comic, imaginative way to respond to a repressively racist culture.

"These young artists are acting out, to lively dance music, a parodic exaggeration of age-old stereotypes of the oversexed female and male. Their exuberant use of hyperbole (phantasmagoric sexual organs, for example), undermines – for anyone fluent in black cultural codes – a too literal-minded hearing of the lyrics." Reading *As Nasty as They Wanna Be* as an effective send-up of racist stereotypes, Gates urged readers to recognize that "censorship is to art what lynching is to justice."[84]

As far as their social impact was concerned, 2 Live Crew worried audiences across the spectrum. The group offended cultural conservatives with their sexual explicitness, but their lyrics also troubled some progressive thinkers, since their images of sexual violence against women were extreme and unrelenting, and they clearly equated black masculinity with an uncompromising heterosexuality. Lisa Jones, in the left-leaning *Village Voice*, lamented the group's misogyny, reporting that she had watched them in concert "push women to the floor, pour water on them, and chant '. . . bitch wash your stinky pussy clean.'"[85] On the other side, Paul Hetrick, Vice-President of Focus on the Family, complained that 2 Live Crew's album contained "87 descriptions of oral sex, 116 mentions of male and female genitalia, and other lyrical passages pertaining to male ejaculation."[86] Meanwhile, the group's defenders argued that the controversy over 2 Live Crew represented a set of racist fears about black male expression, and the assault on the album was part of a sweeping desire to control the speech of African-Americans. In the late 1980s and early 1990s, the press was clearly stoking fears about the threatening force of African-American voices – especially in rap – and the media were accused of using the topic of violence against women to repress the speech of black men.[87] In this context, many African-American feminists deliberately kept silent about the sexism of 2 Live Crew's lyrics, worrying that any critique would simply reinforce the power of the establishment to clamp down on all rap music, and to regulate the performance of black culture more generally. Since sexism was "being used to attack black men, rather than reconstructing power relationships

133

between black men and women," it seemed politically unwise to launch a feminist critique.[88]

The tension between race and gender haunted the trial. One witness explained the importance of 2 Live Crew in terms of black masculinity. Their exaggerated boasts and insults were survival techniques for black people struggling to affirm themselves in a racist culture. And the sexual ribaldry was particularly important for African-American men: "in society, a man's manhood is expressed by money and sex." And if you don't have money, sex allows you to say: "Hey, I'm still a man."[89] The consequences of this kind of masculinity were immediately taken up by the other side. "This is not a loving type of aggressive sexual activity," argued the sheriff's lawyer, "There's one song that makes the analogy that rather than put a woman down with a nine millimeter, he's going to put a woman down with his penis" (152). The sheriff's side claimed that the real aim of the music was its relentless misogyny: "women are always referred to as bitch; simply bitch this, bitch that, bitch everything" (297).[90] Broadly speaking, 2 Live Crew should be censored because "the rights of women and their important and relevant place in the community . . . should not be systematically abused or taken advantage of" (297–98). But as defenders like Gates affirmed, it might be a mistake to take 2 Live Crew too literally. Culturally encoded, their lyrics are insistently playful, performing upendings of convention and a kind of carnivalesque hilarity regarding social relationships. As one witness put it: "no one is [really] saying that . . . you had sex with my mother" (275).

Unlike the trials of *Ulysses* and *Lady Chatterley's Lover*, which understood the cultural field as split between ordinary readers whose experience was shaped by mass culture, and knowledgeable readers whose special skills allowed them to appreciate the subtleties of art – the 2 Live Crew case suggested a struggle among *competing* counter-majoritarian perspectives: the specific struggles of black men, set against feminist apprehensions about a culture of masculine violence and, less prominently, gay concerns about a powerful culture of homophobia. Mass culture still provided the backdrop, since the trial took place amid worries that the whole culture was increasingly open to the violence and sexual explicitness of rap music. But no longer organized by the binary divisions of "high" against "low" or "insiders" against "outsiders," the trial of 2 Live Crew implicitly asked which social group needed most protection: should the law favor potential female or gay male victims of violence or an artistic tradition that performed lightheartedly for a minority racial group? This is, to be sure, a troubling question – especially troubling in the sense that the different imagined responses do not work to the exclusion of one another. One listener might be provoked into violent action by the same lyrics that would delight another with their humor. Indeed, it is even plausible that the same listener might enjoy the joke and also perform the violence.[91] Moreover, since the two sides explicitly set race against gender, they both pointedly failed to imagine the listener as an African-American woman, who was both potential victim and potential admirer, perhaps affected by the performance of 2 Live Crew in *both* damaging and constructive ways. So: faced with competing counter-majoritarian perspectives, what should the courts do?

In the case of 2 Live Crew, they turned to the logic of the avant-garde. During the trial, both sides seemed to assume that advances in artistic technique were of social value and outweighed the dangers of widespread corruption. But they differed strongly in their assessments of 2 Live Crew's inventiveness. The sheriff's lawyer insisted that 2 Live Crew simply recycled profanity: "All it is, is street slang. . . . all of this music, it consists of slang words said on the street every day" (104). There was no creativity there, no inspiration. On the level of instrumentation, too, there was concern that the group relied almost entirely on electronic sampling techniques. David Hobbs, producer of the album, explained that as a rap musician, "You're taking different things from different entities and bringing them all into one. And that's how rap is made" (103). The sheriff's lawyer seized on this notion: "The vast majority of songs that particularly use sexual references are literally – and I hate to be inflammatory about it – stolen from other artists" (153). And it was true: 2 Live

135

Crew's music was composed of riffs taken from past musicians – especially rock, rhythm and blues, and Latin albums – and their lyrics repeatedly relied on allusions to popular culture.[92] Summing up his case, the lawyer claimed that anything artistic about the work belonged to previous artists: "All they've done is borrow [other artists' work] and call it their own and put it through a mixer and call it art. Well, maybe it's art, but it's not their art. Their contribution is nothing other than venom" (203). Thus there were two good reasons why the work should not be protected: first, whatever was artistically valuable in the music was already circulating and did not need the râp recording in order to reach the public; and second, the album could hardly be said to be art at all if what it accomplished was a recycling of existing music.

But in defense of 2 Live Crew, John Leland, a music critic, argued on the stand that all music involved repetition and recombination:

> In the past, you would look at a piece of music as being built out of notes and chords and tones. Those would be the basic building blocks of a piece of music. And hip-hop throws that out, and says the basic building blocks are little chips of other records. . . . We'll create an original work of music; not starting with notes and chords and tones, but we'll create them from other records. The instrumentation is entirely different. (235)

By his own logic, the sheriff would have to accuse Mozart of "borrowing" or "stealing" existing notes, chords, rhythms, and instruments and merely combining them in new ways.[93]

But if total originality was an impossible goal, John Leland argued that there *was* such a thing as musical innovation. He claimed that 2 Live Crew combined old elements in ways that were "incredible," "entirely different," and "really exciting" (237–38). Leading the courtroom through a brief history of rap, Leland described 2 Live Crew as changing the trajectory of contemporary music by fusing two different musical traditions.[94] And whether intentionally or not, Leland's defense of 2 Live Crew borrowed from classic accounts of

136

the avant-garde. Rap, he argued, was an art form that began as marginal, uncorrupted, and critical of the mainstream, but also ahead of its time, an art which the future would eventually recognize and appreciate, and one which would eventually change our very definitions of art itself. Leland's defense of 2 Live Crew's innovations took its place within this larger history of rap, which he told at some length in the courtroom. Rap first began in the West Bronx, Leland told the Court, where a DJ called Cool Herc started playing only "the most exciting piece of the record . . . called the break" (226). Street parties gathered around Cool Herc's music, and other DJs followed suit – all of them acknowledging Cool Herc "as the master guy who invented this music" (229). Of course, the concept of "invention" here is complex: it is in selecting parts of existing recorded music that Cool Herc becomes the origin, the foundation, creating something which everyone recognizes as "a new sound and . . . a new music" (226). But the make-believe of a beginning here was crucial: it marked rap as a new phenomenon, a rupturing of old forms and entrenched expectations. In Leland's telling, too, rap's beginning was important because this was music that started well outside of the mainstream, uncontaminated by capitalism and popular taste: it was first of all an art of integrity. He explained that the earliest rap DJs earned no money from their art, and were willing to "throw away their last ninety-nine cents to buy a copy of some heavy metal record that they thought might have a great beat on it" (230). Rap came not from established institutions, but from the periphery: it was in the world of urban streets and playgrounds that the new form broke into public consciousness, attracting the attention of recognized record labels and concert venues only much later. Gradually rap became more and more accepted until the moment, two years before the trial, when the record industry first awarded a Grammy for rap music. It had been successfully incorporated into the mainstream.[95]

Similar testimony came from a Miami music critic named Greg Baker, who explained that 2 Live Crew had been crucial to the emergence of a particular Florida sound. Like Leland, he made the

case that the value of *As Nasty as They Wanna Be* lay in its departure from convention: "any time music surprises you by breaking
from what you are trained or by what you're used to hearing or
expecting to hear, a traditional musical progression, when that is
broken up in some way, it's startling to you" (205). 2 Live Crew
used lyrics, instrumentation, and rhythm in ways that were ahead
of their time.

The logic of the avant-garde at work here may seem to have
carried us far from the urgent political problems raised by the public debate over 2 Live Crew – racism, misogyny, and homophobia.
Neither race nor gender factored much in either Leland's or Baker's
testimony, and 2 Live Crew's legal team focused the court's attention on the album's role in advancing rap as a musical form. But the
trial began to hint at a link between political minorities and artistic
experimentation.

Carlton Long, a Rhodes scholar and political scientist about
to take up an academic position at Columbia, was the only expert
witness besides Leland and Baker to testify to the social value of
*As Nasty as They Wanna Be*.[96] He told the court that his Oxford
dissertation compared Brixton and Harlem – black communities in
London and New York. As a student of the "black cultural experience," Long's expertise included both art and politics. On the witness stand, he traced a trajectory for rap that focused not so much
on 2 Live Crew's artistic innovations as on the roots of their lyrics
in African-American history. He told the court that the rap group
relied on three poetic techniques: call and response, playing the dozens,
and boasting, all of which had a significant "survival purpose" for
black Americans.[97] But these strategies, he said, remained opaque
to those outside of the African-American community. Doing the
dozens, for example, was "something most black people know about
. . . [while to] most people in the white community, dozens is a
new concept" (267). When asked whether "white people hear this
music in the same way that black people who have had experiences
in the black culture hear the music," Long responded: "No, it's been
my experience that white people, in general, do not hear the music

in the same kind of way" (261). Implicitly, then, Long was unsettling the usual definition of expertise. Obscenity law stipulates that local majorities will not stifle works intelligible only to an enlightened few. But Long suggested that the knowledgeable minority might encompass all African-Americans. Black audiences could *all* be experts on hip hop culture; audiences who were not African-American would need to be educated. Enlightened reading, cultural expertise, specialized knowledge – these were now the province not of a wealthy elite but of a historically disadvantaged minority group. This was a challenge to existing legal models. Since *Ulysses*, obscenity law has typically imagined two audiences for cultural objects: the "average person" ("a legal concept whereby a single perspective is derived from the aggregation or average of everyone's attitudes in the area"),[98] and the expert on a specialized topic who can establish convincing institutional qualifications on the witness stand. Long imagined a kind of combination of the two: a whole minority group, distributed throughout the nation and defined by a specific cultural history, which, thanks to this history, could lay claim to a special expertise.

Long's testimony makes clear how the logic of the avant-garde might share a legal category with oppressed minorities: both can lay claim to interpretive skills that differ from the ordinary interpretive habits of the majority; both draw on the critical perspectives available to outsiders to launch uncomfortable challenges to the mainstream. And in Long's account, it is actually political outsiders who *generate* aesthetic challenges: 2 Live Crew resists the dominant culture by means of unfamiliar artistic techniques which are themselves products of a history of racism and slavery. Thus Long hinted at the inextricability of politics from the logic of the avant-garde: "the music . . . is political, simply in the fact that you have a group of artists who say, I'm going to express myself the way I express myself. I am going to say it the way I talk. I'm not going to fit in, change, try to make myself acceptable to you, it's already acceptable now" (276–77). Blending aesthetic unfamiliarity and political protest, Long suggested that the value of 2 Live Crew depended on their status as outsiders asserting themselves in response to a dominant culture.

After hearing the testimony on both sides, the District Court decided that 2 Live Crew's work was obscene. Judge José A. Gonzalez – a Cuban-American and a Carter appointee – claimed that the album appealed to the prurient interest and offended the community, and he also rejected all of the expert testimony concerning the work's artistic and political value. Indeed, the judge virtually disregarded all of the evidence given by Leland and Baker in the trial, except to say that "neither the 'Rap' nor the 'Hip Hop' musical genres are on trial." Then he turned his attention to a critique of Carlton Long's testimony, dismissing the argument that the album was valuable because it reflected the political history of the African-American community: "While it is doubtless true that [the album] is a product of the group's background, this fact does not convert whatever they say, or sing, into political speech."[99] As for Long's argument that "white Americans 'hear' the Nasty recording in a different way than black Americans," the judge said that he had found "none of these arguments persuasive" because the techniques were not unique to African-Americans: "'Doing the dozens' is commonly seen in adolescents, especially boys, of all races. 'Boasting' seems to be part of the universal human condition." And ultimately, the judge affirmed, the real question was not about outsiders at all: "In an era where the law and society are rightfully concerned with the rights of minorities, it should not be overlooked nor forgotten that majorities also have rights." Not only did the masses have legal rights, according to Judge Gonzalez; they sometimes had good sense: "The Phillistines are not always wrong, nor are the guardians of the First Amendment always right."[100] On populist, majoritarian grounds, the court declared 2 Live Crew obscene.

In May of 1992, the Court of Appeals reversed the District Court's decision. They decided that the original judge's familiarity with contemporary community standards was "sufficient" when it came to the first two prongs of the Miller Test, but not when it came to the question of artistic value. "The record is insufficient . . . for this Court to assume the [judge's] artistic or literary knowledge or skills to satisfy the last prong of the Miller analysis." Judge Gonzalez had clearly disregarded all of the expert testimony he had heard in favor of his own critical judgment. This was unacceptable. "We reject the argument that simply by listening to this musical work, the judge could determine that it had no serious artistic value."[101] The Court of Appeals carefully summarized the testimony of Greg Baker and John Leland, confirmed as experts by virtue of their "hundreds" of articles and huge reading audiences, who had argued for 2 Live Crew's ground-breaking techniques and unanticipated combinations. The law did not acknowledge the specific substance of Long's testimony, the fusion of art and politics, experts and minorities, but it happily recognized the story of avant-garde outsiders, provoking mainstream taste and gradually coming to be recognized by "the people." And so the court eventually decided to protect the voices of a minority group, but it did so in the name of the avant-garde.

## Conclusion

Christopher Nowlin has argued that the use of experts in obscenity trials is evidence of the law's elitist inclinations, its refusals to respect the real and diverse communities of ordinary people whom obscenity laws ostensibly protect. He maintains, too, that obscenity trials have more often ended up in the hands of judges than of juries, further confirmation of the courts' resistance to the people. Nowlin cites *Ulysses* as a particularly egregious example of the elitist assumptions at work in obscenity trials and makes a plea for a more "democratic" approach to obscenity.[102]

Given the history of obscenity law, Nowlin is clearly right to say that obscenity trials are always implicitly about democracy. Contemporary obscenity law itself arises from the conditions of a democratized culture, where widespread access means that texts are reaching vast populations and crossing boundaries of class, age, race, and gender. Obscenity proceedings also repeatedly imagine readers not as individuals or as universals but as social groups characterized by different interpretive strategies: refined elites, innocent school-girls, average men, factory workers, African-American men. Pitting such groups against one another, the courts in the late nineteenth and early twentieth centuries often used an elitist logic to justify their protection of certain works over others. It is true, too, that as obscenity law moved from a struggle between high art and mass culture to a battle between mainstream standards of decency and innovative, challenging art, it continued to hold out a distance between uneducated crowds and knowledgeable aficionados. But where I part ways from Nowlin is in his analysis of the character of artistic expertise itself. I have been suggesting that the courts' increasing reliance on art experts actually marks a shift *away* from elitism. Obscenity law, as I have argued, slowly moved its focus from wealthy elites to the logic of the avant-garde, and as it did so, legal thinkers increasingly understood art not as a sphere accessible to a superior set, but as minority expression that might be disturbing to the cultural mainstream. 2 Live Crew is a useful example here, since the appeals court clearly justified its decision not because the rappers belonged to a high culture elite, but because valuable artistic expression might well be both incomprehensible and unsettling to ordinary audiences.

As obscenity law increasingly adopted the logic of the avant-garde, the courts grew more and more inclined to recognize art experts. But *contra* Nowlin, the experts themselves are often social outsiders and outspoken critics whose "art world" status does not rest on formal credentials or class status. Theodore Dreiser, whose expertise was welcome in the trial of *Ulysses*, had seen his own shocking novel *Sister Carrie* suppressed and bowdlerized. Raymond Williams, one of the literary critics who testified in favor of *Lady Chatterley's Lover*, was a committed socialist whose Marxist-inspired criticism was deeply critical of "high" culture. What made them experts and insiders in the avant-garde logic of the art world was precisely their willingness to act as rebellious social outsiders.

Of course, art experts do not always work in the interest of political minorities, and it would certainly be a mistake to assume that

142

the trial of 2 Live Crew exemplified all obscenity cases in this respect. One might argue, too, that it is trivializing and insensitive to imagine a close relationship between political minorities, who are materially oppressed by cultural and social norms, and artistic minorities, especially those who, in the tradition of avant-garde defiance, willfully and flagrantly reject majority tastes and preferences. But I want to suggest that it is nonetheless true that the logic of the avant-garde may play a constructive role in the fostering of democratic pluralism.

The third prong of the Miller Test, as we have seen, works against the tyranny of the majority: it is with its protection of artistic, literary, political, and scientific value that the court safeguards voices from the margins. Thus artistic merit is one of the specific ways that obscenity law imagines room for the expression of minority preferences and desires. And though it might seem at first a specious comparison, avant-garde artists and political minorities do have something crucial in common. For the avant-garde, it is only by upsetting current taste that new preferences come into public view, and art is useful in that it brings the public into the future. For minority groups in a democracy, it is by moving unsettlingly marginal experiences into the public eye and claiming legitimacy for alternative histories and perspectives that a new and more inclusive society can come into being. For both artists and marginalized groups, in other words, it is by inviting a disconcerting plurality of voices that the collective can be propelled into the future. And when they assume their counter-majoritarian role, the courts actually work to encourage this plurality and dissent against the pressures of popular values. Thus art, progressive politics, and the law all welcome a democratic society transformed by the challenges of marginal voices.

But why does art, in particular, matter to this democratic pluralist vision? Why would it not be both more ethical and more efficacious to emphasize the voices of oppressed and marginalized peoples? The answer lies in the special social function of art in the wake of the avant-garde. Since the beginning of the twentieth century, art has not been defined by the artists or the courts as a

143

particular style or set of conventions. It calls for no particular content; and it does its work in a range of media. Its character shifts with the cultural context, tirelessly finding the margins of experience, the fringes of perception, the edges of belief. What marks the logic of the avant-garde is its *activity of challenging*.

And although the avant-garde might seem too elastic a category – and therefore politically meaningless – I want to suggest that it is precisely the dynamic, shifting content of the avant-garde that gives it its particular political efficacy. In the trial of 2 Live Crew, the court favored the activity of artistic challenging, but rejected the argument that the work was valuable because it was the expression of a social minority. And this, I would argue, was not such an outrageous legal logic. The very contentlessness of the avant-garde allows it to play a *structural* role in relation to democratic invocations of "the people." Chantal Mouffe argues there will always be outsiders in democracies: constitutive of any collective is its sense of its own borders, the boundaries that separate those who belong from those who do not. But the content of the outside can shift, and indeed, it may take shape in the future as categories and groups that we cannot now foresee. The tradition of the avant-garde produces artists constantly willing to put pressure on a oppressively dominant culture, and therefore the art world is a social institution that is perpetually able to shift to adopt the role of the outsider, whoever or whatever that figure might happen to be. Refusing to come to rest in a particular agenda, technique, or approach, the logic of the avant-garde makes room for the outsiders of the future. By contrast, the other political logic that emerged in the trial was markedly rigid: race met gender as if they were antagonists; the binary, adversarial structure of the courtroom provoked and reinforced this conflict, apparently splitting the impact of the album into two distinct and opposing – if unconvincing – halves. For one to win, the other had to lose. And so, while the conventional language of identity politics sets social groups in competition with one another, fighting over limited resources, the logic of the avant-garde is surprisingly supple and inclusive, allowing all outsiders to act as equally contestatory categories, mutually reinforcing in their challenges to the "mainstream." And even more inclusively, it imagines these challenges as beneficial, ultimately, for everyone: the unsettling of dominant views and majority perspectives leads to a vibrant democracy, stimulated and invigorated by marginal and unfamiliar voices.

Oddly enough, the obscenity courtroom turns out to be a fine model of this kind of democratic deliberation. Obscenity trials repeatedly return to the differences among audiences, suggesting that diverse social groups lay claim to different kinds of interpretive competence. In the courtroom, they are compelled to meet, as representatives of 'the people" encounter representatives of the art world who recommend unfamiliar ways of seeing, interpreting, and evaluating, and urge the critical practices of dissenters, experimenters, outliers, and exiles. More often than not, the art world's representatives succeed, changing the minds even of audiences initially appalled by the work. We might think, for example, of the obscenity case against the Cincinnati Arts Center for its show of Robert Mapplethorpe's photographs in 1990. Arts advocates in conservative Cincinnati were "prepared for the worst."[103] One juror explained that he had indeed been shocked initially, but then he had been taught a new way to understand art: "We thought the pictures were lewd, grotesque, disgusting," he acknowledged. "But like the defense said, art doesn't have to be pretty or beautiful."[104]

From *Howl* and *Naked Lunch* to Robert Mapplethorpe and Karen Finley, artists and their allies have been shocked that the law would have the effrontery to enter the realm of art. And they have been just as shocked to discover that they have won in court.[105] So perhaps it is time for artists to face the facts: they are actually remarkably successful at winning obscenity cases. Far from struggling, vulnerable outsiders at the mercy of the "censor-moron," the most rebellious artists do strikingly well within the powerful parameters of the law.

145

# 5

## Originality on Trial

In recent years, legal scholars have argued that the law is well suited to works of modern art but cannot handle the twists and turns of postmodernism. Anne Barron claims that copyright law presumes a "stable, fixed, closed, self-contained" art object, and is therefore unable to recognize multimedia and performance works by postmodern artists who have tried to break down the barriers between genres and between art and life. Copyright law fails in the face of art installations, body art, and earth art, which defy stable concepts of an autonomous art object in favor of a more fluid relationship between art and its sites.[1] Amy Adler makes a similar case for the failures of obscenity law: by putting its emphasis on "serious" artistic value, the landmark case of *Miller v. California* (1973) misses the playful postmodern rejection of serious high art, with its deliberate celebration of "impurity and irreverence."[2]

Adler sketches out the almost insuperable difficulties that have attached to legal attempts to define art: on the one hand, she argues that it would be of no use to rely on experts to establish the boundaries of art because "this standard would not protect undiscovered artists, developing artists, or artists who are 'ahead of their time.'" On the other hand, she suggests that one cannot trust juries and judges because "many contemporary artists are so estranged from lay notions of what constitutes 'art,' courts might refuse to recognize them as artists in spite of wide critical acceptance by the art community." If we cannot trust either the art world or the layperson,

146

what is left? Startlingly little. "Art, by its nature," writes Adler, "will call into question any definition that we ascribe to it." And so "perhaps the only standard left is to defy all standards."[3]

The avant-garde turns out to be a particularly elusive category in Adler's analysis: she claims that postmodernism involves a thoroughgoing rejection of the historical avant-garde, but she also cites Dada as the major inspiration for postmodern art. She maintains that the institutionalized art world misses undiscovered artists who are "ahead of their time," but at the same time she defends the art experts' definitions of art against the layperson's untutored understanding. She understands postmodernism as repudiating avant-garde claims to newness and originality, while suggesting that postmodernism is so radically unpredictable that we could not possibly confine it to existing definitions. I point to these contradictions not to deprecate Adler's argument, but to suggest that it repeatedly leads us back to tensions we have seen before: postmodern art is poised between the desire to be radically new and unfamiliar, on the one hand, and a recognition of the impossibility of being an absolute innovator or outsider, on the other. It is poised, too, between anti-institutional rebellion and the impossibility of attempts to escape institutionalization. Contemporary art is not avant-garde, but then it is not *not* avant-garde, either.

This chapter proposes that controversies over postmodern art tend to continue the logic of the avant-garde, rather than to disrupt it. And it contends that the most effective response to the oppositions identified by Adler is not to choose between the sides but to forge a tense balance. In fact, both the art world and the law, I argue, have *already* worked out that balance, though both institutions are inclined to forget or overlook it, sometimes at their own peril – and ours. Typically, the law does better at understanding the difficult equilibrium that it must strike than the artists do, but the artists do their most effective work, both socially and legally, when they recognize what they have in common with the law. Thus what I want to suggest is that the differences between "modernism" and "postmodernism" do not capture the problem of art's relationship to the law, nor do

147

they resolve it. Instead, I propose to turn our attention to the delicate structural role of art as it has emerged throughout the past century. This is art as democracy's "friendly enemy," an element that is always and necessarily both inside and outside, both new and traditional, both free and restricted, both for and against "the people."

This chapter follows the ins and outs of two legal cases. The first is a customs case brought by Constantin Brancusi, a classic example of a modernist artist; the second a copyright suit against Jeff Koons, a paradigmatic postmodernist. Brancusi won his case, and Koons lost, but not – I will argue – because of the differences between modern and postmodern art forms. Both cases turned on the question of originality. Originality has long been a contested concept in the arts, and the law requires a certain measure of originality to protect works of art in customs and copyright contexts. So: what is originality, exactly? On the one hand, the word evokes revolutionary newness, innovation. On the other hand, it refers to *origins*, implying a movement backward, to the beginning. Originality, as it has traditionally been used in the arts, brings these two meanings together. We typically consider an art work original when it reveals an individual's unique idea or expression: thus it is new in the sense that no one has thought of it before; but it is also original in the sense that its origins can be identified as belonging to a single inspired source. Originality, then, unites the newness of the object with the singleness of its author.

A faith in originality has been understood as the crucial site of difference between modern and postmodern art. Rosalind Krauss argues that the historical avant-garde could not have come into being apart from the "discourse of originality": it was the emphasis on originality that prompted artists to seek the frontiers of artistic production, and it was the high premium on originality that lent significance to avant-garde experimentation.[4] But since the time of Andy Warhol, artists have become accustomed to claiming that there is no such thing as originality at all. In the 1960s, it began to seem impossible to escape the media-saturated, commodified environment to create something entirely new. Indeed, postmodern artists and

148

theorists claimed nothing had *ever* been created out of nothing. Even the materials of art come freighted with cultural meanings: for a sculptor to work in stone or wood was to continue ancient traditions, but to break free from those traditions by working in plastic or fiberglass was not to invent something entirely new, since the materials themselves evoked a preexisting world of mass produced commodities or cutting edge industry. No art work can exist entirely outside of its cultural and historical context, but instead has to borrow from the signs, symbols, materials, and syntax that have already been developed. "All that is left is to imitate dead styles, to speak through the masks and with the voices of the styles in the imaginary museum. But this means that . . . postmodernist art is going to be about art itself in a new kind of way; even more it means that one of its essential messages will involve the necessary failure of art and the aesthetic, the failure of the new, the imprisonment in the past."[5] Furthermore, there is no single individual at the source of artistic production. The artist is herself merely a product of her social and historical environment, a vehicle for the languages, signs, materials, and meanings that have preceded and shaped her. It has come to seem commonplace to say that there are no new objects and no individuals who are the origins of creative works. Rather than standing outside of dominant culture, postmodern artists make use of it, drawing on mass produced contemporary culture in order to criticize, rework, or even to celebrate it. And so contemporary artists flaunt techniques of reuse: appropriation, recontextualization, recombination, and collage. From Jasper Johns and Cindy Sherman to rap groups and L=A=N=G=U=A=G=E poets, postmodern artists have made it clear that their only option is to recombine the objects and meanings that history has left them.

We might expect the avant-gardist Brancusi to embrace a modernist defense of radical innovation and the postmodern Koons to argue that his own work was by necessity composed of recycled elements. But in fact the reverse was true. Brancusi emphasized his debt to tradition, while Koons claimed to be breaking free of all convention to create something dramatically unfamiliar and new. And it is my contention that the real difference between Brancusi and Koons was not a matter of style, medium, or aesthetic theory, but of the artist's *strategy* in court. The implications of this difference were significant indeed. Brancusi's arguments for art's necessary constraints by institutional norms and conventions were so shrewd that they managed to persuade the courts to *change* the law, while Koons's arguments for art's total freedom were so naïve that the law – which could have taken his side – refused to recognize his contribution to society. Brancusi's team cannily worked within the logic of the law, while Koons lost because he continued to insist that art was radically autonomous and should remain absolutely free of the courts' intervention. This chapter therefore offers a warning to artists. Artists on trial who insist on seeing the law as the clumsy apparatus of a hostile and repressive state may be both misled and defeated. Those who work with the notion that art and the law are not so different after all may fare much better: by conceding that art is not so free that it stands above all regulations and norms, and by recognizing that Anglo-American common law provides significant support for innovative expression, they may find that the law serves them better than we have come to expect. Indeed, sharing surprisingly common ground, artists and the courts in democratic contexts have the capacity to reinforce rather than to undermine one another. Artists on trial even have the power, at times, to urge the law to live up to its democratic ideals. So, hardly the beleaguered victims of a hostile state power, as they so often claim, artists on trial can work the law to their own ends – and win.

## Tax Free Modernism: *Brancusi v. United States*

In October of 1926, a brass sculpture was shipped from Paris to New York. It was the work of sculptor Constantin Brancusi, and was officially called *Oiseau*, later known as *Bird in Space* (figure 5.1). The buyer was photographer and art collector Edward Steichen, one of the foremost supporters of the European avant-garde in the United

**Figure 5.1** Constantin Brancusi, *Bird in Space* (1927), silver print. Photo: Bertrand Prevost. Musée National d'Art Moderne, Centre Georges Pompidou, Paris. Photo credit: CNAC/MNAM/Dist. Réunion des Musées Nationaux/Art Resource, NY © 2007 Artists Rights Society (ARS), New York/ADAGP, Paris.

151

States. At the harbor, Steichen's transatlantic purchase encountered an unexpected difficulty. Customs officials refused to allow the object to be categorized as a work of art. And this was no trivial matter: classified as a work of art, the *Bird* could enter the United States tax free, but if it failed to qualify as art, it could be taxed at up to 40 percent of its value. In the case of the *Bird*, customs asserted that the object belonged in the same import category as "Table, household, kitchen, and hospital supplies." It was to be taxed at the full 40 percent.[6]

Steichen, upset by the ruling and the duty he had to pay, voiced his concerns to one of the great patrons of the art world: Gertrude Vanderbilt Whitney. She immediately recognized the cause as a worthy one, and offered to shoulder the full financial burden of a lawsuit against the United States government. As it turned out, her help was not only financial. Canny when it came to public relations, Whitney suggested that Brancusi himself file the suit – rather than Steichen – so that the press and the public would see the action as a battle between a ground-breaking artist and the state. The case would go down in history as *C. Brancusi, plaintiff v. United States, defendant.*[7]

To many in the art world, the whole affair was an affront, but the classification of the *Bird* as a kitchen utensil seemed particularly outrageous. Marcel Duchamp, then living in New York, was one of the few who tried to take advantage of the law's categories, pointing out that if the object was really a "potato masher" then it could not possibly be worth the $600 that Brancusi had charged for it. It would surely bring something more like $35 or $40 on the open market. If it was art, it would be tax free, and if it was a kitchen utensil the tax would be less than $20. The *Chicago Post* responded that Brancusi could charge what he liked for a kitchen utensil, and perhaps the *Bird* was simply an extremely expensive potato masher.[8]

In fact, there was as much antagonism raging against Brancusi in the mainstream press as there was support for him in the art world. The *New York City Sun* insisted that customs' refusal to recognize the *Bird* as art was "a good thing," representing "a healthy independence of French opinion."[9] Trying to foster a national culture, this article tapped into an American anxiety about the innovative new art coming out of Europe. A more common objection targeted the industrial material of the work. It is "a tall, slender, highly polished object, which looks like nothing so much as, say, half an airplane propeller," claimed the *New York American*,[10] and the *Providence Journal* complained that the *Bird* was "nothing more than an oval spindle of bronze," rightly classified by customs officials as "mere junk."[11]

The United States has shown a longstanding commitment to welcoming foreign works of art into the nation by lowering or altogether eliminating import taxes. In part because it considers itself a "new" country – with little cultural heritage of its own – US customs law favors art from overseas.[12] But this commitment was complicated around the turn of the century by the sharp rise in mass produced cultural objects that were saturating the marketplace. Did cheap reproductions deserve the same special import status as works by Michelangelo? The courts and Congress typically concluded in the negative, and they did so on economic grounds. Customs tariffs were supposed to give domestic production a head start against foreign competition, and any object that could be mechanically reproduced could be made just as well at home. American stained-glass makers, for example, strenuously objected to the categorization of imported European stained-glass as art because they were eager "to save the nascent [domestic] industry from being crushed out by foreign competition."[13] The American glass workers deliberately characterized their work as an ordinary craft rather than a high art in order to hold onto their economic edge.

As usual in controversies over the avant-garde, then, the specter of mass culture formed a crucial backdrop. Genuine art, Congress and the courts reasoned, belonged to an altogether different economic category from items of mass production: "stamped with some of the individuality of the artist himself," the work of high art was distinguished from mass culture by its character as "unique," "imaginative," "creative," and "original."[14] Apparently, each art object was so radically exceptional that the question of competition was simply irrelevant. Art is "noncompetitive because a work of art is a work of genius and not the product of a machine. There are no two alike, as in the case of manufactures, but each has its individuality."[15] Some arts advocates went even farther, arguing that imported art was good for the economy: "Free art by multiplying the art objects of the country will develop an artistic taste among the people, which will in turn create a demand for artistic products, and so call into existence new domestic industries which will give employment at high wages to skilled laborers, both men and women."[16] Art's value was that it provoked new cultural activity rather than replicating what was already in existence: "in art the supply has always preceded and created the demand."[17] Where mass culture spun endlessly repetitive – and therefore competitive – copies, art offered original insights, which in turn stimulated further creativity, triggering both economic development and home grown artistic production.

Apparently, when it came to imports, both Congress and the courts depended on a set of presumptions about cultural progress that shared some intriguing characteristics with the logic of the avant-garde: they distinguished art from popular culture; they implied that the nation benefited from the introduction of new art, because it would stimulate the public to adopt new tastes and values; and they assumed an equation between originality and social advancement. But if the state seemed generally predisposed to avant-garde innovation, Brancusi's particular contribution to the avant-garde troubled the distinction between art and mass culture, since the industrial and aerodynamic look of the *Bird* seemed to range it closer to manufacture than to art. Although Brancusi himself testified that he had not used any kind of "polishing machine," an attorney for the government asserted that he was nonetheless merely "a wonderful polisher of bronze. Any polisher can do that" (67). The willingness of the European avant-garde to experiment with materials and styles borrowed from the future-oriented worlds of industry and technology were bringing it perilously close to the mechanized mass production that the American courts took to be the opposite of art.

What made the case seem even more difficult was a 1916 case that had set the most recent legal precedent. *Olivotti v. United States* defined sculpture as an art which carves or models "imitations of natural objects in their true proportions of length, breadth, and thickness, or of length and breadth only."[18] Representational fidelity was written into the legal definition of sculpture. One reporter protested that if the customs officials' approach to sculpture were taken seriously, then "the most perfect work of art" would be "one of the plaster feet that chiropodists use to demonstrate corn and bunion plasters."[19] But the fact remained: customs law had defined sculpture as an art of "imitation." Thus abstract art itself was on trial in the case of *Brancusi v. United States.*

The case came to trial in October 1927. There were four major legal questions that had to be answered. Three were stipulations of the 1922 Tariff Act, which defined the kind of sculpture that could qualify as duty-free art under the law. First, Brancusi's legal team had to establish that the sculpture was not "an article of utility," "nor such as are made wholly or in part by stencilling or any other mechanical process" (112–13). Second, the art work must be "the professional production" of a sculptor. Third, the statute insisted that to qualify as art the work must be "original." And finally there was the fourth, and most difficult, standard, for Brancusi to meet: the result not of the Tariff Act but the precedent set by *Olivotti,* the 1916 ruling that art must replicate the proportions of real objects in the world.

Surprisingly, on all counts, the court in *Brancusi v. United States* found firmly in favor of the avant-garde, overturning the *Olivotti* precedent and allowing the *Bird* to enter the country tax free. But how was it, exactly, that Brancusi's lawyers managed to negotiate an understanding between the courts and the avant-garde? I want to suggest that Brancusi's legal team ingeniously emphasized two remarkable affinities between the art world and common law: the two spheres emerged as sharing a similar relationship to history and to institutionalization that allowed the madness of the avant-garde to seem strangely suited to the sobriety of the courtroom. Particularly central to both was the question of originality. Thanks to some shrewd moves on the part of Brancusi's advocates, what emerged in the courtroom was a complex and subtle understanding of artistic originality peculiarly appropriate to American common law.

The lawyers for the government were so eager to show how far Brancusi had diverged from the "imitation of natural objects in their true proportions" that they spent much of the trial grilling witnesses about the sculpture's failure to represent a bird in a straightforwardly realistic way. Steichen was asked why he called the object a bird. "Does it look like a bird to you?" asked Judge Waite. "It does not look like a bird," Steichen responded, "but I feel that it is a bird, it is characterized by the artist as a bird" (20). In this three-part answer, the witness steadily shifted the basis of artistic authority – transferring it from the world of things in nature ("it does not look like a bird") to the viewer's response ("I feel that it is a bird") to the artist's vision ("it is characterized by the artist as a bird"). Not surprisingly, Steichen's answer did not satisfactorily clear up the point. A second judge intervened in the proceedings to take the same question a step further. Infamously, he asked: "If you saw it in the forest, you would not take a shot at it?" (20). It is this kind of comment that earns the judicial attempt to assess art a bad name. Unperturbed, Steichen confidently affirmed that he would not be at all tempted to shoot at the object. And following him, witness after witness testified that it was a mistake to see the title as a mimetic image of the work or the work as a copy of nature. Jacob Epstein, for example – the scandalous sculptor we met in chapter 2 – argued in his testimony that the title *Bird* was not the equivalent of the object, not its *replacement*, but rather a cue to a new way of reading. He said: "if the artist called it a bird, I would take it seriously if I have any respect for the artist whatever. It would be my first endeavor to see whether it was like a bird" (30). Like Steichen, Epstein put his emphasis not on the object's likeness to the world, but on the artist's conception. And he imagined that the artist's title was there to shape the viewer's understanding of the work.

The courtroom thus witnessed two competing theories of the work's title. On the one hand was the assumption that both the title and the work should be *representational*, the title standing in for the art work, the art work standing in for an object in the world. According to this view, every step in the experience of art should be a repetition of what was already known. This was a chain of substitutions that could work in any direction and any order: title, art work, and real object each operating simply to confirm and replicate the others. And if the work should happen to violate or dislocate that path of substitutions, the viewer could refuse to see the object as art at all. On the other hand, Steichen and Epstein offered the court a theory of art as that which could *transform* the perceptions and assumptions of the audience: the title would teach the viewer to perceive the object in a new and instructive way, and the object, in turn, would prompt a new perception of the world. This was a path not of substitutions but of transformations, and each step built on the one before: first the title, then the art work, then the world, each calling for an unfamiliar experience of the next.

The second theory is clearly closer to the logic of the avant-garde. Art is there not to reaffirm what we already know, but to challenge our perceptions. Thus *Brancusi v. United States* staged a battled between representational art, on the one hand, and the challenges of the avant-garde on the other. And what seems telling in this regard is the unanimous decision of the court, which decided to reject the notion of art as representation, deliberately changing the law to acknowledge that art could include Brancusi's abstract, challenging, and transformative work.

The emphasis on art as an engine of social change was in keeping with a certain understanding of art's distinctiveness that was already – as we have seen – at work in customs law. And this brings us to another of the law's requirements for art: the 1922 Tariff Act's insistence that works of art must be "original." It was this quality that customs cases before *Brancusi* had identified as the crucial hallmark of genuine art, marking it off from ordinary articles of trade. But what exactly did originality entail?

The government's lawyers certainly worked hard to show that Brancusi's work failed to qualify as original. The most significant obstacle to proving originality was that the sculptor had made several

157

versions of the *Bird* and had been planning a whole series to follow. It was true that he was creating them in different media – some marble, some bronze – and with subtly different formal qualities, but opposing counsel argued that the object on trial was simply one of a series of reproductions. Steichen testified that he had personally witnessed Brancusi's laborious work on the *Bird* – including the original conception executed in marble, the plaster cast, and then the filing and polishing of the bronze – but the lawyer for the defense was not satisfied: "In so far as being the second copy or third or fourth, you don't know whether this Exhibit 1 is the first, second, third or fourth of the original model?" Steichen simply stood firm: "It is the only one Brancusi ever made" (25).

Steichen's answer might have been confident, but it is not clear that his confidence was altogether justified. There is something peculiar, surely, in his affirmation of absolute uniqueness when the work had itself been sculpted from two models and would be recreated again and again with minor variations, all bearing the same title. In his own statement for the trial, taken in Paris, Brancusi suggested a different definition of originality. He argued that the bronze *Bird* was original in the sense that it would initiate a series: "it is the only one I have made of this subject and its first replica is not yet finished" (49). Departing from Steichen's definition of originality as uniqueness – "the only one ever made" – Brancusi himself implied that originality involved inaugurating a string of replicas.

Though these theories of originality are strikingly complex and contradictory, their subtleties did not seem to interest the judges, who pronounced in their decision simply that the work was original. The straightforwardness of this ruling might seem surprising, but I want to suggest that the reason for this may lie in a tension within customs law itself.[20] The law as it stood in 1927 defined genuine art as both representational and original. But it is possible to read these two categories as *antithetical*. Mimesis strives to copy the world. It is always a double, a stand-in, an extra. Brancusi's radical abstraction, on the other hand, was strikingly unfamiliar, seeming to cut off its connections to both the world of nature and the world of traditional art.[21] His abstraction therefore undermined his commitment to representation but potentially *reinforced* a faith in his originality. It was precisely the strangeness of the object that made it clear that it was absolutely the artist's own. He was no mere copyist of the world: he was an originator of concepts, an artist whose objects emerged from his head.[22] The spirit of customs law had long been on the side of this version of artistic originality: the artist as inspired genius whose work was unique. On economic grounds, it was more important to establish the art work's radical distinctiveness than to enforce any particular style or tradition.

And although Brancusi's series of *Birds* do not imitate objects in nature, they hint at a different version of mimetic fidelity. As a collection of related works, the very idea for the *Bird* is faithful to *itself* – its numerous replications demonstrate that the work is loyal to a concept, a shape, a figure. If this figure comes from the artist's mind rather than from the world, all the better for the purposes of demonstrating originality. Indeed, a customs court had formulated the difference between genuine art and mere ornament in precisely these terms in 1912: "Ordinarily the ornamentalist in stone imitates that which he actually sees and his work goes no further than to please the eye. The sculptor, on the other hand, reproduces that which is pictured by his imagination; and his production appeals not only to the eye but to the emotions as well. In fine, one copies and the other, in a sense, creates and originates."[23] Strangely, art and mass culture shared the fact of "reproduction," but art reproduced what was in the imagination, while more mechanical craftsmanship reproduced what was already in the world. Thus the very repetition of Brancusi's *Bird* attests to the durability, even the reality, of the artist's original concept.[24] Brancusi's work, we might say, is both mimetic *and* original – because it is the image of its own originality.

But this is not quite the end of the story. Brancusi's legal team soon found that they had to reckon with the opposite problem. Was it possible that the work could be *too* original? If it was completely unlike other art objects, it would cease to count as art at all. After Steichen's testimony, the opposing counsel took up this line of attack,

exaggerating rather than undermining Brancusi's originality, ampli-
fying his oddity to the point that the *Bird* would fail to be recognizable as art. In cross-examination, William Henry Fox, Director
of the Brooklyn Museum, was asked whether the museum contained
any work that looked like Brancusi's *Bird*. When he agreed that Exhibit
1 was "distinct," the lawyer pounced: "Mr. Brancusi's work seems
to stand out alone as far as you are acquainted with the art world,
does it not? . . . Does not the work itself . . . stand out different
from all other sculptures by artists, it is isolated from what we
call art?" (42).

Epstein, himself a sculptor of eccentric work, was asked whether
he was doing work that was like Brancusi's *Bird*. He replied: "Well,
all sculptures are different" (28). Dissatisfied with this nebulous
reply, the lawyer asked the question again: "I asked you if you had
made anything like the Exhibit 1? . . . In all your thirty years?" Epstein
replied that he had not, and this response opened the door to further skepticism about Brancusi's work. The question came again in
a new form: "Do any [other sculptors] do works of this class and
character?" "There are other artists that do work similar," Epstein
responded, "not absolutely like Brancusi, but of that character." The
lawyer seized on this response. "So he stands practically isolated and
alone in this particular class of art?" (30).

Given the logic of American law, the next moment in the trial
may have proved decisive. Epstein formulated a response to this question that was perfectly suited to common-law adjudication. That is,
he produced a *precedent*. Brancusi's work, Epstein explained,

> is related to a very ancient form of sculpture, I should say even to
> the Egyptian. He does not stand absolutely alone. He is related to
> the fine ancient sculpture, like the early Egyptian, three thousand years
> old. If you would like to bring into the court a piece of sculpture,
> ancient sculpture, which I happen to have, I can illustrate. (30)

The sculptor was at once permitted to leave the stand in order to
fetch the object, a three-thousand-year old Egyptian image of a hawk.[25]

Judge Waite, comparing it to Brancusi's *Bird*, asked Epstein to articulate the content of the similarity. Epstein claimed that the likeness lay primarily in the fact that the ancient work was, like the *Bird*, abstract but evocative: "An ornithologist might not find [the similarity]," he said, "I see the resemblance to a bird." The judge appeared convinced: "The wings and feet are not shown, still you get the impression it is a hawk" (31).[26] Egyptian sculpture, like Brancusi's *Bird in Space*, lacked details associated with real birds. It was not anatomically complete, but its simplified contours nonetheless produced an "impression." The ancient sculpture could therefore act as a prototype for abstract art.

At this moment in the trial, the logic of avant-garde originality became strikingly similar to the logic of common law. Anglo-American law seeks to relate each new case to its precedents, setting each in a tradition, but also striving to acknowledge the specificity of the new, the potential for each example to demand a departure from tradition. New precedents are set when the particularities of the case call for a shift or expansion of definitions. Thus common law tries to balance its fidelity to the past with an acknowledgment of the unpredictable newness of the present. Ronald Dworkin argues that "legal claims are interpretive judgments and therefore combine backward- and forward-looking elements."[27] In theory, the avant-garde does the opposite, representing the effort to make a decisive break with tradition and the weight of the past. The law and the avant-garde should therefore find themselves fundamentally at odds, since the artist does her best to cut herself off from history, while common law conscientiously seeks to connect each new case to a cumulative history of legal norms.[28] But Epstein, though himself closely associated with avant-garde experimentation, refused the position that art must rupture its connections from the past. If the *Bird* was to be recognized as an original art work, it must be shown to be new, yes – but not so new that it would cease to belong to the category of art. Connecting abstraction to a very ancient precedent, Epstein affirmed that what had seemed like the shocking, unprecedented new art of the avant-garde actually boasted a venerable history.

With Epstein's testimony, Brancusi's *Bird* assumed a double relationship to history: it was firmly established as an art work by virtue of its link with the past, but as an *original* art work by virtue of its break from the past. Necessarily, it seemed, it had to be both: if it was not "original," it could not qualify as art according to the Tariff Act; but if it was too original, it would not belong to any recognizable definition of art. Thus Epstein proved a remarkably dexterous witness for Brancusi, balancing the logic of the law against the logic of the avant-garde. And this was no cowardly betrayal of principles: Epstein was merely willing to acknowledge a hidden truth about avant-garde experimentation. Instead of insisting that the avant-garde was spectacularly revolutionary, outside of all conventions and norms, he admitted that even the most radically defiant art necessarily takes on a crucial relationship to history. That is, although avant-gardists are proud of their ruptures from all past conventions, in fact each artistic break from the past only counts as a break *with respect to* that past. One of the avant-garde's many paradoxes is that it launches "a long tradition of ruptures with tradition."[29] The avant-garde is never so unprecedented as it likes to claim. Thus "original" art and common-law adjudication suddenly seemed to share the same relationship to history: both emerged as temporal phenomena, bound to convention but willing to accommodate the new.

The fact that the law and the avant-garde artist shared a notion of originality was crucial to Brancusi's case. But what clinched it, I would argue, was another aspect of the kinship between the art world and the law that usually goes unacknowledged: their understanding of themselves as autonomous institutions. The final decision in *Brancusi v. United States* puts its strongest emphasis on an institutionalized art world:

[*Olivotti v. United States*] was handed down in 1916. In the meanwhile there has been developing a so-called new school of art, whose exponents attempt to portray abstract ideas rather than to imitate natural objects. Whether or not we are in sympathy with these newer ideas and the schools which represent them, we think the facts of their existence and their influence upon the art world as recognized by the courts must be considered. (115)

With this decision, customs law added a crucial social element to its longstanding definition of art as the work of individual geniuses; here, whatever spark of creativity there is takes place in "schools" that together form an independent "art world."

And indeed, what emerged in the courtroom proceedings was a remarkably orderly and regulated institution of art. As in any legal case, expert witnesses had to demonstrate their qualifications in order to testify. All of the witnesses for and against Brancusi were grilled on their training, their prizes and diplomas, their time spent writing about or creating art, the galleries and magazines where their work had appeared.[30] The lawyers on both sides worked hard to argue that certain journals, museums, and schools were legitimate sources of expertise on the question of art.[31] And in this context, Brancusi's team had little trouble establishing the professional status of the artist, as the Tariff Act required: certified experts attested to his international reputation, his numerous high-profile shows, his portrayal in recognized arts publications, his place in art history classrooms, and his dedication to the exclusive activity of art-making. Thus, although Brancusi himself had become famous in the US as part of the uninhibited extravagance of the European avant-garde, it could not be denied that he belonged to an organized institution that recognized him as a respected member. To hear the witnesses repeatedly invoking awards and guidelines, recognized authorities and international reputations, it would seem as if the goal of the radical avant-garde was to be conventional, disciplined, and orthodox.

Faced with this institutional solidarity, what choice did the courts have? The judiciary, itself an organized body governed by credentials, norms, procedures, and reviews, simply agreed to recognize the "art world" as a fellow self-regulating institution. "Whether or not we are in sympathy with these newer ideas and the schools which represent them, we think the facts of their existence and their influence upon the art world as recognized by the courts must be considered." However madcap and harebrained it might seem to the average observer, the artistic avant-garde looked to the court something like a self-governing organization that could, with confidence, be left to its own devices.

The art world's institutional autonomy may have been the most important factor established in *Brancusi v. United States*. Let us return for a moment to the Tariff Act's three requirements for art: the object in question must not be an "article of utility"; it must be the professional work of a sculptor; and it must be original. What all three stipulations shared, implicitly, was the notion that art was separate from the rest of the social world: it was distinct from other kinds of commodities and manufacture in that it served no useful purpose; it belonged to its own self-regulating sphere of professional activity; and it could be traced to a concept that emerged from the single artist's imagination. The *Olivotti* definition of art as representation was the only factor that bound art to the world of ordinary life. And it was here that Brancusi's style exerted its significance. Abstract art purposefully worked free from the realm of ordinary objects, and so the *Bird's* abstract style actually completed art's disconnection from the rest of life. Apart from mimesis, every one of the law's conditions for art supported the idea that art was an autonomous sphere, separate from other professions and commodities. And so mimesis had to go. Abstraction was not only the outgrowth of an autonomous art world; it was also a guarantee of that art world's autonomy. Customs law already recognized art as free from usefulness, ordinary labor, and the commercial pressures of the marketplace. Now it would be free from nature too.[32]

In granting the art world its freedom to pursue eccentric and innovative techniques, the law did not concede that the avant-garde was a marginal and counter-cultural sphere. It did not even imagine art as an oppositional and contestatory force. Instead, the customs court cast the art world as a fellow institution, a social body complete with self-determining professional associations, recognized training, and official representatives. Thus while the law separated art from the rest of social life, it readily allowed the art work to be tightly connected to *art itself* – acknowledging the *Bird's* link to a tradition of sculpture reaching back five thousand years, and unreservedly recognizing a network of schools, journals, galleries, and museums as if they bound the many elements of the art world into one. Willingly, in other words, the law hailed the modern art world as a body much like itself, self-sufficient and coherent, with its own rules and guidelines, its own history and its own ruptures from that history. Equally willingly, the art world accepted its special role as a balance of originality and precedent, autonomy and regulation – innovative but not too innovative, and free but not too free.

And that was how the avant-garde entered the country tax free.

## There's No Such Thing as Originality, and It's a Good Thing, Too

If the avant-garde Brancusi managed to persuade the law to change its definition of art, he accomplished this transformation quietly, playing by the rules rather than disrupting them and acknowledging his own institutionalization rather than boasting of a thoroughgoing freedom. My next example is a copyright suit in which the artist adopted the most dramatic rhetoric of avant-garde liberation – and proceeded to lose. He so underestimated the law, in fact, that he managed not only to lose his own case but to persuade the court to set a new and more repressive precedent – with serious consequences for artists in the future.

Like the Brancusi case, this one hinged on the question of originality. Originality, as the Supreme Court has held, is "the sine qua non" of copyright law.[33] But legal scholars argue that the copyright conception of originality is different from that which we saw in customs law, which emphasized uniqueness and genius. The courts in copyright cases offer a much more modest standard, defining as original, for example, compilations of existing materials, maps, and descriptions of ideas already in circulation. The Supreme Court made it clear in 1991 that for copyright protection, the "requisite level of creativity is extremely low; even a slight amount will suffice. The vast majority of works make the grade quite easily, as they possess some creative spark, 'no matter how crude, humble, or obvious' it might be":

> The term "original" . . . means only that the work was independently created by the author, as opposed to copied from other works, and that it possesses at least some minimal degree of creativity; because originality does not signify novelty, a work may be original even though it closely resembles other works, so long as the similarity is fortuitous, not the result of copying; thus, if two poets, each ignorant of the other, compose identical poems, although neither work is novel, both are original and, hence, copyrightable.[34]

Copyright protection thus extends to most works that are not outright piracy.[35] The reasons given for this minimal benchmark are practical: to require significant innovation, as patent law does, would be to set an intolerably high bar for copyright protection.[36] It might mean refusing copyright, for example, to commentaries, textbooks, historical accounts, even descriptions – anything that duplicates knowledge or ideas already in existence. And so, compared with the revolutionary ruptures embraced by the avant-garde, the copyright conception of originality seems cautious and humdrum.

But despite the modesty of its demands, copyright has substantial implications for democracy. Article 1 of the US Constitution authorizes Congress to pass copyright laws in order to encourage citizens to create and invent: "To promote the Progress of Science and useful Arts, by securing for limited times to Authors and Inventors, the exclusive Right to their respective Writings and Discoveries."[37] The idea of allowing authors "exclusive rights" might seem an unlikely spur to "progress," promoting monopolies rather than competitors, but the standard rationale for copyright legislation is that the market alone cannot provide adequate incentives for new ideas. The fruits of intellectual labor – essays, songs, photographs, software – can be reproduced endlessly at almost no cost, and so copyright protection is essential because without it, unrestricted copying by "free riders" would bring the price of any intellectual product down almost to zero. Authors and publishers would then have trouble recovering the initial costs of production. Without copyright protection, in other words, no writer or artist would want to spend time and money producing a work that others would sell for almost nothing, and that in turn would prevent new ideas and art works from being made in the first place.

Neil Weinstock Netanel argues that the Framers of the US Constitution advocated copyright as an exception to First Amendment protections for speech because they were particularly mindful of the dangers of state and private patronage. In most non-democratic societies, authors had to depend on wealthy donors or state powers to sponsor their work, and this dependence stifled critical expression. The Framers thought that authors should be able to speak freely to a large public rather than relying on a single patron. And yet, given the problem of "free riders," market forces alone could not provide sufficient incentives for authors to write and publish their views. For the good of democracy, therefore, the Framers favored the controls on speech afforded by copyright law to stimulate public debate and deliberation. Copyright "constitutes an integral part of a system of collective self-rule in which the norms that permeate our social relations and undergird state policy are determined in the space of broad-based citizen debate, rather than by government or private fiat."[38]

If copyrights are granted for the purposes of progress, they are fixed for only a limited term because, theorists argue, it is bad for democratic dialogue and creativity to allow authors too strict a monopoly on the use of their work. If writers and artists could stifle all later citations, imitations, and derivations, they would severely limit the range of creative resources available to future generations. Disney, to cite a famous example, has borrowed extensively from works in the public domain – including *The Jungle Book*, *Cinderella*, *The*

*Little Mermaid*, *Peter Pan*, *Pinocchio*, and *Alice in Wonderland* – and yet has repeatedly argued that Mickey Mouse should not be free for others to use.[39] This seems illogical and unfair to many copyright critics, who argue that it is only appropriate for copyrights to be temporary, with works eventually entering the public domain, free for all to imitate, build on, and reproduce.[40] In fact, the freedom to make use of preexisting materials is essential to participation in a culture and is therefore a democratic value, as Jack Balkin argues: "Dissenters draw on what they dislike in order to criticize it; artists borrow from previous examples and build on artistic conventions; even casual conversation draws on common topics and expressions. People participate in culture through building on what they find in culture and innovating with it, modifying it, and turning it to their purposes."[41] The democratic logic of copyright, then, is that short term restrictions on public access to original works will stimulate broad, innovative, and diverse kinds of participation in public discourse.[42] Copyright thus emerges as essential to the health of a democracy, promoting progress through a plurality of viewpoints. It is a special exception to the general protections for free speech guaranteed by the First Amendment because, as the Supreme Court ruled, copyright is itself an "engine of free expression."[43]

Now, if we pause for a moment to take stock of the question of originality as it has been theorized in the post-1960s art world and the courtroom, we encounter something of a surprise. The two institutions seem to have reversed their usual roles: while postmodern artists have explicitly abandoned radical innovation in favor of the recycling of conventional forms and meanings, the law reveals itself as dedicated to fostering and supporting plural ideas that are crucial to social progress. The art world has turned to history and tradition, while copyright is committed to novelty, creativity, dissension. In this world turned upside-down, the logic of the avant-garde seems to belong more to the courtroom than to the artist's studio.

But this is a question of emphasis rather than a genuine reversal. As the Brancusi case makes clear, the law and the art world share a structural relationship to history. While art since the beginning of

168

the avant-garde has been associated with shock, radical innovation, and the unsettling of convention, it has never been so free from tradition as the avant-gardists would have had us believe. As we saw with *Bird in Space*, even when an art work breaks from the past, it links itself to that past precisely *as a break*. Like common law, the art world always refers to precedents set in the past. On the other hand, although the law is typically associated with tradition and a deep conservatism, lawyers "adapt, recast – and yes, transform – precedent to speak to a particular case."[44] The courts reach into the past not only to stay faithful to past decisions, but to create new and evolving standards through selection and recombination. Postmodern artists have argued that since nothing is ever really new, the only creative option is appropriation and recombination – the use of old materials in surprising new combinations. Thus Anglo-American common-law adjudication begins to look uncannily like the appropriation artist: both reject the idea of a clean, revolutionary break from tradition; both imagine that the past is inescapable and that the future will be conceived in terms of existing examples. Ronald Dworkin argues that judicial decisions are in fact "creative" in ways precisely analogous to the making of art. In order to describe the law's relationship to history, he imagines a group of writers composing a novel in consecutive stages, what he calls a "chain novel": "Each novelist aims to make a single novel of the material he has been given, what he adds to it, and (so far as he can control this) what his successors will want or be able to add."[45] Like postmodern artists, then, jurists work creatively with existing materials which they reuse and recast to meet the demands of a changing environment.

What is perhaps most surprising is that copyright law has been committed to this "postmodern" notion of creativity at least since 1845, when a Massachusetts court ruled as follows:

In truth, in literature, in science and in art, there are, and can be, few things, which, in an abstract sense, are strictly new and original throughout. Every book in literature, science and art borrows, and must necessarily borrow, and use much which was well known and used before. No man creates a new language for himself, at least if he be a wise man, in writing a book. He contents himself with the use of language already known and used and understood by others. . . . The thoughts of every man are, more or less, a combination of what other men have thought and expressed, although they may be modified, exalted, or improved by his own genius or reflection.[46]

Perhaps the crucial difference between the art world and copyright law is that the courts define quintessentially postmodern techniques of recontextualization, recombination, and collage as *kinds of originality*. Take, for example, the Supreme Court's holding in *Feist* (1991):

> choices as to selection and arrangement, so long as they are made independently by the compiler and entail a minimal degree of creativity, are sufficiently original that Congress may protect such compilations through the copyright laws. . . . Thus, even a directory that contains absolutely no protectible written expression, only facts, meets the constitutional minimum for copyright protection if it features an original selection or arrangement.[47]

It is quite enough, as far as the law is concerned, to put preexisting materials together in thoughtful selections or arrangements. And this notion of "original selection or arrangement" seems nicely to describe the gestures of postmodern artists who take readymade vacuum cleaners, sneakers, or urinals and arrange them in the unlikely space of a museum or gallery – recontextualizing them such that they cannot be understood or put to use in any usual way. The courts may call this "originality" and the art world "appropriation," but the logic is surprisingly similar.

Only a semantic difference, then, cloaks a common set of goals and aspirations. Both the art world and common law value the freedom to create and innovate – but in both contexts, creativity occurs within the boundaries of tradition, and depends on the use of preexisting materials, styles, modes, and meanings. And although individual copyright cases do not typically privilege revolutionary newness in the spirit of the avant-garde, copyright law as a whole *is* intended to stimulate a robust plurality of voices. Netanel argues that avant-garde art would be suffocated without it.[48] Thus what I want to suggest is that, in theory, the logic of the avant-garde and the logic of copyright share a common value: a commitment to the unsettling of oppressively dominant viewpoints. In theory, too, they share a similar democratic function: the provocation of vigorous discussion and the production of an expressive plurality.

In theory. But unhappily, in practice, both the art world and the law have been letting us down in recent years. The postmodern artist on trial, we might think, would readily recognize her kinship with social institutions like the courts, both of them bound to history and convention, both of them committed to a certain social plurality and innovation. But when hauled into court, some of the most quintessentially postmodern artists have boasted of their freedom from all constraints and all norms; they have posed as radical outliers, above or outside the law. And despite their robust critique of originality, they have characterized their own art as a radical break from conventional thoughts and mainstream views. Setting themselves up as the law's antagonists, postmodern artists have sometimes scorned the courts as naïve and conservative, bound to unthinking, repressive institutional norms and unable to recognize the startling, disquieting value of art. They have adopted the rhetoric of the avant-garde in hostile relation to the courts without noticing that the institution of the law is, at least potentially, more friend than enemy.

Meanwhile, the courts have increasingly favored a "bloated" copyright that is bad for both art *and* democracy. When the US Congress first granted copyright protection it limited the author's control to 14 years, renewable for another 14 years if the author was alive to claim it. In the next hundred years, Congress extended the term once, to 28 years, renewable for 14 more. But in the past fifty years, Congress has expanded copyright eleven times, so that an individual "author" now has exclusive rights over her work for her lifetime plus 70 years, while corporate authors have 95 years.

These extensions are retroactive, covering all works currently under copyright as well as those not yet in existence. The Supreme Court has upheld the expanded terms.[49] Thus many commentators have argued that the law is no longer striking the best balance between an author's profits and the public good. Increasingly cast as a private property right rather than as an incentive to new creative endeavor, copyright now belongs to authors' estates long after a work has come into being. This means that the field of creative work that is free for others to draw on is dramatically limited, restricting opportunities for democratic participation in Balkin's sense.[50] It means that heirs who may have created nothing original themselves are being compensated for the work of long-dead creators. And it means that James Joyce's grandson can prevent the publication of scholarly interpretations of *Ulysses* if he does not like them, while Lorenz Hart's estate can refuse to allow biographers to reprint his song lyrics if they plan to mention Hart's homosexuality.[51] How does art fare in this contemporary copyright environment? Sometimes very poorly indeed.

In 1987, the artist Jeff Koons picked up a notecard in an airport souvenir shop. It showed a man and a woman sitting on a bench, holding a row of eight squirming black puppies on their laps (figure 5.2). To Koons, the notecard seemed like typically sentimental kitsch. He wanted to make a sculpture based on the card, perfect for a show he was planning to call "Banality." Koons was at the time one of the biggest stars in the art world. A former commodities trader, he was famous for incorporating advertising and marketing strategies into his work. Glossy billboards announced his shows, and his art included actual Nike posters, images from pornography, and a reworking of tacky souvenirs. But his work was – and is – not merely a celebration of the market: according to Koons and many of his advocates, his art reworks mass culture in order to critique it. Often he appropriates kitsch objects and mass produced commodities – like toys and household products – and then recreates them in surprising materials. One famous example is a toy bunny, cast in stainless steel from an inflatable original.

172

**Figure 5.2**   Art Rogers, "Puppies" © 1980, courtesy Art Rogers.

Koons wanted to use the note card as the basis for a sculpture, but he did not intend to make the art work with his own hands. He tore the copyright notice off the back and sent the card to a wood-carving workshop in northern Italy, asking the artisans there to copy the notecard in three-dimensional sculptural form. He liked the contrast between the trite image and the connotations of wooden sculpture, which is usually associated with sacred icons. In his notes, he indicated that the artisans should make certain changes, but he also directed them to remain faithful to the photo (figure 5.3).

Though the card might have looked like a kitschy piece of commodity culture to Jeff Koons, it was of course the work of a

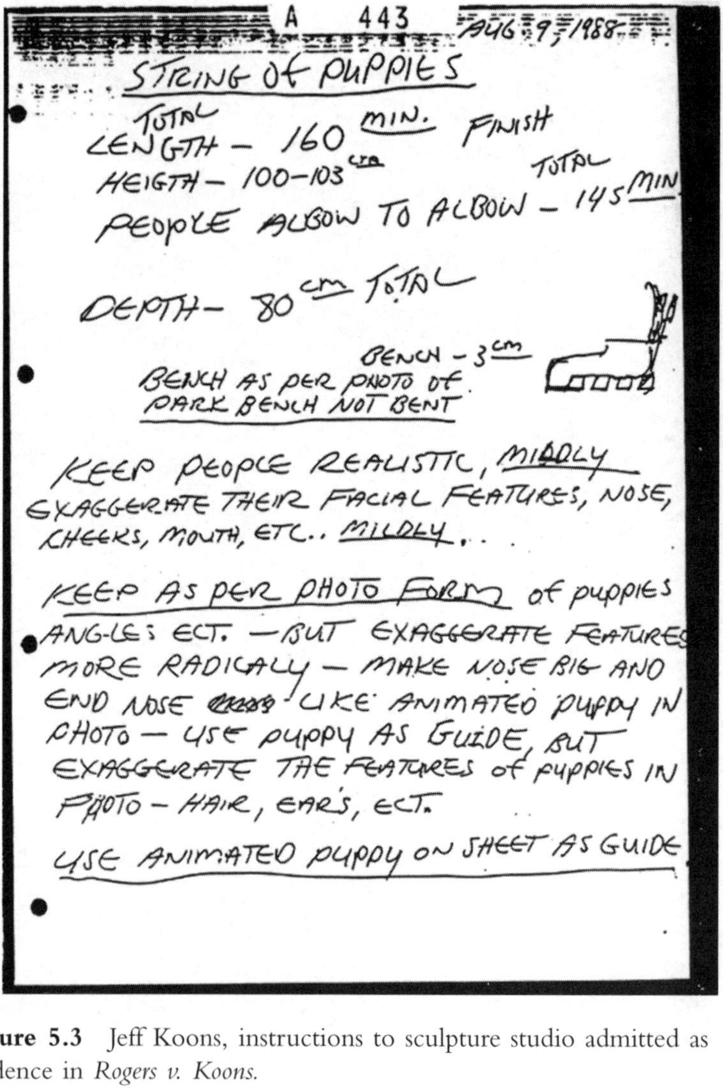
A 443 AUG 9, 1988

STRING OF PUPPIES

TOTAL LENGTH – 160 MIN. FINISH

HEIGTH – 100–103 CM

PEOPLE ALBOW TO ALBOW – 145 MIN TOTAL

DEPTH – 80 CM TOTAL

BENCH – 3 CM

BENCH AS PER PHOTO OF PARK BENCH NOT BENT

KEEP PEOPLE REALISTIC, MIDDLY EXAGGERATE THEIR FACIAL FEATURES, NOSE, CHEEKS, MOUTH, ETC.. MILDLY...

KEEP AS PER PHOTO FORM of puppies ANGLES ECT. — BUT EXAGGERATE FEATURES MORE RADICALLY — MAKE NOSE BIG AND END NOSE LIKE ANIMATED PUPPY IN PHOTO — USE PUPPY AS GUIDE, BUT EXAGGERATE THE FEATURES of PUPPIES IN PHOTO – HAIR, EAR'S, ECT.

USE ANIMATED PUPPY ON SHEET AS GUIDE

**Figure 5.3** Jeff Koons, instructions to sculpture studio admitted as evidence in *Rogers v. Koons.*

particular person, a professional photographer named Art Rogers, who was – and still is – working in northern California. In 1980, a friend asked Rogers to take a picture of a new litter of eight German Shepherd puppies. He decided that the best way to photograph them would be in the arms of their owners, and he carefully posed them to give the image what he called a feeling of "joy and pride."[52] In 1984 he sold the image to Museum Graphics, a company that produces notecards and postcards.

When Art Rogers opened the *LA Times* one day in 1989 to see that his work was the basis of a sculpture priced at almost $200,000 (figure 5.4) he brought a suit for copyright infringement. The case came to court in 1990 and was decided by a judge alone, without a jury. Koons lost the initial suit and then lost again in two appeals.

**Figure 5.4**   Jeff Koons, *String of Puppies* (1988), courtesy Jeff Koons.

Though postmodern artists like Andy Warhol and Robert Rauschenberg had also been sued in the past for appropriations of professional photography, the parties in all previous suits had agreed to settle out of court. Thus *Rogers v. Koons* was the first case of its kind to yield a published opinion.

Surprisingly for a famous postmodern artist, Koons borrowed his most heartfelt defenses from the rhetoric of the avant-garde. First, he insisted that a strong artist was ahead of his time, providing "leadership" "in global culture" (A151). Second, he took pride in his solitary daring, refusing to be grouped with any school of artists or any arts institution, saying, "I am my own man in my own shoes" (A178). Third, he rejected the notion that financial rewards had meaning for him:

> "It's about my generosity to my public and how much I want to give to my public. . . . It's not about trying to find people to buy my work. . . ."
> "There is already more demand for it than you can satisfy?"
> "Other than myself continuing to push myself to be courageous and to lead my community." (A296)

Koons also insisted that art meant *freedom*:

> One of my major goals is to let artists know, and it always has to be hammered in, that art can be absolutely anything, absolutely anything the artist desires, as long as they are strong enough to carry that out. It can be anything. It's a totally undefined profession. It is total liberation. And they should have to embrace that liberation. (A299)

Finally, Koons distinguished his own, exceptional and valuable conceptual art from the work of ordinary artisans and commercially popular artwork. "I saw this note card as part of mass culture. It was a commercially presented image. I saw it as resting in the collective sub-consciousness of people (regardless whether the card had actually ever been seen by such people)" (A791):

To me it is not art. To me it is a post card. It is something that is
reproduced over and over and over again to penetrate into a culture.
What I liked about it was just a sense of familiar. I mean it is just a
familiar kind of sense. Just like one of these black and white post
cards with maybe just a little something off, that's it. It is not a signed
limited edition or anything. It is not numbered, like 1 of, you know,
5,000 or 1 of 10 million. It is just part of the public domain. (A305–6)

Setting the solitary, autonomous, and "totally liberated" artist against
the bulk production of mass culture, Koons claimed that Rogers'
work was part of the public domain. In other words, from the perspective of the avant-garde, *mass culture does not deserve copyright
protection*. The artist should be free to use it without permission
precisely because it is banal.

The art experts who added their voices to the chorus in Koons's
defense also borrowed their rhetoric from the avant-garde, suggesting that his art was so extraordinary, new, and distinctive, indeed
so outside of the conventional spheres of commerce and law, that
it could not properly be judged by any commonplace standards. A
curator from the Baltimore Museum argued that she found it
"appalling that an important sculptural work by an artist of Koons's
stature would be said to have an improper or illegal connection to
an ordinary and conventional picture like the Rogers notecard" (A897).
A representative from San Francisco Museum of Modern Art
claimed to be "surprised that someone could claim that such a unique,
important sculptural work of art could be considered a violation
of a very ordinary photograph" (A826). And the director of the
Sonnabend Gallery stated that Koons "is a great artist . . . he has
a particular vision and a personal, unique style for presenting his
vision" (A809).

Thus both Koons and the experts who wrote affidavits in his defense
expressed shock that Rogers' ordinary work could have anything
to do with the "great" art of Jeff Koons. And they made it clear
that they felt it was wrong – "surprising" and "appalling" – for
the law to consider Koons a proper subject of a run-of-the-mill

177

copyright suit. Koons was too much a leader, too special a voice, too "important" to be constrained by the rules that pertained to those who were engaged in low, mainstream cultural activity like the mass production of sentimental notecards. Imagining a chasm between ordinary commercial representation and the work of great artists, Koons's side suggested that the two worlds were always and necessarily separate: while the ordinary person might be hauled into court for copying another's work, the artist should be free to explore his unique and distinctive vision.

Rogers countered that Koons had carefully copied his creative idea for the purposes of his own commercial gain, adding nothing to the public store of thoughts and expressions. Both artists, in other words, were claiming originality for themselves and *un*originality for the other. So: which of the two was contributing more to the health and vigor of democracy – the commercial photographer who had conceived of the scene in the first place or the cutting-edge artist who intended to use the photograph to comment on the banality of contemporary life?

Rogers' legal team had no difficulty establishing that photography in general could be original: in 1884, a battle over copies of a photograph of Oscar Wilde went to the Supreme Court. Though the justices acknowledged that it was commonplace to assume that "a photograph is the mere mechanical reproduction of the physical features or outlines of some object, animate or inanimate, and involves no originality of thought or any novelty in the intellectual operation connected with its visible reproduction in shape of a picture," the court in this case affirmed "the existence . . . of intellectual production, of thought, and conception on the part of the author."[53] As this decision makes clear, it is the labor of the mind – intellectual work – that copyright law specifically acknowledges and compensates. But the evidence of intellectual labor does not need to be extraordinary: it includes quite commonplace choices, including "posing the subjects, lighting, angle, selection of film and camera, evoking the desired expression, and almost any other variant involved."[54]

In the *Rogers* case, the court flatly rejected Koons's argument that the mass produced note card was part of the public domain, too unoriginal to earn the protection of copyright:

> Substantial creative effort went into both the composition and production of "Puppies". . . . At the photo session, and later in his lab, Rogers drew on his years of artistic development. He selected the light, the location, the bench on which the Scanlons are seated and the arrangement of the small dogs. He also made creative judgments concerning technical matters with his camera and the use of natural light.[55]

Koons's contention that the photo was too trite, too ordinary, too *familiar* to earn the court's protection was a misunderstanding of the legal definition of originality. It did not have to be revolutionary; it merely had to involve some thoughtfulness about selections and arrangements.

But to establish that one has a valid copyright is not quite enough to win a copyright case. Rogers' legal team had to show that Koons had indeed copied the photograph, and also that there was "substantial similarity" between the notecard and the sculpture. This was no small matter, given that Koons had made changes to the medium, color scheme, size, and facial expressions. Then, even if those facts could be established, Koons's side could still argue that he had used Rogers' photograph for the purpose of criticism or parody – a classic "fair use" exception to the usual standards of copyright.[56]

These three considerations – the evidence of copying, the problem of substantial similarity, and the question of fair use – formed the bulk of the dispute in the trial. Evidence of copying was the easiest to establish. Admitted into evidence were a number of Koons's faxed orders to his studio, which seemed like quite a smoking gun: "work must be just like photo"; "Details – Just Like Photo!" "keep woman's big smile"; "Girl's nose is too small. Please make larger as per photo"; and "Paint realistic as per photo, but in blues" (Rogers' brief, 8).[57]

The second point was more contentious: was there really a "substantial similarity" between a small, black-and-white notecard and a cartoon-colored sculpture that was larger than life? Koons's side wanted a jury to decide, but Rogers' team explained that there was no need:

> The well-established test in this circuit for substantial similarity, which the district quoted and applied, is "whether an average lay observer would recognize the alleged copy as having been appropriated from the copyrighted work" . . . Jim Scanlon's friend, an average lay observer, had actually mistaken the sculpture for a "colorized" version of the photograph. . . . [The] similarity extends to minute details, e.g., the position of each person and each puppy, the wrinkles in the Scanlons' clothes, and even the angles of the points of Jim Scanlon's shirt collar, are the same. (Rogers' brief, 19–20)

Koons's side disagreed, pointing out that there was another test typically used by the courts, which asked whether "the ordinary observer . . . would regard their aesthetic appeal as the same." Koons's side contended that the "expression" of the two works was fundamentally dissimilar:

> there are significant differences in the two works which have nothing to do with the change in medium. The blue, cartoon faces on the dogs and the exaggerated features on the couple were deliberately added to bring out the critical aspects of the work. The colors, the larger than life scale, the flowers in the hair all evidence a new artistic conception. The District Court could not properly decide the factual issue of copying and ignore the total, combined effect each separate change and each additive element have on the final work. Based on the testimony . . . a jury could reasonably find that the photograph conveyed love and warmth while the sculpture conveyed frightening detachment, an entirely different mood and artistic conception. (Koons's brief, 7–8)

Koons emphasized that while the note card did communicate a feeling of "joy and pride," the sculpture was larger than life-sized, goofy, caricatured, and even "nightmarish." Antonio Homem of Sonnabend Gallery stated in his deposition that "Jeff used a sentimental 'cliché' description of a domestic scene and transformed it into a kind of miraculous vision of something hypnotic and quite unrelated to reality as we know it" (A808). If the case concerned the originality of "expression," then surely Koons had dramatically altered the mood and feeling – the "aesthetic appeal" – of the original? Moreover, it was a crucial fact that the sculpture had not even been brought into the courtroom. Instead, a photograph of the sculpture was standing in for the work itself, suggesting a deceptively pronounced similarity between the two works. If the court had allowed Koons to bring the sculpture before a jury, they might well have seen a significant discrepancy between the two works.

The third question was the most difficult of all: numerous experts testified that Koons's work was critical and parodic, and thus constituted a fair use of the note card. Parody earns special protection under copyright law because authors of original works are unlikely to grant permission to parodists to mock their creations, but without ridicule, the arts and political discourse would suffer.[58] This was the basis for Koons's strongest defense: "For the general viewer Koons is criticizing the social systems which breed greed, self indulgence, and conspicuous consumption" (A903); "Koons is interested in emotional cliches. He is interested in exposing the insincerity in them" (A917); "the intent of the transformation is . . . to comment critically both on the incorporated object and the political and economic system that created the object" (Koons's brief, 12). Koons's legal team underscored this fair use defense by arguing that the sculpture in no way limited the market for Rogers' original, since the two works spoke to different audiences: those who bought the Rogers post card would be eager for an experience of sentimentality, whereas those who purchased or viewed Koons's work would be seeking the critical, satirical experience offered by postmodern appropriation art.

Rogers countered that if Koons was criticizing the larger society, there was no need to copy a very specific note card to launch his generalized critique. Why steal Rogers' arrangement and poses at all? Indeed, Koons was violating any standard definition of parody: "By definition a parody or satire must depend for its point, whether it be humor or social commentary, at least in part, on the audience's familiarity with the original" (Rogers' brief, 29). Since Koons was not parodying Rogers in particular, his decision to copy the photograph could not rightly be considered fair use:

> Shorn of the rhetoric, Koons's basic argument here – which was never presented below – is that copyright law must yield to his desire to produce and sell sculptures that depict other artists' copyrighted expression, not to parody or satirize their work even in part, but to comment on or criticize society in general. The argument fails because absent a satiric purpose to make a point, in least in part, by comparison with a well-known original, there is no need for Koons's sculptures to "conjure up" the original's protected expression. . . . It is not "conjured up." It has simply been appropriated. (Rogers' brief, 3)

Since Rogers' work was relatively obscure and since Koons did not cite his use of it, no audience would automatically think of the note card when faced with Koons's sculpture. They might grasp the critique of consumer society, but they would not understand the work as *parody*. Koons responded by pointing out that Rogers' note card was famous enough: it had not only been published, it had been mass produced, thereby becoming as "well known" as any object of parody needed to be. Koons also argued that it was a misreading of the copyright statute to claim that a parody must "conjure up" the original: the statue "does not impose any such limitation on the meaning of 'comment' or 'criticism.' . . . the terms should be defined flexibly (by their common meaning) *so as to encourage creativity*" (Koons's brief, 11–12, my emphasis).

Koons lost on all three of these issues. The court found his copying "in bad faith, primarily for profit-making motives." Judge Cardamone found that the two works were substantially similar, and had the "same aesthetic appeal": "Koons's copying of Rogers' work was the essence of the photograph. . . . Koons went well beyond the factual subject matter of the photograph to incorporate the very expression of the work created by Rogers." And as for fair use,

> the copied work must be, at least in part, an object of the parody, otherwise there would be no need to conjure up the original work. . . . By requiring the copied work be an object of the parody, we merely insist that the audience be aware that underlying the parody there is an original and separate expression, attributable to a different artist.[59]

Some scholars argue that this decision set a distressing precedent for appropriation artists in the future.[60] No longer could an artist choose to rework a common object in order to comment on consumer desire, mass production, or the power of advertising. Now she would have to be sure of two things: first, that the original object was explicitly cited or so generally known that audiences would recognize it as the artist's target; and second, that it was the major focus of the artist's critique.

Legal theorist Jeannie Suk points out that the precedent set in the *Rogers* case is pernicious because it will help to discourage a whole range of subtle literary rewritings and artistic appropriations that use existing works to comment on social injustice, convention, and cliché. For example, in the copyright case against Alice Randall's *The Wind Done Gone* − a sequel to *Gone With the Wind* told from the perspective of Scarlett O'Hara's half-sister, a slave − the court decided in favor of Randall. But they did so, in the aftermath of *Rogers*, because the novel was so clearly a parody of the original. Suk writes:

> To find that *The Wind Done Gone* was a parody of the underlying work, rather than a work that criticized or commented on subjects outside of the underlying work, the court downplayed the book's originality and emphasized the extent to which it simply attacked *Gone with the Wind*. If the court had emphasized the originality of the work's transformative commentary on, say, slavery, canonicity, or history, it would have been more difficult to permit the work as parodic fair

use. . . . In other words, which is more original and valuable to the public: an attack on the famously trite *Gone with the Wind*, or a reflection, through transformative engagement with the familiar work, on the nature of American slavery, literary voice, and cultural construction?[61]

By limiting the definition of parodic fair use, the court is now actually inclined to safeguard only the most obvious, restricted kinds of aesthetic transformations: unambiguous parodies. Concerned that the court's narrow understanding of fair use will dramatically limit the kinds of rewritings and reappropriations that enrich the public sphere, Suk points out that lawyers should know better: "If anything, lawyers should appreciate literary rewriting because we know that applying precedent is not a mechanical act, but one that involves transformation and even originality. Lawyers know that in the production of texts, copying and originality coexist, each nourishing the other." In the end, Suk suggests, by defining fair use as narrow and obvious parody, the courts failed to acknowledge the central, subtle insight of both postmodernism *and* the long tradition of copyright law – namely that "borrowing is [both] inseparable from, *and constitutive of*, originality."[62] Strangely, then, both the court and the postmodern artist seemed to forget what we thought they know about originality: that original work depends on responses, reworkings, criticisms, and imitations of what is already circulating.

Intriguingly, in *Rogers v. Koons*, the court also forgot its tradition of deference to the arts and art experts. Koons had claimed that the court ought not to make aesthetic judgments. "The chilling effect on creative art . . . by a judge who may not know or appreciate art is obvious" (Koons's brief, 33). He quoted Oliver Wendell Holmes's famous assertion: "It would be a dangerous undertaking for persons trained only in the law to constitute themselves final judges of the worth of pictorial illustrations, outside the narrowest and most obvious limits."[63] Judge Cardamone responded: "the decision-maker, whether it be judge or jury, need not have any special skills other than to be a reasonable and average lay person."[64] Thus the judge turned his back on a longstanding legal willingness to respect expertise in the arts and its defense of difficult, challenging, unpopular art – a tradition that, as we have seen, includes *Ulysses*, *Lady Chatterley's Lover*, *Bird in Space*, Robert Mapplethorpe, and 2 Live Crew. Judge Cardamone explicitly chose instead the ordinary observer, precisely the representative of the mainstream rejected by the artistic avant-garde.

The question, then, is *why*? Why did the courts set a new precedent that would appear to limit the range of legitimate rewritings to a narrow and unimaginative few? Indeed, why would they choose to breach their longstanding commitment to the protection of creativity, no matter how humble, meager, or crude, by ruling against a well respected artist, praised by his peers and valued by galleries, museums, and arts publications? These questions become even more urgent, and more perplexing, when we consider the details of the dispute. Why, for example, did both the District and the Circuit Courts summarily refute Koons's argument that the sculpture should be brought before a jury before it was assumed to be "substantially similar" to the photograph? The court's contention that the note card and the sculpture offered the "same aesthetic appeal" seems surprising, if not absurd, and its conclusion that Koons had copied the "essence" of the photograph's expression seems incongruous, given the starkly different mood and feeling of the two works. And even more surprisingly, why did the court feel qualified to judge contemporary art works, despite a long legal tradition of allowing the art world to speak for itself?

Although the rhetoric of the avant-garde emphasizes freedom – and often to productive ends – I want to suggest that too grandiose a set of claims about emancipatory art can end up forestalling the sympathy of democratic institutions. If artists understand themselves as above the law, too sophisticated to be confined by mere legal reasoning, too emancipated to follow the rules that apply to everyone else, and therefore free to act as they choose, the art world begins to look like a dramatically anarchic social force. While the revolutionary avant-garde might well favor such a role for art, it is certainly understandable why the courts do not. It would hardly be reasonable for the courtroom to valorize and protect a group of people who set themselves against the law on principle.

But I do not want to claim that the only option is a standoff between the repressive courts and the liberated artists. It is the classic posture of the avant-garde to claim a freedom from all rules, all conventions, all institutions, all restraints. To the extent that this posture helps to produce stimulating and thought provoking dissent, it is a democratically useful stance. But the notion of an *absolute* freedom is a myth, and it is not only false, it is self-defeating. Artists who claim that they are justified in breaking the law because laws are always needlessly restrictive will not fare well in the courts, which, after all, wield substantial power, and are perfectly capable of punishing artistic illegalities. Koons lost, in the words of Louise Harmon, because he "was saying only one thing: As an artist, he was above the law. And we all know: law trumps art."[65]

Yet the artist who wants to win a court case does not have to abandon the rhetoric of freedom altogether. What works best in the courtroom, as Brancusi made clear, are arguments for a specific *kind* of freedom, the kind of freedom offered by avant-garde experimentation and welcomed by theorists of democratic pluralism – the freedom to innovate, to dissent, and to create, or, as the law might have it, the freedom to promote collective progress through original thoughts and expressions. Koons might have argued that his work explored the social roles of kitsch and mass production by engaging with mass culture, helping to encourage a public understanding of the relationship between "high" and "low" art and investigating the very question of originality; or he might have shown how the transformation of existing materials has always been crucial to artistic production, and emphasized the specific transformations accomplished by *String of Puppies* and their conceptual purpose. He might have explained how Rogers' photograph set the scene for the production of a work that had an entirely different meaning and function. Instead, he and his advocates favored the most radical avant-gardist claims: that the artist was so radically autonomous, so unfettered by the

demands of the public and the state, that he need not please anyone but himself. Koons and his supporters thus missed a strategic
chance to display their value to democracy.[66]

Koons's avant-garde rhetoric may have hurt him in another way
as well. He readily invoked the classic posture of a conflict between
art and mass culture. But if the familiar argument is that the artist
is the friendless outsider, bravely willing to challenge the dominant
culture, in this case that account seemed flimsy indeed. Koons was,
after all, the consummate art world insider, making hundreds of thousands of dollars for each piece of work, flaunting his relationship to
commercialism, and boasting numerous high profile shows, while poor
Rogers was struggling to make ends meet with his photography
studio. It might be true that in the largest sense, Rogers participated
in the dominant culture, while Koons belonged to the critical
fringe, but faced with their competing claims in court, the court
was hard pressed to see Koons as the beleaguered little guy. Judge
Cardamone's decision emphasized Koons's relative wealth, power, and
arrogance: "The copying was so deliberate as to suggest that defend-
ants resolved so long as they were significant players in the art business, and the copies they produced bettered the price of the copied
work by a thousand to one, their piracy of a less well-known artist's
work would escape being sullied by an accusation of plagiarism."[67]

If Koons lost his case in part because he persuaded the courts that
he was indifferent to legal norms and blithely willing to step on those
poorer and less famous to build himself up, there is a final – and
more subtle – reason for the failure of his avant-garde posturing. As
we have seen, Jeff Koons was widely taken as a classic exemplar of
postmodern reuse and recombination – indeed, was on trial at that
very moment for the typically postmodern act of appropriation. But
although he was clearly dedicated in his work to the rejection of
originality and artistic individuality, and to the reuse of mass culture, when he was under legal scrutiny, he did what many other
artists in the past few decades have done: he continued to embrace
the rhetoric of the avant-garde long after its historical demise.
He adopted the posture of the heroic, emancipatory, innovative, and

solitary avant-garde artist – precisely the object of his own artistic critique. This produced a curious contradiction. How was it that Koons could be, on the one hand, innovative and revolutionary, and on the other, a critic of innovation and revolution? The experts who wrote in his favor tried to reconcile these two opposing motives. What made Koons unique, distinctive, and innovative, they claimed, was precisely his reuse of prosaic objects from contemporary culture. He was ground-breaking in his selection of the most ordinary and most familiar objects. Koons "uses palpable kitsch to help us see beneath the surface, to that which is less digested – our prejudices, lusts, needs – our addiction to that which we have been instructed to desire by advertising and media" (A902). "His fetish for finish gives the banal an exquisite appearance, making the ordinary, elevated by such refinement, a sure sign of decadence" (A913). What the court was expected to assess, then, was an artist who bravely produced the new – by reproducing the old.

If this was not paradoxical enough, according to experts in the art world and articles from journals like *Artforum* and *Art News* that were part of the trial's proceedings, the point of Koons's art was to expose the trite familiarity and predictability of mass culture by reusing a trite and predictable image. He copied in order to reveal the banality of copying. One academic essay that was admitted into evidence characterized Koons's work as part of a "new art" precisely because it was an ingeniously cynical response to a culture saturated in advertising and commodified imagery: "Stripped of any pretenses to heroic individual style, the new art would insist that all that was possible now was a flat recycling of imagery and style from degraded pop culture."[68]

In this context, we can set the courts' logic of originality side by side with that offered by the art world in *Rogers v. Koons*. The law is out to protect a certain minimal creativity: "the quantity . . . that need be shown is modest – only a dash of it will do." And the court confirmed that Rogers had demonstrated at least a dash of originality, including his "posing of the subjects, lighting, angle, and selection of film and camera." But if Rogers' photo could be shown to be original, then Koons's appropriation of the photo to reveal its *un*originality would become not only illegal, but ludicrous and nonsensical. In other words, Koons claimed that what made his work new, unique, and distinctive was his talent for revealing how clichéd and familiar images like Rogers' were. But if the law understood Rogers to be producing original work, then what could possibly be interesting about Koons's critical comment on its unoriginality?

In fact, the kind of originality that the art world set out to critique is not of great interest to the courts. None of the judges required Rogers' work to be a totally new and elemental creation generated by an individual genius. No one claimed that Rogers had invented the camera, or that Koons appropriated his photographic techniques. Instead, the courts agreed that the photographer's work was original if he made choices about which film and lenses to use, about contrasts between light and shadow, and about the development of the film. So what the court recognized as originality postmodernism acknowledges too – selection and recombination, the artists' choices from among a set of preexisting variables. But far from winning Koons his case, the kinship between postmodern art and copyright law might well have lost it for him. Koons lost because he tried to *combine* postmodern irony with avant-garde authenticity. His lawyers challenged the courts to recognize the techniques of postmodernist duplication and appropriation as "new and legitimate." The art world experts speaking on his behalf acted as if the postmodern critique of originality was itself cutting edge. There were two problems with this position: first, Koons adopted the mantle of the heroic and original artist in order to reject it; and second, the account of originality as heroic individual style had never persuaded the courts in the first place. Indeed, far from being concerned about protecting the sanctity of individual genius, the courts have wanted to prevent free-riding piracy, the intentional theft of works already in existence at a low cost – and, more broadly, a future doomed to duplication and repetition rather than progress. On both counts, Koons seemed to miss the point: he embraced the ease of free-riding as a privilege accorded to authentic artists, who need not be troubled by such legalistic details; and he claimed his right to copy a work already in existence on the grounds that art could do what it liked with mass culture, thereby endorsing the very nightmare of unending duplication which stops democratic participation and pluralism in its tracks.

Koons claimed a profound originality for his own postmodern appropriation, while refusing to acknowledge the "dash" of originality that distinguished Rogers from other photographers. This was not only a paradoxical position, but a naïve one, since it failed to recognize that originality had always been a limited and partial category; artists had never accomplished a thoroughgoing break with the past, nor had the courts ever believed that they should. And so we might say that the courts refused to accept the postmodern critique of originality as avant-garde, because they had already written that critique into law. Koons's critique of triteness and banality, as far as the law was concerned, was already trite and banal.

## Conclusion

Some legal scholars assert that the Second District Court was so appalled by Koons's "conduct" that it missed the genuine importance of appropriation art as a valuable contribution to our collective store of ideas and expressions.[69] One could make precisely the opposite argument for Brancusi: that his advocates behaved so well in the courtroom that the judges managed to overlook the fact that the law was not actually on his side. But while it is certainly likely that Koons's blustery overconfidence and Brancusi's polite deference played a crucial role in their legal outcomes, my own argument is more specific than a nod to general "conduct" would suggest. I want to conclude by suggesting that both cases hinged on the difference between the *rhetoric* of the avant-garde and the *logic* of the avant-garde. The rhetoric of the avant-garde is the language of radical and authentic outsiders who are beholden to no one, who must bravely defy all state, popular, and corporate power in order to achieve a genuine and thoroughgoing freedom. The logic of the avant-garde, on the other hand, involves a recognition that art only ever achieves a bounded freedom – implicated as it is in social institutions, in the complexities of the cultural field, and in history – and that it does its best as a dissenting agent of democratic pluralism when it acknowledges its role as both insider and outsider, both friend and enemy, willing to break from convention and yet always and necessarily indebted to the past. Where the rhetoric of the avant-garde assumes a deep and impassable gulf between the art world and the law, the logic of the avant-garde reveals profound and unspoken commonalities between them: both counter-majoritarian institutions with a commitment to dissent, pluralism, and innovation.

When two artists choose between the logic and the rhetoric of the avant-garde in court, the results are suggestive. Brancusi's willingness to adopt the logic of the avant-garde prompted the court to act in a surprisingly avant-gardist spirit of its own – to overturn a recent precedent in favor of the new art. Koons's antipathy to the law and his refusal to compromise the radical rhetoric of the avant-garde provoked the court to close ranks, to seek its most conservative ground, and to recast the postmodern art of appropriation as the very outlier that Koons had made it out to be. Thus although one might accuse Brancusi of being cravenly co-opted, while Koons heroically upheld the flag of the purist avant-garde, one might just as well say that Brancusi was both an honest and a canny strategist, while Koons seemed to forget just how much he was caught up in norms, institutions, and historical precedents. And however tempted we might be to think of Brancusi as a sell-out – a traitor to the revolutionary spirit of the avant-garde – we might want to remember, too, that he was an anti-conventional artist who managed to change the law.

# Conclusion

## *Artists, Academic Writing, and the Classroom*

A surprising range of artists have continued to play the unsettling role of the avant-garde well after the end of the historical avant-garde movements. And the logic of the avant-garde, as we have seen, has intertwined itself quite persistently with the logic of democracy. At first the two seem like stark antagonists – the democratic majority, bound together by laws and parliaments, mainstream media and common sense, as opposed to the elitist outsider, repudiating institutions and traditions, popular media and mainstream tastes. If both sides need each other to define their differences, they also seem locked in a perpetual conflict. But the role of the artist in the liberal democratic context turns out to be more complex and more unexpected than a settled stand-off between two hostile camps. As we saw in controversies over public art objects, artists take on a structural role as democracy's outsiders – unsettling, deviant, unfamiliar, foreign – and so reveal the boundaries around "the people," the lines drawn between those who belong and those who do not. Artists and theorists have argued that those boundaries do not emerge spontaneously and authentically from the majority itself, but are rather constructed, fortified, and naturalized by both longstanding traditions and the spread of a homogenizing mass culture. And so, by tirelessly setting themselves against both conventional wisdom and currents of mainstream opinion, the avant-garde is that force which, for a century and more, has insistently tested democracy's boundaries, probing its exclusions, its willingness to close out strangers to majority

192

tastes and values − among them, socialists and Jews, agnostics and anti-nationalists, intellectuals and African-Americans, sexual outsiders and experimental visionaries, those who speak in strange languages and in unfamiliar, disorienting ways.

But these artistic outsiders are not simply exiles and pariahs in democratic societies. We saw how the liberal democratic state made use of the radically challenging, nonconformist artist when its own principles and values were under attack. Struggling to establish itself as a champion of freedom and diversity, the US during the Cold War relied on unsettling artists to publicize the idea that democracy was hospitable to dissident and minority voices, that the majority did not tyrannize over the margins. To be sure, elected officials at the time were doing their best to squelch unsettling, unfamiliar voices in the name of the majority, and so the logic of the avant-garde became the clandestine and cynical tool of powerful strategists. And yet, this strange story of avant-garde propaganda also reveals the same tension we saw at work in public arts controversies: a tension between democratic collectives and dissident freedoms − one that always haunts democratic states, and especially those at war. Thus although the artist's nonconformity might be put to use for sinister ends, the avant-garde, even as a tool of the state, poses a serious and ongoing question about the feasibility of freedom within democracy.

It is not only in cases of propaganda that the democratic state has integrated the logic of the avant-garde. We saw how the courts in liberal democracies play their own structural role as counter-majoritarian forces, and so, like the art world, set themselves up as protectors of strange, unpopular, and critical perspectives. It makes a certain sense, then, that the Anglo-American judiciary has written the value of avant-garde challenges into the very framework of obscenity law. But this means that the logic of the avant-garde is hardly a simple antagonist of the state it so often shuns. In the courtroom, the artist emerges as both a democratic outsider *and* as an institutional insider, as both free from the state *and* as co-opted by it: spoken for by experts from the art world but judged, ultimately, by non-specialist judges and juries; outside of the mainstream

193

yet supported by state institutions. Turning the logic of the avant-garde outside in, the courts bring the rebellious outcast into the enclosure of the law.

Common-law adjudication and avant-garde art share a surprisingly significant set of structures and aspirations: both are, at least in principle, committed to fostering a plurality of perspectives, especially critical and innovative ones; both are relatively independent, self-organizing institutions that set themselves against the tyranny of the majority; and both implicitly bind themselves to a model of history that depends on patterns set in the past while also inviting openings to the future. We saw how much the law and the art world shared, in customs and copyright contexts, and we saw, too, how mistaken – and how perilous – it is for artists in the courtroom to cast themselves as profoundly uncompromising outsiders, bound by neither norms nor traditions and resolutely hostile to an oppressive state, since the courts foster and maintain not only their values but their best creative resources.

And yet, the artist's assimilation by the state does not strip the avant-garde of its unsettling power. The logic of the avant-garde continues to play a crucial role in societies pressed by the imperatives of homogeneity, normalization, and collective unity: it resists the pressure to conform to mainstream tastes; it seeks to emancipate audiences from habits of submission and acceptance; and it persistently seeks the limits of belonging. Acting as a permanent, intentional minority, the institution of the avant-garde will play a necessary social role as long as democratic majorities threaten to muffle or dispossess the margins. But the avant-garde is not simply an enemy of the majority, either; since its inception in the late nineteenth century, it has set itself against the power of a profit-driven mass culture to standardize, to enforce a sense of collective belonging through the policing of the "normal." It has resisted the tyranny of mainstream culture for the sake of democratic freedom. In good paradoxical fashion, the logic of the avant-garde rejects the people in the name of the people.

Is the logic of the avant-garde limited to the art world? Recent debates over academic writing suggest that a similar logic has emerged in the context of the university too. Like artists, academics – especially in the humanities – are often accused of elitism and inscrutability, of displaying insider exclusivity, speaking in codes intelligible only to those admitted to the inner circle.[1] Like artists, academics often seem far outside of the mainstream, resistant to common sense and skeptical of mass culture. And like artists, many academics are proud of the difficult challenges of their work, their capacity to unsettle conventional habits and assumptions, to trigger new ways of thinking and living.

In January of 1999, when the journal *Philosophy and Literature* announced that it was awarding its "Bad Writing" prize to a sentence written by philosopher and gender theorist Judith Butler, a heated debate erupted in the mainstream press. The prize-winning sentence, from the journal *Diacritics*, reads: "The move from a structuralist account in which capital is understood to structure social relations in relatively homologous ways to a view of hegemony in which power relations are subject to repetition, convergence, and rearticulation brought the question of temporality into the thinking of structure, and marked a shift from a form of Althusserian theory that takes structural totalities as theoretical objects to one in which the insights into the contingent possibility of structure inaugurate a renewed conception of hegemony as bound up with the contingent sites and strategies of the rearticulation of power."[2] Denis Dutton, the editor of *Philosophy and Literature*, published an op-ed piece in the *Wall Street Journal*, in which he argued that this sentence "beats readers into submission and instructs them that they are in the presence of a great and deep mind. Actual communication has nothing to do with it."[3] Butler responded with her own op-ed in the *New York Times*, asserting, in the spirit of the avant-garde, that "scholars are obliged to question common sense, interrogate its tacit assumptions and provoke new ways of looking at a familiar world."[4] Flurries of letters followed. Some defended Butler for refusing "the culture of the sound bite" and for spurning "moralisms and banalities."[5] Philosopher Martha Nussbaum accused her of deliberately spinning mystifications to build up her own authority, and abandoning "real" politics in the process.[6] A letter to the *Times* made the case that Butler's style produced a culture of cozy insiders delighted to exclude the masses: "obscure prose serves more to protect [scholars'] own comfortable assumptions than as a tool of social change."[7]

Provocations and banalities, elitist insiders and radical outsiders, common sense and impenetrable novelty: all of this sounds familiar from battles over avant-garde art works. Some scholars actually draw a link between the historical rise of the artistic avant-garde and the need for a set of academic disciplines that could account for its difficulty and its strangeness. Cultural criticism not only strives to be avant-garde in the sense that it challenges popular wisdom; its terms have themselves developed out of an attempt to explicate the shocks of the artistic avant-garde.[8] Other commentators suggest that professors try but fail to achieve the disruptive force of the avant-garde: academics cannot live up to the work of Pound, Mallarmé, Faulkner, and H.D., according to Mark Bauerlein, because "genuine displacement comes about through an original and stunning expression containing arresting thoughts and feelings, not through the collective idiom of an academic clique smoothly imitated by a throng of aspiring theorists."[9] Whether the commentators are favorable or unfavorable, then, what is worth noting here is that the debate about abstruse academic language returns, again and again, to the question of the avant-garde.

And yet, the challenges of the humanities and the challenges of the arts are not precisely the same. One important factor that distinguishes the institution of the research university from the art world is the classroom.[10] Of course, I do not mean to say that educational processes are missing from the art world, or that artists never teach. Creative artists are often employees of universities, and many artists would never be able to make ends meet if it were not for teaching positions in academic contexts. But for the moment, let's assess the logic of the avant-garde and the university as *institutions* – social bodies that are relatively continuous, self-regulating, and normative.

Thus we may pass over the fact many individuals cross between the two contexts in order to focus on the different regulations, expectations, and structuring factors that shape each institutional body. From this perspective, it becomes clear that the relationship between research and teaching in the university profoundly shapes its institutional character. Academics in research universities are expected to perform two functions: for the purposes of publication, they are required to produce original research, which involves pushing the boundaries of established explanations, adding to the common store of knowledge, or challenging existing theories; for the purposes of teaching, they are expected to introduce students to ideas, facts, and ways of thinking that they would not have encountered before and gradually to build up their store of specialized knowledge and skills so that they may themselves contribute, eventually, to the cutting edge of scholarly production. And so, besides producing challenges and innovations in a research program, a typical research academic might teach introductory lectures and undergraduate seminar courses. In other words, the research university calls for scholarly innovation in the spirit of the avant-garde, but it also asks researchers to construct mediating bridges between non-specialist beginners and the forward-looking challenges of the avant-garde.

Judith Butler calls this process "translation," and literary critic Gerald Graff argues that scholars should ideally be "bilingual," able to move flexibly between vernacular and specialized languages for the purposes of constructing links between what is already known and the new, the unfamiliar, the challenging.[11] The metaphor of the foreign language is certainly apt in a debate over the abstruse technicalities of academic writing. But it seems to imply that the two idioms – one avant-garde, one popular – remain separate, distinguishable, belonging to different cultures, with a gap between them. Let me propose two alternative metaphors. First, the feedback loop. We have ample evidence that that which was once foreign can become familiar. This is equally true in the art world and in the university. Just as shockingly avant-garde art can have become comfortably mainstream in a few decades – Impressionist painting, for example, or montage in film – so too can intellectual innovations seep into mass culture and can even begin to seem like second nature. Cultural studies scholar Michael Warner writes: "My students have trouble reading eighteenth-century prose that was a model of clarity in its time, but they take as self-evidently clear such terms as *objective* and *subjective* – terms denounced as hideous neologistic jargon when Coleridge used them."[12] As the foreign feeds into the familiar, transforming the grounds of our discourse, what had been familiar becomes foreign. A second way to capture the relationship between mass culture and the avant-garde would be the *spectrum*. Though the avant-garde typically challenges mainstream presumptions and tastes in the name of a radical new future, its innovations are often assimilated piecemeal, becoming gradually familiar rather than remaking the world with a single transformative blow. Similarly, some academic jargon that was once limited to a few intellectuals is now part of the common currency of journalism and popular culture but does not necessarily bring its full intellectual context with it. We might think of the term *deconstruction*, which has a difficult and technical meaning in the work of Jacques Derrida but has now come simply to mean critique in popular parlance. Is it familiar or foreign? For the moment, it is a little of both.

If the avant-garde artist and the avant-garde researcher share the urge to challenge mass culture in ways that often come to be assimilated into that culture, what distinguishes them is their institutional emphasis – their normative sense of purpose. The logic of the artistic avant-garde involves finding the limits of mass culture and then exposing those limits, purposefully breaking from common sense and convention. It institutionalizes the fracturing of the cultural field, seeking out the mainstream in order to perform a rejection of it. Though the research university also challenges mass culture, what it institutionalizes is not the break but the loop and the continuum. If we understand the classroom as a mediating apparatus between familiar and foreign, between conventional wisdom and the avant-garde, the research university emerges as an institution that incorporates both the mainstream and challenges to that mainstream, accommodating both vernacular, popular, common culture *and* unsettling, difficult, disruptive critiques of that culture. It in fact does much of its daily work precisely in the interstices between the two: privileging mainstream terms and models for beginning students but gradually incorporating ever more unfamiliar terms for those who are farther along in the pedagogical program. The university takes non-specialists and, little by little, turns them into experts. But it also trains most of those who will be professionals outside of the academy, including those who will work in the culture industry producing the very mass culture that academics work to unsettle, including journalists, scriptwriters, pundits, editors, and bloggers. In the process, it brings its own, insider culture to those who begin as outsiders, while it also disseminates its oppositional, challenging outsider culture to those comfortably inside the mainstream. Institutionally speaking, insiders and outsiders perpetually switch places in the transformative space of the university.

While the logic of the avant-garde is alive and well in research universities, then, what organizes academia as an institution is its mediating character. This means that a wide range of styles will work equally well to carry out academia's institutional purpose, and indeed, that academics *must* speak in more ways than one. To launch cutting edge challenges to conventional wisdom, the strangest and most unfamiliar concepts might well take shape in uncomfortable, demanding ways; but the pressure to make those ideas comprehensible to beginning students will mean drawing on models and terms taken from the most common, most habitual, most comfortably mainstream culture. And between the poles on the spectrum is the advanced major or the beginning graduate student – poised, by necessity, between mass culture and the avant-garde.

This characterization of academia might make it look like a more democratic institution than the artistic avant-garde. Dedicated to bridging the gap between outside and inside, the university seems more actively involved in the processes of social transformation than artist-rebels with their hectic gestures of defiance. And yet, the university enforces its own norms, and of course its own exclusions: hardly open

199

to all comers, the research university in particular serves only a narrow band of the wider public. By contrast, the avant-garde's interventions into the wider cultural field are intended to transform the *entire* public arena, to unsettle the dominance of oppressively normalizing forces for the sake of all outsiders. The artistic avant-garde seeks to lodge its disruptions at the heart of public discourse for the sake of freedom itself. And in a democracy, that is no small challenge.

# Notes

## CHAPTER 1 DEMOCRACY MEETS THE AVANT-GARDE

1 Vitaly Komar and Alexander Melamid, "Blue Landscapes, Bewitching Numbers, and The Double Life of Jokes: An Interview with Komar and Melamid," in JoAnn Wypijewski, ed., *Painting by Numbers: Komar and Melamid's Scientific Guide to Art* (Berkeley: University of California Press, 1997): 40.

2 Hon. Henry Hyde, "The Culture War," *National Review* (April 30, 1990); reprinted in Richard Bolton, ed., *Culture Wars: Documents from the Recent Controversies in the Arts* (New York: New Press, 1992): 191. Peter Hirsch, in Clara Weyergraf-Serra and Martha Buskirk, eds., *The Destruction of Tilted Arc: Documents* (Cambridge, MA and London: MIT Press, 1991): 123.

3 Frederick Hart, "Contemporary Art is Perverted Art," *Washington Post* (August 22, 1989): A19.

4 Vaclav Havel, statement for Arts Advocacy Day (March 18, 1990), reprinted in Bolton, 156–57.

5 Since "bohemian" calls up images of sexual license and deliberate social marginalization, Hart's implication is that the artistic break followed a social and sexual desire for nonconformity. "Avant-garde" puts the artistic impulse first.

6 See Renato Poggioli, *The Theory of the Avant-Garde*, trans. Gerald Fitzgerald (New York: Harper and Row, 1971): 8–15.

7 Giorgio de Chirico, *The Mystery of Creation* (1938), quoted in Jean-Luc Daval, *Avant-Garde Art, 1914–1939* (New York: Rizzoli, 1980): 14.

8 F. T. Marinetti, *Selected Writings*, ed. R. W. Flint (London: Secker and Warburg, 1972): 114. Alfred Stieglitz, letter to *Blind Man* 2 (May 1917): 15.

9 Pierre Bourdieu, *The Rules of Art: Genesis and Structure of the Literary Field*, trans. Susan Emanuel (Stanford: Stanford University Press, 1996): 21.

10   See Matei Calinescu, *Five Faces of Modernity: Modernism, Avant-Garde, Decadence, Kitsch, Postmodernism* (Durham, NC: Duke University Press, 1999): 112.

11   Richard Huelsenbeck, "En avant Dada," in Robert Motherwell, ed., *The Dada Painters and Poets: An Anthology* (Boston: G. K. Hall, 1981): 45.

12   Alfred Jarry, "Questions du théâtre," *Oeuvres complètes.* 8 vols (Monte Carlo: Editions du Livre, 1948), vol. 1: 218.

13   F. T. Marinetti, "Fondazione e manifesto del futurismo," *Le Figaro* (February 20, 1909), my translation.

14   Peter Bürger, *Theory of the Avant-Garde*, trans. Michael Shaw (Minneapolis: University of Minnesota Press, 1984): 52–54.

15   Mark Hudson, "What's Really Shocking about Modern Art," *Daily Telegraph* (December 7, 2005): 29; Anthony Julius, *Transgressions: The Offences of Art* (Chicago: University of Chicago Press, 2002): 198–202; Wendy Steiner, "The Culture Wars: Art in 20th Century Has Always Been 'Shock of the New'," *Los Angeles Times* (October 10, 1999): M1, M6.

16   Roberta Smith, "Why Attack Art? Its Role is to Be Helpful," *New York Times* (May 13, 2004): E1; Nicholas Serota, "Who's Afraid of Modern Art?" *The Richard Dimbleby Lecture*, BBC TV (November 23, 2000); Ted Weiss, Statement to the House Committee on Postsecondary Education (April 4, 1990): reprinted in Bolton, 166; Jacob K. Javits, in Weyergraf-Serra and Burkirk, 97–98; David Gergen, "Who Should Pay for Porn?" *US News and World Report* (July 30, 1990): 80; George Will, "Brooklyn's Artsy Dogers," *Washington Post* (February 22, 2001): A19; Ilene Chaiken, writer, and Tony Goldwyn, director, "Limb from Limb," in *The L Word*, season 1, episode 13 (April 11, 2004), produced by Ilene Chaiken, Showtime.

17   The hugely popular Thomas Kinkade, for example, is widely praised for his "inspiration" and "compassion," and is said to be the "world's most collected living artist." Thomas Kinkade and Robert Goodwin, Interview, *Larry King Live*, CNN (New York: July 1, 2006). "Beloved by middlebrow America but reviled by the art establishment," "he sells his art in malls rather than appearing in museums and art galleries." Nicholas K. Geranios, "Truly, Home Is Where the Art Is," *Los Angeles Times* (May 24, 2006): E10. See also Susan Orlean, "Art for Everybody," *New Yorker* (October 15, 2001): 124–30.

18   After the Dixie Chicks spoke out against President Bush's war in Iraq, Bruce Springsteen praised them for resisting the "pressure coming from the government and big business to enforce conformity of thought" (www.news.bbc.co.uk/1/hi/entertainment/music/2981853.stm: posted April 28, 2003; accessed September 2006). For Koons, see chapter 5.

19   Brigid Doherty, "The Work of Art and the Problem of Politics in Berlin Dada," *October* 105 (summer 2003): 75.

20   See, for example, Edward Lucie-Smith, *Art of the 1930s: The Age of Anxiety* (London: Weidenfeld and Nicolson, 1985): 166–201; and Lloyd Goodrich, *Pioneers of Modern Art in America: The Decade of the Armory Show, 1910–1920* (New York: Praeger, 1963). Wyndham Lewis and the other Vorticists were an exception in Britain, and it is misleading to see the avant-garde too strictly in national terms. Roger Fry's exhibition at London's Grafton Galleries, "Manet and the Post-Impressionists," provoked huge outcry in 1910–11, but also profoundly shaped the work of British artists; similarly, the famous Armory Show in New York in 1913 brought the European avant-garde to the United States and prompted American artists to work in radical new ways. Marcel Duchamp moved to New York, and Gertrude Stein and Ezra Pound lived in Europe.

21   James M. Markham, "Bullet-Proofed 'Guernica' Goes on Display in Spain," *New York Times* (October 24, 1981): 11.

22   Boal's "forum theatre" method involved transforming the audience's relationship to drama: first, actors would perform a social or political problem, allowing it to develop into a crisis; then they would invite spectators to offer solutions based on their own experience, replacing the actors onstage as the sources of action. Boal has taken his methods worldwide: he now calls his work "legislative theatre." See Augusto Boal, *Theatre of the Oppressed* (1974), trans. Charles A. and Maria-Odilia Leal (New York: Theatre Communications Group, 1979): 156; and Augusto Boal, *Legislative Theatre*, trans. Adrian Jackson (London and New York: Routledge, 1998).

23   Quoted in Lynda Morris, "Recollection: Joseph Beuys," *Art Monthly* 284 (March 2005): 43.

24   Lisa Ito, "Art for Oust's Sake," *Butalat: The Philippine's Alternative Weekly Magazine* V (July 24–30, 2005): n.p.

25   For example, here is George W. Bush: "Iraqi democracy will succeed – and that success will send forth the news, from Damascus to Teheran – that freedom can be the future of every nation." "Remarks," Speech for the 20th Anniversary of the National Endowment for Democracy (United States Chamber of Commerce, November 6, 2003).

26   Alexis de Tocqueville, *Democracy in America*, trans. Harvey C. Mansfield and Delba Winthrop (Chicago and London: University of Chicago Press, 2000): 369.

27   Ibid., 588.

28   Ibid., 410, 674.

29   Alan Ryan describes this position as follows: "To the objection that majority rule may be inconsistent with liberty, the sophisticated reply is essentially that the authority, as distinct from the power, of the majority is intrinsically self-limiting. We cannot claim the right to vote, for instance, on terms that

violate others' rights. On this view, a Bill of Rights does not limit the majority's authority so much as spell out what its authority is." "Liberalism" in *A Companion to Contemporary Political Philosophy*, eds. Robert E. Goodin and Philip Pettit (Oxford: Blackwell, 1998): 307. Etienne Balibar also makes an impassioned case for what he calls *égaliberté*: "*There are no examples* of restriction or suppression of liberties without social inequalities, nor of inequalities without restriction or suppression of liberties." "Droits de l'homme et droits du citoyen: La dialectique moderne de l'égalité et de la liberté," *Actuel Marx* (1990): 22.

30 This argument for the opposition between democracy and liberalism is made most famously by political philosopher Carl Schmitt, *The Crisis of Parliamentary Democracy*, trans. Ellen Kennedy (Cambridge, MA: MIT Press, 1985). Despite Schmitt's own fascism, his arguments have been important points of reference for progressive political theorists recently, who have taken the distinction between liberalism and democracy less as an impossibility than as a productive tension. See especially Chantal Mouffe, *The Democratic Paradox* (London: Verso, 2000): 36–59.

31 J. S. Mill, *On Liberty*, in *The Basic Writings of John Stuart Mill*, ed. J. B. Schneewind (New York: Modern Library, 2002): 69.

32 John Dewey, *The Public and its Problems: An Essay in Political Inquiry* (1927) (Chicago: Gateway Books, 1946): 115, 126.

33 David Manning White, "Mass Culture in America: Another Point of View," in Bernard Rosenberg and David Manning White, eds., *Mass Culture: The Popular Arts in America* (New York: Free Press, 1957): 17.

34 For a fascinating account of jazz as an art form decried by both elitists and socialists horrified at the rise of a popular but also corporatized consumer culture, see Matthew Mooney, "An 'Invasion of Vulgarity': American Popular Music and Modernity in Print Media Discourse, 1900–1925," *Americana: The Journal of American Popular Culture* 3 (spring 2004) (www.americanpopularculture.com/journal/articles/spring_2004/mooney.htm; accessed June 2006).

35 Bernard Rosenberg, "Mass Culture in America," in Rosenberg and White, 9.

36 Theodor Adorno and Max Horkheimer, "The Culture Industry: Enlightenment as Mass Deception," in Adorno and Horkheimer, eds., *Dialectic of Enlightenment* (London: Verso, 1979): 127.

37 Thomas Frank, *The Conquest of Cool: Business Culture, Counterculture, and the Rise of Hip Consumerism* (Chicago: University of Chicago Press, 1997).

38 Jürgen Habermas, *The Structural Transformation of the Public Sphere: An Inquiry into a Category of Bourgeois Society*, trans. Thomas Burger (Cambridge, MA: MIT Press, 1989): 195.

39  "In 1947, 80 percent of daily newspapers were independently owned; in 1989 only 20 percent were independently owned. Most of the business of the nation's eleven thousand magazines was controlled by twenty companies in 1981; by 1988, that number had fallen to three. Books are much the same. . . . Music is even more concentrated. . . . The same is true in film. . . . Cable and television are no better. . . . '[D]espite more than 25,000 outlets in the United States, 23 corporations control most of the business in daily newspapers, magazines, television, books, and motion pictures.' . . . The top six have more annual media revenue than the next twenty combined." Lawrence Lessig, *The Future of Ideas* (New York: Vintage, 2001): 117.

40  See, for example, Barbara O'Brien, *Blogging America: Political Discourse in a Digital Nation* (Wilsonville: William James, 2004).

41  Cass Sunstein, *Republic.com* (Princeton: Princeton University Press, 2001): 8, 16.

42  Cass Sunstein, *Why Societies Need Dissent* (Cambridge, MA and London: Harvard University Press, 2003): 28.

43  Bonnie Honig, *Political Theory and the Displacement of Politics* (Ithaca, NY: Cornell University Press, 1993): 2. Sunstein agrees: "my emphasis on dissent goes against the grain of contemporary political theory. In recent decades and more, the emphasis has been on the need for consensus." Sunstein, *Why Societies*, 8.

44  Mouffe, 15–16. See also Chantal Mouffe, "The End of Politics and the Rise of the Radical Right," *Dissent* 42 (fall 1995): 498–502; and "Deliberative Democracy or Agonistic Pluralism?" *Social Research* 66 (fall 1999): 745–58.

45  Jane Mansbridge, "Using Power/Fighting Power: The Polity," in *Democracy and Difference: Contesting the Boundaries of the Political*, ed. Seyla Benhabib (Princeton: Princeton University Press, 1996): 48.

46  Jane Mansbridge, "The Making of Oppositional Consciousness," in *Oppositional Consciousness: The Subjective Roots of Social Protest* (Chicago: University of Chicago Press, 2001): 4.

47  Patricia Cormack, *Sociology and Mass Culture: Durkheim, Mills, and Baudrillard* (Toronto: University of Toronto Press, 2002): 118.

48  Anthony Arblaster, *The Rise and Decline of Western Liberalism* (Oxford: Blackwell, 1984): 82.

49  David Banash argues that the process can also work the other way: advertising and fragmented newspaper reading formed the basis for avant-garde techniques of collage. "From Advertising to the Avant-Garde: Rethinking the Invention of Collage," *Postmodern Culture* 14.2 (2004): 33 pars (www.iath.virginia.edu/pmc/; posted June 25, 2004; accessed September 2006).

50  Howard S. Becker, *Art Worlds* (Berkeley: University of California Press, 1982): 36.

51 As two sociologists of Impressionist art argue: "Long-term control in any institutional system requires control over marginal as well as respected members of the system." Harrison C. White and Cynthia A. White, *Canvases and Careers: Institutional Change in the French Painting World* (New York: John Wiley, 1965): 103.

52 Institutions vary enormously in scale and power – the term is capacious enough to refer to a parliament, an education system, a global market, "a family, a ceremony, or a game." Mary Douglas, *How Institutions Think* (Syracuse: Syracuse University Press, 1986): 46.

53 Ibid. Scholars argue that institutions profoundly shape both individuals and societies, molding actions, norms, expectations, identities, and even knowledge. Some have defined institutions as specific material forms – constitutions, bureaucracies, legislatures, courts, labor unions, political parties – while others have broadened the definition to include norms, routines, values, and habits. Recently theorists have begun to integrate the two: institutions are "not monolithic entities but are composed of *interrelated* but distinct components, particularly rules, beliefs, and norms, which sometimes manifest themselves as organizations." Avner Greif, *Institutions and the Path to the Modern Economy: Lessons from Medieval Trade* (Cambridge: Cambridge University Press, 2006): 14.

54 Hans Richter, *Dada: Art and Anti-Art* (New York and Toronto: McGraw-Hill, n.d.): 50.

55 Tristan Tzara, "Dada Manifesto" (1918), in Motherwell, 78–79.

56 Richter, 48.

57 Ibid., 12.

58 Ibid., 13.

59 Georges Ribemont-Dessaignes, "History of Dada," in Motherwell, 109.

60 Margaret Spillane, "The Culture of Narcissism," *The Nation* (December 10, 1990): reprinted in Bolton, 302.

61 Jessie Gray, in Weyergraf-Serra and Buskirk, 121.

62 Sunstein, *Republic.com*, 131.

63 Artists who have set themselves against consumerism and corporatism are too numerous to name, but we might think of the Situationists in Paris in the late 1960s, socialists influenced by the historical avant-gardes who argued that late capitalism had so effectively seemed to turn the world into a set of consumable appearances that it had estranged human beings from themselves: they called for acts of vandalism and sabotage as creative interruptions of the status quo. Artists who have wanted to challenge the law include numerous writers and visual artists who have defied existing obscenity standards: from D. H. Lawrence and Henry Miller to feminist Karen Finley and web artist Barbara Nitke. As for the force of majority values, the 1960s Black Arts

Movement was an attempt to throw off the weight of white, Western traditions in favor of a self-confident African-American art. In 1967, Charles H.
Fuller wrote: "art born out of oppression can not be explained in the terms
of the unoppressed, since the condition of the oppressor does not allow him
to deal with a form that might conceivably make the oppressed his equal."
"Black Writing is Socio-Creative Art," *Liberator* (April 1967): 9.

64  See chapter 2.
65  Not everyone agrees that this system functions as intended. Though most democratic constitutions have followed the model of checks and balances, there
are some scholars who argue that these institutional balancings are as likely
as a more straightforward majoritarian rule to lead to tyrannical political control. See John Ferejohn and Pasquale Pasquino, "Rule of Democracy and Rule
of Law" and José Maria Maravall, "The Rule of Law as a Political Weapon,"
in José Maria Maravall and Adam Przeworski, eds., *Democracy and the Rule of
Law* (Cambridge: Cambridge University Press, 2003): 242–60 and 261–301.
66  To give just one recent example of a bureaucratic invocation of the logic of
the avant-garde: the state-run Arts Council England issued a "manifesto" to
"encourage artists working at the cutting edge" and "radical thought and action."
Peter Hewitt, "Ambitions for the Arts 2003–2006" (London: Arts Council
England, 2003): 3.
67  Tocqueville, 98, 274.
68  For example, both the *Ulysses* trial in America and the trial of *Lady
Chatterley's Lover* in England were test cases of obscenity which called for shifts
in the legal standard for literature. See chapter 4.
69  *Memoirs v. Massachusetts*, 383 US 413 (1966). See also *Bleistein v. Donaldson
Lithographing Co.*, 188 US 239, 251 (1903).
70  As Dean Roscoe Pound wrote in 1921: "the court proceeds by analogy of
rules and doctrines in the traditional system and develops a principle for the
cause before it according to a known technique. Growth is insured in that
the limits of the principle are not fixed authoritatively once for all but are
discovered gradually by a process of inclusion and exclusion as cases arise."
Quoted in Richard B. Cappalli, *The American Common Law Method*
(Irvington-on-Hudson: Transnational Publishers, 1997): 91.
71  Bourdieu, *Rules of Art*, 301.


CHAPTER 2  THE PEOPLE V. THE ARTS

1  James C. Nicola, New York Theater Workshop's artistic director, in Jessie
McKinley, "Theater Addresses Tension over Play," *New York Times* (March
16, 2006): E1; see also Philip Weiss, "Why These Tickets Are Too Hot for

New York" *The Nation* (April 3, 2006): 13–18. The show began its New York run at the Minetta Lane Theatre in October 2006.

2   Katherine Viner, interviewed by Brian Lehrer, *On the Media*, WNYC radio (March 23, 2006).

3   "We did not 'poll' anyone. We did not hold 'focus groups.' No 'wealthy Jewish donors' pressured us. We were never threatened." James C. Nicola and Lynn Moffatt (www.nytw.org/rachel_corrie.asp; accessed May 2006).

4   Viner.

5   The specific avant-garde movements most often associated with Epstein are Cubism, Futurism, and Vorticism.

6   *The Nation* (February 14, 1920), quoted in Jacob Epstein, *Let There Be Sculpture: An Autobiography* (London: Michael Joseph, 1940): 28.

7   Letter from Muirhead Bone, reprinted in Terry Friedman, *The Hyde Park Atrocity: Creation and Controversy* (Leeds: Henry Moore Centre, 1988): 149; L. R. W. Nevinson, an artist, called Epstein "by far the greatest sculptor in the world," *Daily News* (May 21, 1925): 8.

8   Friedman, 148.

9   Memorandum sent by Muirhead Bone to the Rt. Hon. Viscount Peel, First Commissioner of Works (November 29, 1925), in Epstein, 294.

10   Friedman, 9.

11   Quoted in Friedman, 32.

12   Frank Dicksee, President of the Royal Academy. "Another Attack on 'Rima.' Artists Appeal for the Removal of Epstein's Monument," *Evening Standard* (November 18, 1925): 4.

13   Letter from George Hubbard, *Daily Mail* (May 21, 1925): 9.

14   Letter from R. W. Bennett, *Daily Mail* (May 25, 1925): 10.

15   "The Hyde Park Atrocity," *Daily Mail* (May 22, 1925): 8.

16   A prominent actor told the press: "I dislike the modern worship of ugliness, and if it comes to a question of ugly-ugly and pretty-pretty, I prefer the pretty-pretty" ("Another Attack on 'Rima' "). The *Daily Mail* complained: "It is unfortunate that so many of our 'highbrows' seem to imagine that art is only good when it is ugly." "The Hyde Park Atrocity," *Dail Mail* (May 22, 1925): 8. And one irate Londoner wrote to *The Times* to say: "we wanted something to appeal to the man, the woman, the child 'in the street,' and if it had been achieved we would have cared little if it had been 'pretty-pretty' to the art critic" (May 26, 1925): 17.

17   "The Hyde Park Atrocity: Mr. Epstein's Panel," *Daily Mail* (May 23, 1925): 10.

18   "Bird Sanctuary Panel," *Daily News* (May 21, 1925): 8.

19   The petition read: "[*Rima* is] by universal consent so inappropriate and even repellent in character that the most fitting course open to the authorities for

so woeful a lapse of judgment would be to remove it bodily from its present position with as little delay as possible." Quoted in Stephen Gardiner, *Epstein: Artist Against the Establishment* (London: Michael Joseph, 1992): 256.

20   *Rima* had gathered support, the second petition claimed, from "nearly all the greatest artists." "A Counter-Blast for 'Rima,'" *Evening Standard* (November 19, 1925): 4. Epstein told the *Daily News* that Dicksee's view was not even representative of the whole Royal Academy. "Epstein and Dicksee," *Daily News* (November 19, 1925): 5.

21   "Another Attack on 'Rima.'"

22   Letter from Sybil Thorndike, *The Times* (May 25, 1925): 15.

23   "Mr Epstein and Hyde Park," *The Spectator* (May 30, 1925): 880.

24   *The Nation* (November 28, 1925), quoted in Gardiner, 257.

25   "Bird Sanctuary Panel," *Daily News* (May 21, 1925): 8.

26   Friedman, 10.

27   *The Hidden Hand, or The Jewish Peril* (February 1924): 22–23.

28   Evelyn Silber and Terry Friedman, "Epstein in the Public Eye, 1917–30," in *Jacob Epstein: Sculpture and Drawings*, eds. Evelyn Silber and Terry Friedman (Leeds: Henry Moore Centre, 1989): 221.

29   Anti-Semitism frequently underpinned popular responses to the modern in art and science. This satirical limerick is one example: "I don't like the family Stein./There is Gert, there is Ep, there is Ein./ Gert's writings are punk./ Ep's statues are junk,/Nor can anyone understand Ein." *Saturday Review* (November 1928), quoted in Gardiner, 258.

30   Letter from A. L. Kennedy, *The Times* (May 23, 1925): 12; Gardiner, 258.

31   Letter to the *Morning Post* (November 24, 1925); Gardiner, 258.

32   Quoted in Elizabeth Baker, "The Primitive Within: The Question of Race in Epstein's Career," in Silber and Friedman, 44.

33   Carl Schmitt, *The Crisis of Parliamentary Democracy*, trans. Ellen Kennedy (Cambridge, MA: MIT Press, 1988): 9.

34   "Until now there has never been a democracy that did not recognize the concept 'foreign' and that could have realized the equality of all men" (ibid., 11).

35   "By constantly challenging the relations of inclusion-exclusion implied by the political constitution of 'the people' – required by the exercise of democracy – the liberal discourse of universal human rights plays an important role in maintaining the democratic contestation alive. On the other side, it is only thanks to the democratic logics of equivalence that frontiers can be created and a demos established without which no real exercise of rights would be possible." Chantal Mouffe, *The Democratic Paradox* (London: Verso, 2000): 10.

36   Ibid., 13.

37  For a remarkable account of the political implications of style, see Rebecca L. Walkowitz, *Cosmopolitan Style: Modernism Beyond the Nation* (New York: Columbia University Press, 2006).

38  See Ernst Gellner, *Nations and Nationalism* (Ithaca, NY: Cornell University Press, 1983).

39  David Caute, *The Dancer Defects: The Struggle for Cultural Supremacy during the Cold War* (Oxford: Oxford University Press, 2003): 74.

40  "Mr Epstein and Hyde Park," *The Spectator* (May 30, 1925): 880–81.

41  "The Hyde Park Atrocity: Take It Away!" *Daily Mail* (May 25, 1925): 9–10.

42  "Mr Epstein and Hyde Park," 880.

43  "The Epstein Panel. Minister on Suspending Judgment," *Daily Mail* (May 28, 1925): 4.

44  "The Hyde Park Atrocity: Mr. Epstein's Panel," 10.

45  See, for example, John Dewey, *Democracy and Education: An Introduction to the Philosophy of Education* (1916) (New York: Free Press, 1944); Paulo Freire, *Pedagogy of the Oppressed* (1968), trans. Myra Bergman Ramos (New York: Continuum, 1988); and E. D. Hirsch, Jr. *Cultural Literacy: What Every American Needs to Know* (New York: Vintage, 1988).

46  The Royal Parks website notes that "It is difficult to understand why this bird-bath, in commemoration of the writer and naturalist Hudson, received such criticism in 1925" (see www.royalparks.co.uk; accessed May 2001).

47  Suzanne Delahanty, member of the NEA panel that had nominated Serra, from her testimony in the hearings about *Tilted Arc*. See Clara Weyergraf-Serra and Martha Buskirk, eds., *The Destruction of Tilted Arc: Documents* (Cambridge, MA and London: MIT Press, 1991): 83.

48  Art critic Douglas Crimp, in Weyergraf-Serra and Buskirk, 221.

49  Letter of August 18, 1981, from Chief Judge Re to Gerald P. Carmen, administrator of the GSA in Washington, in Weyergraf-Serra and Buskirk, 26.

50  Serra alleges that Re was the ringleader of this campaign. Re himself does not claim to have solicited letters of protest, though he did enclose a number of letters demanding the removal of the sculpture with his own letter of November 5, 1984 to Ray Kline, acting administrator of the GSA (Weyergraf-Serra and Buskirk, 5, 27–28). I will argue later that the judiciary has been particularly friendly to works of art, but the case of Judge Re suggests that when acting outside of the courtroom – in a personal capacity – judges may be as hostile to the avant-garde as the most populist of politicians.

51  Testimony from these hearings is collected in two recent volumes, Weyergraf-Serra and Buskirk, *The Destruction of Tilted Arc*, and Sherrill Jordan, ed., *Public Art, Public Controversy: Tilted Arc on Trial* (New York: American

Council for the Arts, 1987). Neither text offers a complete transcript of the hearings.

52  Quoted in Weyergraf-Serra and Buskirk, 3.

53  During the hearing a couple of witnesses complained that the sculpture acted as a shield for drug-dealers and terrorists, but the official body responsible for commissioning the sculpture had been satisfied that the *Arc* presented no danger to the public.

54  "In 1967 Barbara Rose and Irving Sandler published the results of a large survey that they had conducted among New York artists. Responding to the question, 'Is there an avant-garde today?' most of these artists answered 'no.' In addition to the impossibility of shocking the middle class, always a desideratum of the historical avant-garde, an artistic underground seemed untenable because there was no escaping media attention and the public's voracious appetite for the new." Bruce Altschuler, *The Avant-Garde in Exhibition: New Art in the 20th Century* (New York: Harry N. Abrams, 1994): 9.

55  Shirley Paris, in Weyergraf-Serra and Buskirk, 126.

56  Jessie Gray, in ibid., 121.

57  Benjamin Buchloh, in ibid., 92.

58  Victor Ganz, in Jordan, 112.

59  Harriet Dorsen, in ibid., 87.

60  Claes Oldenburg, in Weyergraf-Serra and Buskirk, 78.

61  Quoted from an interview with William Wilson, "The Matter of Serra's 'Arc' de Trauma," *Los Angeles Times* (June 30, 1985): AC80.

62  Letter from William Diamond to Dwight Ink (May 1, 1985), in Weyergraf-Serra and Buskirk, 144.

63  Elyse Grinstein, in Jordan, 67.

64  Donald W. Thalacker, in ibid., 120.

65  William Rubin, in ibid., 100–1.

66  Dwight Ink, "Decision on *Tilted Arc*," in ibid., 164.

67  For a fuller treatment of *Tilted Arc* as a site-specific object in a public space, see my article, "The Paradox of Public Art: Democratic Space, the Avant-Garde, and Richard Serra's *Tilted Arc*," *Philosophy and Geography* 5 (February 2002): 51–68. See also Gregg M. Horowitz, "Public Art/Public Space: The Spectacle of the *Tilted Arc* Controversy," *Journal of Aesthetics and Art Criticism* 54 (winter 1996): 8–14. Horowitz argues that the Reagan-appointed Diamond imagined the space of the plaza without the *Arc* as a usable, pleasant public area. But there was ample evidence that it had never actually been a hospitable public site, and that the pitiless production of alienating urban environments was actually the fault of conservative government policy, not of Richard Serra's art work.

68 Serra advocates even cast doubt on the small number of detractors at the hearing: "Of the ten thousand employees in the subject building, approximately fifty-five people spoke in favor of its relocation. This modest number is significant because the employees were already at the site of the hearings and could easily take time off to testify." Of the 115 who spoke out to keep the sculpture, by contrast, many had to travel some distance to make their case. Memo from Donald Thalacker to Dwight Ink (May 9, 1985), in Weyergraf-Serra and Buskirk, 152–53.

69 Hirsch, in ibid., 123.

70 Norman Steinlauf, in ibid., 111.

71 Annette Michelson, in ibid., 95.

72 William Toby, in ibid., 119.

73 Tony Rosenthal, in Jordan, 139.

74 Peter Levine, "Lessons from the Brooklyn Museum Controversy," *Philosophy and Public Policy Quarterly* 20 (summer 2000) (www.puaf.umd.edu/IPPP/reports/vol20sum00/lessons.html; accessed September 2006).

75 Michael Warner, *Publics and Counterpublics* (New York: Zone Books, 2002): 135.

76 John Ryan and Deborah A. Sim, "When Art Becomes News: Portrayals of Art and Artists on Network Television News," *Social Forces* 68 (March 1990): 881, 886–87.

77 The predictability of shocking art comes up just about every year in discussions of Britain's prestigious Turner Prize. Here is a typical comment from 2005: "there has been the predictable scoffing dissent, the huffing and puffing. . . . But this ritual carping feels more tired and disingenuous than ever." Mark Hudson, "What's Really Shocking about Modern Art," *Daily Telegraph* (December 7, 2005): 29.

78 Sociologists since Emile Durkheim sometimes argue that crime plays a comparable social function. According to Randall Collins, for example: "The main object of a crime-punishment ritual . . . is not the criminal but the society at large. The trial reaffirms belief in the laws, and it creates the emotional bonds that tie members of society together again. . . . The criminal is an outsider, an object of the ritual, not a member of it." *Sociological Insight: An Introduction to Non-Obvious Sociology* (1982) (Oxford: Oxford University Press, 1992): 111. The avant-garde has the advantage of a more self-conscious and deliberate relationship to society than the criminal.

79 Richard Serra, in Weyergraf-Serra and Buskirk, 5.

80 Quoted in Jordan, 160.

81 Jerald Ordover, in ibid., 141.

82 Marion Javits, reading a statement by Jacob Javits; William Rubin; Donald Thalacker, letter to Dwight Ink, in ibid., 98, 102, 154.

83 Steven Davis, in Jordan, 102.

84 Philosopher Michael Kelly argues that Serra's work was not genuinely public because Serra "deliberately ignored or even defied" the publics who used the plaza. "[T]he minimum – and, I should think, noncontroversial – point is that to be public, art must be created with a recognition on the artist's part of the people who constitute the 'public' of public art, whoever they are." Kelly's suggestion seems controversial indeed if we take seriously the avant-garde's deliberate critical resistance to the acceptance of a passive, media-produced public taste that is neither authentic nor spontaneous. "Public Art Controversy: The Serra and Lin Cases," *Journal of Aesthetics and Art Criticism* 54 (1996): 17.

85 Dwight Ink was the first of many. He recommended that the Art-in-Architecture program be modified, "so that GSA tax-supported art is recognized as enhancing the environment for the public. . . . This will require a more meaningful and formal involvement of the local community in the planning and selection process." In Weyergraf-Serra and Buskirk, 172.

86 Warner, 72.

87 Marta Malina Moraczewska, "Let it be Seen," *Index on Censorship* 33 (2004): 211–17.

88 Ibid. See also Elzbieta Matynia, "Feminist Art and Democratic Culture: Debates on the New Poland," *PAJ: A Journal of Performance and Art* 27 (January 2005): 1–20.

89 See Jonathan Jones, "Art, Anger, Ambiguity in Bloody Image," *Los Angeles Times* (January 25, 2004): M.5; Eric Silver, "Sharon Backs Art-Wrecking Ambassador," *Independent* (London, January 19, 2004): 13; David Smith, "Ambassador Outrages Guests with Art Attack," *Observer* (London, January 18, 2004): 22; and Calem Ben-David, "Diplomat as Performance Artist," *Jerusalem Post* (January 21, 2004): 13.

90 Ben-David, 13; and Silver, 13.

91 The Swedish government supported the artists and caused a diplomatic disagreement between the two nations.

92 Gayatri Sinha, "No Go for Show at National Gallery," *The Hindu* (September 3, 2000) (www.hinduonnet.com/2000/09/03/stories/14032184.htm; accessed September 2006). R.V.V. Ayyar, the Culture Secretary who had closed the show, stated: "If it had been exhibited in a private gallery, I would have had no problem. But this is a government body and we have to appreciate its difficulties." See Anshul Avijit, "Clipped Wings," *India Today* (September 18, 2000): 63.

93 Surendran Nair, "Curbing Icarus' Flight," *Flair: The Express Magazine* (September 18, 2000), n.p.

94 See www.LAHCOWS.org (accessed September 2006).

213

CHAPTER 3 PROPAGANDA FOR DEMOCRACY:
THE AVANT-GARDE GOES TO WAR

1 Lion Feuchtwanger, "Some Useful 'Enemy Aliens'; But Anniversary of Nazi Book Burning Finds Them Bound by Red Tape," *New York Times* (May 11, 1942): 14.

2 The USA PATRIOT Act is an obvious example: it limits individual freedoms, allowing government heightened powers to detain suspected terrorists, to investigate citizens' bank accounts, to perform wiretaps and searches, and to scan library, medical, and education records. The rationale for the Act, passed by both parts of the legislature and signed into law by the executive, was that it would "unit[e] and strengthen America." The implicit logic here is that a strongly united democracy means fewer individual freedoms, and more individual freedoms mean a weaker, more fragmented democracy. *Uniting and Strengthening America by Providing Appropriate Tools Required to Intercept and Obstruct Terrorism (USA PATRIOT) Act of 2001* (Public Law 107–56).

3 The US Department of Defense itself issued a report in September 2004 warning that hypocritical US policies had alienated people in the Middle East: "The information campaign – or as some still would have it, 'the war of ideas,' or the struggle for 'hearts and minds' – is important to every war effort. In this war it is an essential objective, because the larger goals of US strategy depend on separating the vast majority of non-violent Muslims from the radical-militant Islamist-Jihadists. But American efforts have not only failed in this respect: they may also have achieved the opposite of what they intended. . . . Muslims do not 'hate our freedom,' but rather, they hate our policies. . . . [W]hen American public diplomacy talks about bringing democracy to Islamic societies, this is seen as no more than self-serving hypocrisy . . . motivated by ulterior motives, and deliberately controlled in order to best serve American national interests at the expense of truly Muslim self-determination." *Report of the Defense Science Board Task Force on Strategic Communication* (September 2004), Office of the Under Secretary of Defense for Acquisition, Technology, and Logistics. Washington, DC 20301–3140: 47–48.

4 J. Edgar Hoover himself authorized a wiretap for the Los Angeles motel room where Brecht's mistress and collaborator, Ruth Berlau, planned to stay (www.foia.fbi.gov/foiaindex/brecht.htm; accessed September 2006).

5 *Los Angeles Examiner* (October 31, 1947).

6 Eric Bentley, *Thirty Years of Treason: Excerpts from Hearings Before the House Committee on Un-American Activities, 1938–1968* (New York: Viking, 1971): 209.

7   There are a number of accounts by those who refused to name names during the HUAC hearings, including Nancy Schwartz's *The Hollywood Writers' Wars* (New York: Knopf, 1982); Victor S. Navasky, *Naming Names* (New York: Hill and Wang, 1980); and Paul Buhle and Dave Wagner, *Hide in Plain Sight: The Hollywood Blacklistees in Film and Television, 1950–2002* (Houndmills: Palgrave Macmillan, 2003).

8   Bentley, 222–23.

9   Ibid., 209.

10  Bertolt Brecht, *The Jewish Wife and Other Short Plays*, ed. Eric Bentley (New York: Grove Press, 1965): 77–78, 99.

11  Brecht, frustrated with Lang, pictured him as a greedy and shameless panderer to popular taste: "He sits behind his boss-desk, with all the airs of a dictator and old moviehound, filled up with drugs and resentments at any good suggestion, collecting 'surprises,' little bits of suspense, filthy lies and sentimentalities, and collects licenses for the 'box office'." Bertolt Brecht, journal entry from October 16, 1942 (my translation), in *Werke*, ed. Werner Hecht (Frankfurt: Suhrkamp, 1988): vol. 27, 126.

12  Gert Gemünden suggests that although Lang made some decisions that upset Brecht (including cutting out a scene in which Czech hostages make anti-Semitic statements just moments before their execution), the screenplay ultimately bore out some of Brecht's most important intentions. "Brecht in Hollywood: 'Hangmen Also Die' and the Anti-Nazi Film," *TDR* 43 (winter 1999): 72, 74 *n*.1.

13  James K. Lyon, *Bertolt Brecht in America* (Princeton: Princeton University Press, 1980): 33.

14  Sidney Fay, a scholar and friend of Ruth Fischer, wrote: "It was an unusual step to put a young woman in her early twenties, and not even a German citizen, in command of the largest Communist Party organization in the Reich. . . . [M]any of the rank and file of the Party distrusted the old leaders, and wanted to avoid having the organization become an instrument in the hands of a small clique or a tool to be used by Russian agents." See Fay's preface to Ruth Fischer's book, *Stalin and German Communism: A Study of the Origins of the State Party* (1948) (New Brunswick: Transaction Books, 1981): xvii.

15  Fischer writes: "[Stalin's] methods, the ruthless extermination of every opposition, became the studied model of every pimpled Nazling" (ibid., 644), and she describes the support Stalinism and Nazism offered to one another (656). Stalin himself explained his reasons for punishing Fischer and Maslow in a speech called, "The Fight against Right and Ultra-Left Deviations" (January 22, 1926); translated in J. V. Stalin, *Works* (Moscow: Foreign Languages Publishing House, 1954), vol. 8, pp. 1–10.

16  Bentley, 65, 73.

17  Ibid., 61, 63.

18  Quoted in Albrecht Betz, *Hanns Eisler: Political Musician*, trans. Bill Hopkins (Cambridge: Cambridge University Press, 1982): 197.

19  It is intriguing that Ruth Fischer saw her brother Hanns as a Soviet spy and turned him in along with Gerhart: Hanns's ties to Stalin were never strong, and he managed to persuade the US press in the 1940s that he was altogether apolitical. In his HUAC testimony, he insisted: "I couldn't combine my artistic activities with the demand of any political party, so I dropped out" (Bentley, 78). He told the press that his sister had "completely and deliberately invented" "all her suposed 'revelations' about myself [*sic*]." (Undated memo by Hanns Eisler. Feuchtwanger Memorial Library, Specialized Libraries and Archival Collections, University of Southern California.) In order to justify their grant to Eisler, the Rockefeller Foundation argued to itself that though "his music had been taken up by the Left," he simply stood for an antifascist kind of progressivism in the arts (letters and memos between Alvin Johnson of the New School and John Marshall of the Rockefeller Foundation, discussing Eisler's application for a grant in 1940). Johnson later complained that he had probably been "blacklisted" by the Rockefeller Foundation "on account of Hanns Eisler," who "was non-political but did tunes the revolutionaries sung, as you and I sing the melody of God Save the King and call it America." (Record group 1.1, box 259, series 200, folder 3095, Rockefeller Foundation Archives, Rockefeller Archive Center, Sleepy Hollow, New York.) But it was also true Hanns maintained his ties to Gerhart, and his musical work certainly never strayed far from politics.

20  Fischer, 617–18.

21  Quoted in Martin Esslin, *Brecht: The Man and His Work* (Garden City: Doubleday, 1961): 156–57.

22  William Hauptman, "The Suppression of Art in the McCarthy Decade," *Artforum* (October 1973): 48–52.

23  Margaret Lynne Ausfeld and Virginia M. Mecklenburg, *Advancing American Art* (Montgomery: Montgomery Museum of Fine Arts, 1984): 17.

24  Fischer, 624.

25  "Benton Says Soviet Sows Propaganda," *New York Times* (April 23, 1947): 16.

26  See Russell Lynes, *Good Old Modern: An Intimate Portrait of the Museum of Modern Art* (New York: Athenaeum, 1973): 295.

27  Taylor D. Littleton, "'The Life of Our Design': Advancing American Art," *National Forum* 76 (spring 1996): 24–25. Another article claimed: "If you know how to read them, modern paintings will disclose the weak spots in US fortifications, and such crucial constructions as the Boulder Dam." Quoted

in Frances Stonor Saunders, *The Cultural Cold War: The CIA and the World of Arts and Letters* (New York: New Press, 1999): 253.

28 Ausfeld and Mecklenburg, 19.

29 Littleton, 25.

30 Vivien Raynor, "A 'Scandalous' Show Returns," *New York Times* (April 15, 1984): C22. A review in Paris had it that the "vigor" of the American show was a surprise, one "which has very successfully changed the summary idea which has generally been held." *Les Arts* (November 22, 1946). In Prague, the success of the US show prompted Moscow to respond with the *Soviet Exhibition of Works of National Artists*. The Czech press gave a much more favorable account of the art from the US. One Prague newspaper explained that "the exhibited works [from the Soviet Union] are more remarkable for their size than for their artistic value." In Latin America, the US show was similarly well received. Ausfeld and Mecklenburg, 16, 17.

31 Alfred Barr, "Is Modern Art Communistic?" *New York Times Magazine* (December 14, 1952): SM22.

32 Saunders, 259.

33 Ibid., 257.

34 Rockefeller wanted his foundation "to report annually to the Secretary of the Interior on the details of its operations." The trustees of the Foundation included Winthrop Aldrich, ambassador to Great Britain, Chester Barnard of the State Department, and John Foster Dulles, later Secretary of State and brother of CIA mastermind Allen Dulles. See Raymond B. Fosdick, *The Story of the Rockefeller Foundation* (New York: Harper and Row, 1952): 28, 309–10. Edward H. Berman explains that the close ties between the charitable foundations and the nation's leaders were not surprising, since they all belonged to a small elite coterie. *The Influence of the Carnegie, Ford, and Rockefeller Foundations on American Foreign Policy: The Ideology of Philanthropy* (Albany: SUNY Press, 1983): 32.

35 As Tom Braden explained, "The idea that Congress would have approved of many of our projects was about as likely as the John Birch society approving Medicare." Quoted in Eva Cockcroft, "Abstract Expressionism, Weapon of the Cold War," *Artforum* 12 (June 1974): 40.

36 "The Communist Party of the United States, in fact, at that moment, was practically a branch of the Justice Department." Howard Fast, quoted in Saunders, 191.

37 One of the writers who first identified Ab Ex as a group was Clement Greenberg, who argued that these painters brought together two trends that had been separate in the European tradition: "the flattening-out, abstracting, 'purifying' process of cubism" and "a violent and extravagant temperament." "Art," *Nation* (June 9, 1945): 657.

38  One figure who represented capitalism held a swastika along with symbols of the Democratic and Republican parties in his hands. Annette Cox, *Art-as-Politics: The Abstract Expressionist Avant-Garde and Society* (Ann Arbor: UMI Research Press, 1982): 17.

39  A number of the Ab Ex painters had received assistance from the WPA during the Depression, but during and after World War II found themselves struggling to stay alive. Pollock almost finished life as a carpenter, and Rothko had to work odd jobs to keep body and soul together.

40  Lawrence de Neufville, quoted in Saunders, 263.

41  Donald Jameson of the CIA, in Saunders, 260. Jameson was right: the Ab Ex painters saw themselves either as political radicals or as entirely apolitical, eschewing all affiliations with the state. Many began with a sympathy with socialism that later turned to disenchantment, but even those artists who had been disappointed by the left did not explicitly embrace US policy, preferring to boast of their autonomy and freedom from all ideology. Cox, 70.

42  Saunders, 262.

43  Ibid., 268–69.

44  Ibid., 267.

45  Art historian Kirk Varnedoe writes that the Pollock publicity marked a watershed in the history of art. A "special dance was tentatively forming between the mass-audience system of *Time* and *Life* and the evolving small-audience world of advanced art. In that process, Pollock was not simply a cheapened victim of philistine publicity, but instead (or also) its accomplice. . . . [H]e became famous for being famous." *Jackson Pollock* (New York: Museum of Modern Art, 2002): 19.

46  Brian Sewell, "The Fall and Fall of Jack the Dripper," *Evening Standard* (London: March 11, 1999): 34. See also Jane Frances Healy, *Painting Pollock: The Creation of a Cultural Hero in Post-World War II America*, unpublished PhD dissertation (University of Minnesota, 1991).

47  These are the words of the CIA's Donald Jameson, in Saunders, 260.

48  Dwight D. Eisenhower, "Freedom in the Arts," recorded address to MoMA on its 25th anniversary (October 19, 1954), in the *Museum of Modern Art Bulletin* (1954).

49  US House. 80th Cong., second sess. February 18, 1947. Washington: GPO, 1948.

50  William Hauptman, "The Suppression of Art in the McCarthy Decade," *Artforum* (October 1973): 52.

51  Richard M. Nixon, "Special Message to the Congress about Funding and Authorization of the National Foundation on the Arts and the Humanities" (December 10, 1969), in *Public Papers of the Presidents: Richard M. Nixon, 1969* (Washington, DC: Government Printing Office, 1970): 1020.

52  The National Foundation for the Arts and the Humanities had gotten its original impetus from Kennedy, and was later established by Johnson, both of whom supported a new federal arts body at least in part for Cold War reasons. As Arthur Schlesinger explained in an influential memo to Kennedy: the arts are "of obvious importance . . . in transforming the world's impression of the United States as a nation of money-grubbing materialists." Michael Brenson, *Visionaries and Outcasts: The NEA, Congress, and the Place of the Visual Artist in America* (New York: New Press, 2001): 15.

53  Republican Congressman Paul Fino of New York complained in 1968 that "Aid to individuals is liable to turn out to be nothing more than a subsidy for hippies, beatniks, junkies, and Vietniks." He bemoaned the tax dollars that had been spent "to subsidize anti-Vietnam movies made by European Communists" and "anti-white plays written by black nationalists like LeRoi Jones." Quoted in ibid., 82.

54  Matthew C. Moen, "Congress and the National Endowment for the Arts: Institutional Patterns and Arts Funding, 1965–1994," *Social Science Journal* 34 (1997): 185.

55  Richard M. Nixon, "Message to the Congress Transmitting Annual Report of the National Endowment for the Arts and National Council on the Arts" (April 22, 1974). John Woolley and Gerhard Peters, *The American Presidency Project* (www.presidency.ucsb.edu/ws/?pid=3488; accessed September 2006).

56  See Donna M. Binkiewicz's fine book, *Federalizing the Muse: United States Arts Policy and the National Endowment for the Arts 1965–1980* (Chapel Hill: University of North Carolina Press, 2004): 164.

57  Richard Jensen, "The Culture Wars, 1965–1995: A Historian's Map," *Journal of Social History*; Supplement, Vol. 29 (fall 1995): 17.

58  Not only did he serve as President of the Museum of Modern Art in the 1940s and 1950s, but he also became special advisor on Cold War strategy to Eisenhower in 1954 and chaired the Planning Coordination Group, which managed a whole range of national security decisions, including the hidden cultural operations of the CIA. Saunders, 261.

59  Nixon's close friend and advisor, Leonard Garment, suggested that the new President wanted to use the arts to astonish and also placate Rockefeller's more liberal constituency, because they expected him, based on his HUAC record, to act like a repressive philistine: "Nixon was facing months and probably years of thunder on his left. . . . I had an intuition that if we made the case that a dollar of intervention in the arts would buy multiple dollars of political peace, Nixon might agree." Leonard Garment, *Crazy Rhythm: My Journey from Brooklyn, Jazz, and Wall Street to Nixon's White*

*House, Watergate, and Beyond* . . . (New York: Random House, 1997): 128, 162–63.

60 Stephen Ambrose also makes this analogy in *Nixon: The Triumph of a Politician 1962–1972* (New York: Simon and Schuster, 1989): 439.

## CHAPTER 4   OBSCENITY AND THE DEMOCRATIZATION OF CULTURE

1   D. H. Lawrence, letter to Morris Ernst (November 10, 1928), in *The Selected Letters of D. H. Lawrence*, ed. James T. Boulton (Cambridge: Cambridge University Press, 2000): 414. C. Carr, "War on Art," *Village Voice* (June 5, 1990).

2   Though we might imagine societies have always fought to restrict the circulation of obscene texts and images, prosecutions of sexually explicit representations have only been going on seriously for about a century and a half. For hundreds of years before this, art had been the target of state censorship for religious and political dissent, but it had rarely come under attack by the law for disturbing sexual morals. Some notable exceptions include the Romantic poets, sometimes understood to be precursors to the historical avant-garde. George Gordon Byron's *Don Juan* and Percy Shelley's *Queen Mab* were both found obscene in Britain. For censorship in the earlier periods, see Janet Clare, *Art Made Tongue-Tied By Authority: Elizabethan & Jacobean Dramatic Censorship* (Manchester: Manchester University Press, 1999); Fredric Hemming, *Theatre & State in France, 1760–1905* (Cambridge: Cambridge University Press, 1984); and Jane Moody, *Illegitimate Theatre in London, 1787–1843* (Cambridge: Cambridge University Press, 2000). For the relationship between Romanticism and the avant-garde, see Renato Poggioli, *The Theory of the Avant-Garde* (New York: Harper and Row, 1968): 43–59.

3   Walter Kendrick, *The Secret Museum: Pornography in Modern Culture* (Harmondsworth: Penguin, 1987): 57.

4   Lynn Hunt, "Introduction," *The Invention of Pornography: Obscenity and the Origins of Modernity, 1500–1800*, ed. Lynn Hunt (New York: Zone Books, 1993): 12–13.

5   For a typical expression of anxiety about pornography on the internet, see Ryan Singel, "Internet Porn: Worse Than Crack?" *Wired News* (November 19, 2004) (www.wired.com/news/technology/0,1282,65772,00.html; accessed October 2006).

6   "Mr. Comstock's Work," *New York Times* (November 13, 1887): 3.

7   *New York Herald* (November 13, 1887): 4.

8  *The World* (November 17, 1887): 8.

9  For a fascinating look at this case by a sociologist focusing on class norms, see Nicola Beisel, "Morals Versus Art: Censorship, the Politics of Interpretation, and the Victorian Nude," *American Sociological Review* 58 (April 1993): 145–62.

10  This example comes from an 1894 civil case that involved the sale of a number of works of classic literature, including *The Decameron, The Arabian Nights, Gargantua and Pantagruel,* and *Tom Jones.* Judge O'Brien balked at the absurdity of including canonical works under the rubric of obscenity: "It is very difficult to see upon what theory these world-renowned classics can be regarded as specimens of that pornographic literature which it is the office of the Society for the Suppression of Vice to suppress. . . . What has become standard literature of the English language, – has been wrought into the very structure of our splendid English literature – is not to be pronounced at this late day unfit for publication or circulation and stamped with judicial disapprobation as hurtful to the community." *In re Worthington Co.* 30 NYS 361 (S.Ct. 1894). In a 1909 battle over the sale of the works of Voltaire, the court felt obliged "to recognize that the genius of Voltaire has enriched many fields of knowledge. . . . Differ as men may as to the views of Voltaire on many questions, none can deny the great influence of his work in promoting justice and humanity and the reign of reason in public affairs." *St. Hubert Guild v. Quinn,* 64 Misc. 336, 118 N.Y.S. 582 (Sup. Ct. 1909).

11  For example, although judges are typically appointed to their positions for life, they can be impeached and removed by legislatures. They are bound by some legislative actions and have no power to overrule them, as when a two-thirds majority of the US Congress as well as the President agree to amend the Constitution. Moreover, trials themselves include representatives of the citizenry in the form of juries.

12  Wilbur C. Rich, "The Warren Court and American Politics (review)," *Rhetoric & Public Affairs* 4 (fall 2001): 578. Rich disagrees with this claim.

13  Michael J. Klarman, "What's So Great about Constitutionalism?" *Northwestern University Law Review* 93 (1998): 161; and Suzanna Sherry, "Too Clever by Half: The Problem of Novelty in Constitutional Law," *Northwestern University Law Review* 95 (spring 2001): 921–31. See also Corinna Barrett Lain, "Countermajoritarian Hero or Zero? Rethinking the Warren Court's Role in the Criminal Procedure Revolution," *University of Pennsylvania Law Review* 152 (2004): 1361–452.

14  *United States v. Carolene Products Company,* 304 US 144 (1938).

15  John Hart Ely, *Democracy and Distrust: A Theory of Judicial Review* (Cambridge, MA: Harvard University Press, 1980), 100–1, 103.

16  *Chambers v. Florida* 309 U.S. 227, 241 (1940).

17  See, for example, Justice Black's concurring opinion in *Kingsley Pictures Corp. v. Regents*, 360 U.S. 684 (1959). For differences between the US and Britain on the specific legal matter of freedom of expression, see Eric Barendt, *Freedom of Speech* (New York: Oxford University Press, 2005).

18  *Regina v. Hicklin*, 3 L.R.-Q.B. 360 (Eng. 1868).

19  See Frederick F. Schauer, *The Law of Obscenity* (Washington, DC: Bureau of National Affairs, 1976): 8, 16, 27, 71.

20  See, for example, Edson McClellan, "Comment: Sharpening the Focus on Daubert's Distinction Between Scientific and Nonscientific Expert Testimony," *San Diego Law Review* 34 (1997): 1719–85.

21  The role of expert witnesses in the courtroom has long been troubling, and it has only grown more so in recent decades, as lawyers have introduced experts more frequently: they are seen as "mercenaries, prostitutes or hired guns, witnesses devoid of principle who sell their opinions to the highest bidder." L. Timothy Perrin, "Expert Witness Testimony: Back to the Future," *University of Richmond Law Review* 29 (December, 1995): 1389. There are a number of thorny questions that attach to experts, including the fact that juries may have to decide between experts on two sides of the issue, and so, to quote Justice Blackmun, "One can only wonder how juries are to separate valid from invalid expert opinions when the 'experts' themselves are so obviously unable to do so." Dissenting opinion in *Barefoot v. Estelle*, 463 U.S. 880 (1983). But in the obscenity trials of the late nineteenth century, the question was whether or not experts had any place in decisions about obscenity at all.

22  *Commonwealth v. Landis*, 8 Phila. 453 (1870). A few years later, another judge concluded that "the question of obscenity or indecency is one falling within the range of ordinary intelligence and so does not require an expert in literature or art to determine." *People v. Muller*, 96 NY 408 (1884).

23  "Pictures of a Doubtful Kind," *New York Times* (December 18, 1883): 3. Some courts showed an inclination to weigh the claims of experts more seriously. One 1909 decision concluded with the words of a famous historian, W. E. H. Lecky, and stated firmly that "It is no part of the duty of courts to exercise a censorship over literary productions." *St. Hubert Guild v. Quinn*, 64 Misc. 336, 118 N.Y.S. 582 (Sup. Ct. 1909).

24  Quoted in Vera Brittain, *Radclyffe Hall: A Case of Obscenity* (London: Femina Books, 1968): 91.

25  *Bleistein v. Donaldson Lithographing Co.*, 188 U.S. 239, 251 (1903).

26  Brief for claimant-appellee in *United States of America v. One Book Entitled Ulysses*. In Michael Moscato and Leslie Le Blanc, eds., *The United States of America v. One Book Entitled Ulysses by James Joyce: Documents and*

Commentary – A 50-Year Retrospective (Frederick: University Publications of America, 1984), 404.

27 Barbara Leckie, "'Short Cuts to Culture': Censorship and Modernism; or, Learning to Read *Ulysses*," *European Joyce Studies* 14 (2002): 10.

28 "Conboy Recites from *Ulysses* and Girl Flees," *New York Daily News* (May 18, 1934); in Moscato and Le Blanc, 449.

29 *United States v. One Book Called "Ulysses,"* 5 F. Supp. 182 (S.D.N.Y. 1933).

30 Morris Ernst, *The Best is Yet* (New York: Harper and Brothers, 1945), 116.

31 Judge Woolsey was not in fact the first to break with *Hicklin* in this way, though he is the most famous. Learned Hand had called this element of *Hicklin* into question as early as 1913 in *United States v. Kennerley*, 209 F. 119, 120 (S.D.N.Y. 1913).

32 *United States v. One Book Called "Ulysses,"* 5 F. Supp. 182 (S.D.N.Y.1933).

33 He also cast doubt on "those who pose as the more highly developed and intelligent." *United States v. One Book Entitled "Ulysses" by James Joyce*, 72 F.2d 705 (2d Cir. 1934).

34 See, for example, Marisa Anne Pagnattaro, "Carving a Literary Exception: The Obscenity Standard and *Ulysses*," *Twentieth Century Literature* 47 (summer 2001): 217–40; and Paul Vanderham, *James Joyce and Censorship: The Trials of Ulysses* (New York: New York University Press, 1998).

35 Schauer, 144. This was not a thoroughgoing shift, and the question of elites did continue to appear in obscenity cases.

36 Hand wrote, for example, "*Ulysses* is rated as a book of considerable power by persons whose opinions are entitled to weight." *United States v. One Book Entitled "Ulysses" by James Joyce*, 72 F.2d 705 (2d Cir. 1934).

37 See, for example, Paul Cézanne, who had this to say about *les professeurs*: "they are all bastards, castrati, sons-of-bitches; they've got no guts at all!" Quoted in Philip Nord, *Impressionists and Politics: Art and Democracy in the Nineteenth Century* (New York: Routledge, 2000): 90. Mark Rothko was similarly emphatic on this point: "I hate and distrust all art historians, experts and critics. They are a bunch of parasites, feeding on the body of art. Their work not only is useless, it is misleading." Quoted in Mark Rothko, *Writings on Art*, Miguel López-Remiro, ed. (New Haven and London: Yale University Press, 2006): 132.

38 See Learned Hand, "Historical and Practical Considerations Regarding Expert Testimony," *Harvard Law Review* 15 (1902): 40–58.

39 As the Supreme Court held in 1968, "Providing an accused with the right to be tried by a jury of his peers gave him an inestimable safeguard against the corrupt or overzealous prosecutor and against the compliant, biased, or eccentric judge. If the defendant preferred the common-sense judgment of a jury to the more tutored but perhaps less sympathetic reaction of

the single judge, he was to have it." *Duncan v. Louisiana*, 391 U.S. 145 (1968).

40   Brian Martin, *Confronting the Experts* (Albany: SUNY Press, 1996): 6–7.

41   Steven Mark Levy explains that the courts have been less able to establish expertise in the arts than in other fields: "art experts are not subject to any licensing system and are not required to meet any minimal standards." Levy argues that the courts have traditionally favored "Formal education, such as a degree in art history, museology, science or related fields." There are exceptions, however: "In a case involving the authenticity of Salvador Dali prints . . . the court specifically held that practical experience is an adequate substitute for academic qualifications." "Liability of the Art Expert," *Wisconsin Law Review* (July/August 1991): 600, 601, 615.

42   To give just one example: testifying in the Cincinnati trial against an exhibition of Mapplethorpe photographs, Janet Kardon, who had directed the Institute of Contemporary Art in Philadelphia, gave a formalist analysis of the photograph. She pointed out the "almost classical" composition of the man with the bull-whip inserted into his anus, and the "oppositional diagonals" that organized the photograph of one man urinating into the mouth of another. The jury found in favor, citing "artistic value." Elizabeth Hess, "Art on Trial: Cincinnati's Dangerous Theater of the Ridiculous," in *Culture Wars: Documents from the Recent Controversies in the Arts*, ed. Richard Bolton (New York: New Press, 1992): 277.

43   The earliest judicial objection seems to have come in 1894, when a judge worried that "to condemn a standard literary work because of a few of its episodes, would compel the exclusion from circulation of a very large proportion of works of fiction of the most famous writers of the English language." *In re Worthington Co.* 30 NYS 361 (S.Ct. 1894).

44   *Halsey v. New York Society for the Suppression of Vice*, 234 N.Y. 1, 136 N.E. 219 (1922).

45   "If a person should write an essay upon the subject of honesty, and fill it with notes containing filthy and obscene stories, and could then pass it through the mails on the ground that it was an essay on honesty, the way would be easy to a disregard of the statute." *United States v. Bennett*, 24 F. Cas. 1093 (1879).

46   "Sincerity and literary art are not the antitheses of obscenity, indecency, and impurity in such manner that one set of qualities can be set off against the other and judgment rendered according to an imaginary balance supposed to be left over on one side or the other. . . . Indeed, obscenity may sometimes be made even more alluring and suggestive by the zeal which comes from sincerity and by the added force of artistic presentation." *Commonwealth v. Isenstadt*, 318 Mass. 543; 62 N.E.2d 840 (1945).

47  *The People of the State of New York v. Viking Press, Inc., and Helen Schiller,*
    147 Misc. 813; 264 N.Y.S. 534 (Magis. Ct. 1933). The same novel fared
    less well in Massachusetts: *Attorney General v. Book Named "God's Little Acre,"*
    326 Mass. 281, 93 N.E. 2d 819 (1950).

48  *United States v. One Book Called "Ulysses,"* 5 F. Supp. 182 (S.D.N.Y. 1933).

49  Sir Theobald Matthew, quoted in "Publishers Urge More Uniform Law on
    Obscenity," *The Times* (London, May 13, 1958): 6.

50  "We think the same immunity should apply to literature as to science, where
    the presentation when viewed objectively, is sincere, and the erotic matter
    is not introduced to promote lust and does not furnish the dominant note
    of the publication." *One Book Entitled "Ulysses" by James Joyce,* 72 F.2d 705
    (2d Cir. 1934). Javier Romero claims that the whole-book standard has intro-
    duced a problem of vagueness in cases that involve the internet, since it has
    become difficult to define the "whole." "Comment: Unconstitutional
    Vagueness and Restrictiveness in the Contextual Analysis of the Obscenity
    Standard: A Critical Reading of the Miller Test Genealogy," *University of
    Pennsylvania Journal of Constitutional Law* 7 (October, 2005): 1207–28.

51  All references to the trial of *Lady Chatterley's Lover* will cite H.
    Montgomery-Hyde's excellent edition of the proceedings, *The Lady
    Chatterley's Lover Trial: Regina v. Penguin Books, Limited* (London: Bodley Head,
    1990). In the trial, literary critic Raymond Williams testified: "I think one
    could fairly say that he [Lawrence] is one of the five or six major literary
    figures of modern Europe – of Europe in this century" (204). And when
    asked where he would place Lawrence "in all contemporary literature,"
    E. M. Forster replied: "I would place him enormously high . . . when com-
    pared with all novels which come out the novels he wrote dominate
    terrifically" (160). Oddly enough, F. R. Leavis, Lawrence's great champion,
    refused to testify because he felt that *Lady Chatterley* was an inferior novel.
    See Rachel Bowlby, " 'But She Would Learn Something from Lady
    Chatterley': The Obscene Side of the Canon," in *Decolonizing Tradition: New
    Views of Twentieth-Century "British" Literary Canons,* ed. Karen R. Lawrence
    (Urbana: University of Illinois Press, 1992): 124.

52  In 1954, five relatively obscure obscenity cases caught the British public's
    attention: in some of these cases the courts had severely punished works by
    reputable publishers, while in others they had allowed seamy pornographers
    to get away without penalty. As a number of voices complained, an incon-
    sistent law might well be worse than no law at all. After several years of
    debate, committee work, and consultations with authors, publishers, and arbiters
    of public morality, Parliament passed the Obscene Publications Act.

53  The US case was *Grove Press v. Christenberry,* 175 F. Supp. 488 (1959 U.S.
    Dist.). Overturning the decision of the Postmaster General and the lower

court, the court of appeals' reasoning rested largely on the same two factors we saw at work in *Ulysses*. "The Postmaster General has no special competence or technical knowledge on this subject which qualifies him to render an informed judgment entitled to special weight in the courts." The court added that the experts were virtually undivided about the value of the novel: "Publication of the Grove edition was a major literary event. It was greeted by editorials in leading newspapers throughout the country unanimously approving the publication and viewing with alarm possible attempts to ban the book." The court of appeals was also careful to assess the novel as a "whole": "Even if it be assumed that these passages and this language taken in isolation tend to arouse shameful, morbid and lustful sexual desires in the average reader, they are an integral, and to the author a necessary part of the development of theme, plot and character. The dominant theme, purpose and effect of the book as a whole is not an appeal to prurience or the prurient minded."

54   For more on the distinction between modernism and the avant-garde, see Jochen Schulte-Sasse's introduction to Peter Bürger, *Theory of the Avant-Garde*, trans. Michael Shaw (Minneapolis and London: University of Minnesota Press, 1984): xiv–xv. For a compelling account of modernism's relationship to a pornographic mass culture, see Allison Pease, *Modernism, Mass Culture, and the Aesthetics of Obscenity* (Cambridge: Cambridge University Press, 2000).

55   Or, as defending counsel Gardiner put it, "the whole [class] attitude is one which Penguin Books was formed to fight against, which they have always fought against, and which they will go on fighting against – this attitude that it is all right to publish a special edition at five or ten guineas, so that people who are less well off cannot read what other people do" (268).

56   After protracted debate in the press and the House of Commons, in 1959 Parliament had finally agreed to allow expert witnesses in obscenity trials for the first time. See "Obscenity Bill Prospects," *The Times* (London, December 17, 1958): 8; and "Clause on Expert Evidence Added to Obscenity Bill," *The Times* (London, March 19, 1959): 16.

57   The names and identities of the jurors are not recorded, but we know from descriptions of the courtroom that three were women and one was an Orthodox Jewish man.

58   Griffith-Jones complained that he was "barred from calling any evidence" about anything other than "the literary and other merits of the book." The only witness he did call was Detective Inspector Monahan, who simply described Penguin's delivery of the book to the authorities (70).

59   At the time, Katherine Anne Porter criticized *Lady Chatterley* as "sickly sentimental" rather than honest. "A Wreath for the Gamekeeper," *Encounter* 14 (February 1960): 72.

60  Colin Welch, "Black Magic, White Lies," *Encounter* 16 (February 1961): 79.

61  The judge also immediately contradicted himself: "you will read this book just as though you had bought it at a bookstall and you were reading it in the ordinary way" (86).

62  Or as the witness Graham Hough put it: "No man in his senses is going to write a book of three hundred pages as mere padding for thirty pages of sexual matter" (93).

63  From the testimony of Professor Vivian de Sola Pinto (254).

64  Hector Alastair Hethrington, editor of the *Guardian* (240, 255).

65  Literary critic Helen Louise Gardner (119).

66  The New Critics were in fact a miscellaneous group whose ideas cannot be reduced to a single program. The major thinkers widely associated with this movement – I. A. Richards, William Empson, John Crowe Ransom, Allen Tate, Yvor Winters, Cleanth Brooks, R. P. Blackmur, W. K. Wimsatt Jr., René Wellek, and Kenneth Burke – differed in significant ways over methods, presumptions, and aims. For an introduction to some of the general practices and presumptions of the New Criticism, see Cleanth Brooks, "New Criticism," in *Princeton Encyclopedia of Poetry and Poetics* (Princeton: Princeton University Press, 1974): 567–68.

67  Gerald Graff, *Professing Literature: An Institutional History* (Chicago: University of Chicago Press, 1989): 173.

68  John W. Stevenson, "In Memoriam: Cleanth Brooks," *South Atlantic Review* 59 (September 1994): 163–64. For New Critical textbooks, see especially Cleanth Brooks and Robert Penn Warren, *An Approach to Literature* (1936), *Understanding Poetry* (1938), and *Understanding Fiction* (1943).

69  Carl Woodring, *Literature: An Embattled Profession* (New York: Columbia University Press, 1999): 41.

70  I. A. Richards, *Practical Criticism* (1929) (New York: Harvest Books, 1956): 295.

71  Allen Tate, "The Function of the Critical Quarterly," in *Essays of Four Decades* (Wilmington, DE: Intercollegiate Studies Institute, 1999): 45–55. Robert Penn Warren attacked "Common-manism," which undermined the "human capacity to move towards excellence, to define ourselves in a communal aspiration." "Knowledge and the Image of Man," in *Robert Penn Warren: A Collection of Critical Essays*, ed. John L. Longley (New York: New York University Press, 1965): 240.

72  For the *Rima* case, see chapter 2.

73  *Roth* distinguished the artistic treatment of sex – a matter of "public concern" that might be dealt with seriously in controversial ways – from obscenity, which had nothing to offer but the provocation of "itching,

morbid, or lascivious longings." *Roth v. United States*; *Alberts v. California*, 354 U.S. 476 (1957).

74  *Miller v. California*, 413 U.S. 15 (1973).

75  See Edward J. Main, "The Neglected Prong of the Miller Test for Obscenity: Serious Literary, Artistic, Political, or Scientific Value," *Southern Illinois University Law Journal* 11 (1987): 1159–77.

76  See chapters 2 and 3.

77  In *Roth*, Justice Harlan explained that the states should have the right to define offensiveness so that the country as a whole would respect a diversity of judgments: "The fact that the people of one State cannot read some of the works of D. H. Lawrence seems to me, if not wise or desirable, at least acceptable. But that no person in the United States should be allowed to do so seems to me to be intolerable, and violative of both the letter and spirit of the First Amendment." See *Roth v. United States*, 354 U.S. 476 (1957).

78  *Pope v. Illinois*, 481 U.S. 497 (1987).

79  Justice Blackmun, dissenting in ibid.

80  *Pope* is sometimes understood to elevate the "reasonable" person standard too far above the experts. Edward deGrazia, "Girls Lean Back Everywhere: The Law of Obscenity and the Assault on Genius," *Cardozo Arts and Entertainment Law Journal* 11 (1993): 851. But, in fact, the cases that have followed *Pope* – including obscenity trials of Robert Mapplethorpe, 2 Live Crew, and Karen Finley – have incorporated testimony from experts that has proven highly persuasive to judges and juries. And the fact that the reasonable person is expected to listen to the experts – and potentially to learn from them – reveals again the balance between the art world and "the people" that the law has been favoring since *Ulysses*.

81  2 Live Crew, "Put Her in the Buck," *As Nasty as They Wanna Be* (Miami: Skyywalker Records, Inc., 1989).

82  See Nelson George, *Hip Hop America* (Harmondsworth: Penguin, 1998): 132, 176.

83  "Scholar Gates Recalls Yale Days in Campus Talks," *Yale Bulletin and Calendar* (February 11, 2000) (www.yale.edu/opa/v28.n20/story10.html; accessed September 2006).

84  Henry Louis Gates, Jr. "2 Live Crew, Decoded," *New York Times* (June 19, 1990): A23.

85  Quoted in William Eric Perkins, "The Rap Attack," in *Droppin' Science: Critical Essays on Rap Music and Hip Hop Culture*, ed. William Eric Perkins (Philadelphia: Temple University Press, 1996): 25.

86  Ibid.

87  As Tricia Rose writes: "The way rap and rap-related violence are discussed in the popular media is fundamentally linked to the larger social discourse

on the spatial control of black people." See "Hidden Politics: Discursive and Institutional Policing of Rap Music," in Perkins, 237.

88  "[A] number of female rappers were asked to comment on the 2 Live Crew and the sexist content of their lyrics. . . . MC Lyte, Queen Latifah, Sister Souljah, and Yo-Yo refused to criticize their male colleagues – not necessarily because they did not find the lyrics offensive, but because they were acutely aware of the dominant discursive context in which their responses would be reproduced. Cognizant that they were being constructed in the mainstream press as a progressive response to regressive male rappers, these female rappers felt that they were being used as a political baton to beat male rappers over the head." Tricia Rose, *Black Noise: Rap Music and Black Culture in Contemporary America* (Hanover: Wesleyan University Press, 1994): 149–50.

89  From the trial transcript of *Skyywalker Records, Inc. v. Nick Navarro*, 739 F. Supp. 578 (1990): 273–74. Hereafter, all citations from the transcript will simply refer to page numbers.

90  Overall, the lawyer argued, "the references to women and the attitude to contact between men and women is always in the most degrading, dehumanizing, horrifying terms" (297).

91  Curiously, the implicit legal question seems to have less to do with obscenity, "appealing to the prurient interest," and more with hate speech – "words that are persecutorial, hateful, and degrading; that promote a message of racial or religious or other trait-based inferiority; and that target a historically oppressed group." But the US is the only common law country that does not criminalize hate speech, and so it was the sexual content of the lyrics that allowed the Broward County sheriff's office to charge obscenity. See Judge Helen Ginger Berrigan, "Speaking Out about Hate Speech," *Loyola Law Review* 48 (spring 2002): 1; and Mari J. Matsuda, "Legal Storytelling: Public Response to Racist Speech, Considering the Victim's Story," *Michigan Law Review* 87 (August 1989): 2347.

92  One of the more prominent examples from *As Nasty as They Wanna Be* was a pair of lines taken from the film *Full Metal Jacket*: " 'How much do I get for ten dollars?' 'Anything you want.' " When the group admitted that the line came from a movie they'd seen together, the sheriff's lawyer pounced: "So the idea wasn't yours. It was from a whole other source; is that correct?" (89–90).

93  On this count, the judge needed no persuasion, and he tried to squelch the sheriff's side. "That argument's been around for a million years. Especially music. So that's not an issue here" (137–38).

94  "People in New York thought of [rap] as taking small bits of records and sort of throwing them at one another and letting them collide in the most explosive way possible. . . . Miami has a different kind of dance tradition than

229

New York. The huge Cuban population is really largely responsible for disco. . . . Two Live Crew . . . picked up on that and they were also playing at a tremendous tempo . . . at a time when New York records were moving fairly slowly" (238–39).

95  "A Grammy testifies that . . . this is valid music" (246).

96  The sheriff called no expert witnesses.

97  Call and response, he argued, was a form of "group bonding" that had come originally from Africa: "in this tradition, you had one person basically introduce a theme or an idea to a group, and the group would all respond, and that response would be an affirmation" (252). Playing the dozens was a legacy of slavery: "it's an insult game . . . it's a game of one-up-manship, where I say something about you, and you actually respond. You respond with something which is different, but also it's a criticism of me, but yours has to be better than what was just served to you" (267). Long explained that "Doing the dozens could help you develop the kind of thick skin you needed to survive in society" (270). Boasting served a similar purpose: "If you're dealing from the position of the disadvantaged or impoverished, to talk about how good you are, it's incredibly important because you're really trying to put yourself on the level that other people take for granted" (273).

98  *Skyywalker Records, Inc. v. Nick Navarro*, 739 F. Supp. 578 (1990).

99  Ibid. This was something of a misreading: Long had not argued that all speech by African-Americans was automatically political, but rather that the particular political *value* of the album could be grasped only by an audience knowledgeable about African-American cultural codes.

100  Ibid.

101  *Luke Records, Inc. v. Nick Navarro* 960 F.2d 134.

102  Christopher Nowlin, *Judging Obscenity: A Critical History of Expert Evidence* (Montreal: McGill-Queen's University Press, 2003): especially 55–66.

103  Bolton, 269.

104  Quoted in deGrazia, 816.

105  In the case of *Naked Lunch*, for example, Norman Mailer claimed that he "didn't see any hope of winning" and "was startled when we won." Quoted in Edward deGrazia, "DeGrazia and Ginsberg: A Remembrance of their Struggles Against Censorship," *Cardozo Life* (fall 1998): (www.cardozo.yu.edu/life/fall1998/degrazia/index.shtml; accessed September 2006).

## CHAPTER 5   ORIGINALITY ON TRIAL

1  Anne Barron, "Copyright Law and the Claims of Art," *Intellectual Property Quarterly* 4 (2002): 370.

2  Amy M. Adler, "Note: Post-Modern Art and the Death of Obscenity Law," *Yale Law Journal* 99 (April 1990): 1364.

3  Ibid., 1377, 1378, 1365.

4  Rosalind E. Krauss, *The Originality of the Avant-Garde and Other Modernist Myths* (Cambridge, MA: MIT Press, 1985): 157–58.

5  Fredric Jameson, "Postmodernism and Consumer Society," in *The AntiAesthetic: Essays on Postmodern Culture*, ed. Hal Foster (Port Townsend, WA: Bay Press, 1983): 115–16.

6  The trial proceedings have recently been published in Margit Rowell, ed., *Brancusi v. United States: The Historic Trial, 1928* (Paris: Adam Biro, 1999). All subsequent citations from the trial will refer to this edition.

7  "Brancusi vs. United States," *New York Herald Tribune* (December 25, 1963): 5.

8  Anna Chave recounts this exchange in *Constantin Brancusi: Shifting the Bases of Art* (New Haven and London: Yale University Press, 1993): 201.

9  *New York City Sun* (February 24, 1927), quoted in Rowell, 133.

10  *New York American* (October 22, 1927), quoted in ibid., 136.

11  *Providence Journal* (February 27, 1927), quoted in ibid., 134.

12  Patty Gerstenblith argues that "Because the dominant culture in North America identifies almost exclusively with the European background, considerable efforts are made to ensure access to the European heritage. This access, though threatened by the restrictions that art-source nations have increasingly placed on export of their cultural property, has been facilitated by a virtual lack of United States import controls and significant tax advantages. The inward flow thus continues virtually unabated. At the same time, the United States has made no attempt to restrict export of cultural property from its shores, a phenomenon that may be the result of a belief in free markets, or perhaps of a belief that we have little cultural property worth protecting." "Identity and Cultural Property: The Protection of Cultural Property in the United States," *Boston University Law Review* 75 (May 1995): 562. This reasoning is explicit in a Second Circuit Court of Appeals decision from 1916, which held "That Congress, realizing the importance of works of art to a comparatively new country, has in all the later tariff acts discriminated in favor of paintings and statuary cannot be denied." *United States v. Tiffany & Co.* 160 F. 408 (1908).

13  *United States v. Perry*, 146 U.S. 71 (1892).

14  *Consmiller v. United States*, 3 Ct. Cust. 298 (1912).

15  H. R. Doc. No. 1505, 60th Cong., 2nd Sess. 1713–14 (1908).

16  H. R. Doc. No. 1505, 60th Cong., 2nd Sess. 7209 (1908).

17  Letter from Kenyon Cox, an artist, read at the Congressional hearings over new tariff regulations for art: H. R. Doc. No. 1505, 60th Cong., 2nd Sess. 7210 (1908).

18 *Olivotti v. United States*, 7 Ct. Cust. Appeals, 46 (1916). The court followed definitions of sculpture from the *Standard Dictionary* and the *Century Dictionary*.

19 Hortense Saunders in the *Times* of Warren, Pennsylvania (October 28, 1927): quoted in Rowell, 137.

20 One of the few works of legal scholarship to analyze this case argues that what secured the decision for Brancusi was simply that Judge Waite was already predisposed to reject the standard set by *Olivotti*. Walter J. Derenberg and Daniel J. Baun, "Congress Rehabilitates Modern Art," *New York University Law Review* 34 (November 1959): 1228–53.

21 For a thoughtful commentary on the relationship between mimesis and originality, see Jeffrey Malkan, "What is a Copy?" *Cardozo Arts and Entertainment Law Journal* 23 (2005): 419–63.

22 In the words of the Director of the Brooklyn Museum, William Henry Fox, the work came "from an abstract idea" (40).

23 *Consmiller v. United States*, 3 Ct. Cust. 298 (1912).

24 Here I am following Jean Baudrillard. Since modernist art no longer provokes us to believe that it can call up either material or transcendent truth through representations, art objects cease to work together as if they were all fragments joining together to invoke a universal whole. Art therefore becomes a "succession of moments," discrete and discontinuous. And once the representation of the world is no longer the object of art, then works of art "are only able to follow each other and then to refer by virtue of their difference and their discontinuity in time, to a quite different model, to the *subject-creator-himself*." Thus the modern artist takes on an identity through a signature gesture – a gesture which, ironically, by virtue of its repetition, permits the conception of the artist as unique. In this way, modern art becomes entirely bound up in the series. "Gesture and Signature: Semiurgy in Contemporary Art," *For a Critique of the Political Economy of the Sign*, trans. Charles Levin (St. Louis: Telos Press, 1981): 104.

25 Epstein was himself a serious collector of ancient Egyptian, classical, and African sculpture. I have been unable to trace the whereabouts of the particular figure that was brought into the New York courtroom. Among the items listed in Ezio Bassani and Malcolm McLeod, *Jacob Epstein Collector* (Milan: Associazione Poro, 1989), #857, #890, and #891 seem likely candidates.

26 In the court record, this statement ends with a period rather than a question mark, which suggests that it was not posed as a question. But Epstein answered "Yes" as if it had been a question asked of him. The published version of the trial changes the period into a question mark.

27 Ronald Dworkin, *Law's Empire* (Cambridge, MA: Harvard University Press, 1986): 225. There is significant debate about the binding nature of precedent

among legal scholars, but most acknowledge both the value of legal stability and predictability, on the one hand, and the law's flexibility to adapt to new circumstances, on the other. For some more recent analyses of *stare decisis*, see Michael Stokes Paulsen, "Abrogating Stare Decisis by Statute: May Congress Remove the Precedential Effect of Roe and Casey?" *Yale Law Journal* 109 (2000): 1535–602; and Christopher J. Peters, "Foolish Consistency: On Equality, Integrity, and Justice in Stare Decisis," *Yale Law Journal* 105 (1996): 2031–115.

28  Roger Traynor writes: "Even if [a judge] confronts a truly unprecedented case, he still arrives at a decision in the context of judicial reasoning with recognizable ties to the past; by its kinship thereto it not only establishes the unprecedented case as a precedent for the future, but integrates it in the often rewoven but always unbroken line with the past." "Reasoning in a Circle of Law," in *Precedents, Statutes and Analysis of Legal Concepts*, ed. Scott Brewer (New York and London: Garland Press, 1998): 344.

29  Pierre Bourdieu, *The Rules of Art: The Genesis and Structure of the Literary Field*, trans. Susan Emanuel (Stanford: Stanford University Press, 1996): 301.

30  Epstein testified: "I won my way into the Gallery of Beaux Arts by competition with the entire class. . . . You are not admitted unless you show yourself competent on some work" (27). The critic Forbes Watson was asked whether he had seen Brancusi's work "as matter for his professional writing" (35). Fox gave so much evidence of his experience in the arts that Judge Waite interrupted the proceedings: "You need not go any further into his qualifications" (40). And on the other side, Brancusi's lawyers implied that Thomas H. Jones, at the tender age of 35, was too young to be taken seriously as an expert (64).

31  One witness was invited to confirm that *A Short History of Art*, by André Blum and Robert Tatlock, was "an authority on the subject of the new art" (67). Another was asked why the Brooklyn Museum had not chosen to buy a Brancusi when it had the opportunity (40). Yet a third was questioned about whether the sculptor's work had shown in "recognized galleries" (33).

32  Ultimately, the court's language strongly suggested that art no longer needed to be connected to nature. The decision describes the *Bird* as "A piece of sculpture, not bearing any striking resemblance to a living object, the original product of a professional sculptor . . . and a work of art, by reason of its symmetrical shape, artistic outlines and beauty of finish" (111).

33  *Feist Publications, Inc. v. Rural Telephone Service Company, Inc.* 499 U.S. 340, 345 (1991).

34  Ibid. The court's emphasis on the author as the site of originality has led some scholars to argue that copyright law depends on a specifically *romantic* notion of art. Writers at the end of the eighteenth century shifted away from

a longstanding idea of books as vehicles for imitation and received ideas, and began to see their work "as the intellection of a unique individual." Martha Woodmansee, "The Genius and the Copyright: Economic and Legal Conditions of the Emergence of the 'Author,'" *Eighteenth-Century Studies* 17 (1984): 434. See also Martha Woodmansee and Peter Jaszi, eds., *The Construction of Authorship: Textual Appropriation in Law and Literature* (Durham, NC and London: Duke University Press, 1994).

35  "All that is needed . . . is that the 'author' contributed something more than a 'merely trivial' variation, something recognizably 'his own.'" *Alfred Bell and Co., Ltd. v. Catalda Fine Arts, Inc.* 191 F.2d 99 (1951).

36  "In time a standard of novelty would have to be debased or distorted, else copyright as a system would lose all viability." Benjamin Kaplan, *An Unhurried View of Copyright* (New York: Columbia University Press, 1967): 43.

37  US Constitution, article I, § 8, cl. 8

38  Neil Weinstock Netanel, "Copyright and Democratic Civil Society," *Yale Law Journal* 106 (1996): 358.

39  See Lawrence Lessig, *Free Culture: How Big Media Uses Technology and the Law to Lock Down Culture and Control Creativity* (New York: Penguin, 2004): 21–24; and Bob Levin, *The Pirates and the Mouse* (Seattle: Fantagraphics Books, 2003).

40  See, for example, Lawrence Lessig, *The Future of Ideas: The Fate of the Commons in a Connected World* (New York: Random House, 2001); and Siva Vaidhyanathan, *Copyrights and Copywrongs: The Rise of Intellectual Property and How it Threatens Creativity* (New York: New York University Press, 2001).

41  Jack M. Balkin, "Digital Speech and Democratic Culture: A Theory of Freedom of Expression for the Information Society," *New York University Law Review* 79 (April 2004): 4–5.

42  Scholars often argue that the law strikes a delicate balance between "authors," on the one hand, who are granted exclusive rights over their works so that they will have an incentive to write and invent, and the public, on the other, who benefit from access to an array of competing viewpoints and creative possibilities. But these may be mutually reinforcing values: authors are granted an incentive to produce because the public needs to hear a wide range of voices. As the Supreme Court held, "The monopoly created by copyright . . . rewards the individual author in order to benefit the public." *Sony Corp. of America* v. *Universal City Studios, Inc.*, 464 U.S. 417, 429 (1984). There are two major alternatives to this school of thought. One favors the "moral rights" of an author "to reap the fruits of his or her own labor." According to this view, there should be no public domain, and copyrights need never expire. Marshall A. Leafer critiques this in *Understanding Copyright Law* (New York: Matthew Bender, 1999): 16–18. The second favors the view that copyright inhibits creativity. "Copyleft" activists advocate the free sharing of software

as a condition of free speech. See Richard Stallman, "What is Copyleft?" (www.gnu.org/copyleft/copyleft.html; accessed September 2006).

43 *Harper and Row Publishers, Inc. v Nation Enterprises*, 471 U.S. 539, 588 (1985).

44 Jeannie Suk, "Note: Originality," *Harvard Law Review* 115 (May 2002): 2003.

45 Dworkin, 229.

46 *Emerson v. Davies* 8 F. Cas. 615, 619 (C. C. D., Mass., 1845).

47 *Feist Publications, Inc. v. Rural Telephone Service Company, Inc.* 499 U.S. 340, 345 (1991).

48 "As numerous studies have concluded, corporations regularly eschew avant-garde or controversial expression, tending rather to support cultural production that reflects mainstream interests and tastes, as befits a vehicle of public relations." Netanel, 360.

49 *Eric Eldred v. John D. Ashcroft*, 537 US 186 (2003).

50 Lessig writes: "more content is controlled by law today than ever in our past." *The Future of Ideas*, 110.

51 D. T. Max, "The Injustice Collector: Is James Joyce's Grandson Suppressing Scholarship?" *The New Yorker* (June 19, 2006): 34–43; and Shauna C. Bryce, "Recent Development: Life Plus Seventy: The Extension of Copyright Terms in the European Union and Proposed Legislation in the United States," *Harvard International Law Journal* 37 (spring 1996): *n*. 103.

52 These are words used by Rogers' legal team to represent his work. *Rogers v. Koons*, 960F.2d 301 (2nd Cir., 1992): A658–59. All subsequent references to the legal proceedings, apart from the decision, will refer simply to page numbers.

53 *Burrow-Giles Lithographic Co. v. Sarony*, 111 U.S. 53 (1884).

54 *Rogers v. Koons*, 960F.2d 301 (2nd Cir., 1992).

55 Ibid.

56 "Fair use" is the legal freedom to use copyrighted material for a range of purposes, including education, news reporting, research, parody, and criticism. "Fair use" exceptions to copyright law are often justified on democratic grounds. New authors need to be able to quote from others' works and build on their insights for the purposes of deliberation and the pursuit of knowledge. "Without referring to or freely quoting from original works, newspaper editorials, book reviews, and satirical television shows could not do their work. If students had to ask permission from publishing companies for every quotation they used in term papers, education would grind to a halt." Vaidhyanathan, 26.

57 Rogers' side conceded that "Rogers cannot protect the 'theme' or 'idea' of a couple holding eight puppies," but they argued that this was not the point: "Koons chose to copy the precise way Rogers expressed the idea down to the exact details of the pose, including 'variation of light to dark' among

235

the puppies, which he expressly told his artisans to imitate" (Rogers' brief, 23–24).

58 "The doctrine of fair use . . . permits courts to avoid rigid application of the copyright statute when, on occasion, it would stifle the very creativity which that law is designed to foster." *Iowa State Univ. Research Found., Inc. v. American Broad. Cos.*, 621 F.2d 57, 60 (1980).

59 *Rogers v. Koons*, 960F.2d 301 (2nd Cir., 1992).

60 Lynne A. Greenberg objects to the language of the *Rogers* decision, which she claims is "overbroad in its indictment of, and hostility toward, appropriation." "The Art of Appropriation: Puppies, Piracy, and Post-Modernism," *Cardozo Arts and Entertainment Law Journal* 11 (1992): 25. See also "Notes: Beyond *Rogers v. Koons*: A Fair Use Standard for Appropriation," *Columbia Law Review* 993 (October 1993): 1473–526.

61 Suk, 1996–97.

62 My emphasis. Ibid., 2002–3, 1994.

63 *Bleistein v. Donaldson Lithographic Co.*, 188 U.S. 239 (1903).

64 *Rogers v. Koons*, 960F.2d 301 (2nd Cir., 1992).

65 Louise Harmon, "Art, Law, and the Killing Jar," *Iowa Law Review* 79 (1994): 411.

66 To be fair, Koons's legal team was never given a full chance to air their arguments, since they were denied a jury trial. The District Court decided that no issues of fact were at stake in the case. Koons appealed, claiming that the facts in dispute included the assertion that Koons's act of copying had been in bad faith, that he had intended to profit by his use of the note card, and that he had indeed duplicated the "essence" of the photograph (Koons's petition for rehearing, 6–10).

67 *Rogers v. Koons*, 960F.2d 301 (2nd Cir., 1992).

68 Kirk Varnedoe and Adam Gopnik, *High and Low: Modern Art and Popular Culture*, reprinted in Brief and Addendum for Koons; or see paperback ed. (New York: Harry N. Abrams, 1993): 389.

69 See, for example, Greenberg; and "Notes: Beyond *Rogers v. Koons*."

## CONCLUSION: ARTISTS, ACADEMIC WRITING, AND THE CLASSROOM

1 Few commentators attack scientists for using a technical language that is impenetrable to non-specialists, but humanists are perhaps vilified for using specialized language because they are supposed to be reaching everyone, "transmitting a cultural heritage." Jonathan Culler, "Introduction: Dressing Up, Dressing Down," in *Just Being Difficult? Academic Writing in the Public Arena*,

eds. Jonathan Culler and Kevin Lamb (Stanford: Stanford University Press, 2003): 2.

2   Judith Butler, "Further Reflections on the Conversations of Our Time," *Diacritics* 27 (spring 1997): 13.

3   Denis Dutton, "Language Crimes – A Lesson in How Not to Write, Courtesy of the Professors," *Wall Street Journal* (February 5, 1999), W11.

4   Judith Butler, "A 'Bad Writer' Bites Back," *New York Times* (March 20, 1999): A15.

5   Brian Brennan, "Fish Wrap Language," *New York Times* (March 3, 1999), A16; Timothy J. Clark, "Ugly May be Better," *New York Times* (March 3, 1999): A16.

6   Martha Nussbaum, "The Professor of Parody," *New Republic* (February 22, 1999): 37–45.

7   Stanley N. Kurtz, "'Bad Writing' Has No Defense," *New York Times* (March 24, 1999): A26.

8   See, for example, Peter Brooks, "On Difficulty, the Avant-Garde, and Critical Moribundity," in Culler and Lamb, 132.

9   Mark Bauerlein, "Bad Writing's Back," *Philosophy and Literature* 28 (2004): 190. See also Marjorie Perloff, "The Intellectual, the Artist, and the Reader," *PMLA* 112 (October 1997): 1129–30.

10  I refer to the "research university" here because the debate about difficult writing focuses on academics engaged in active scholarly publishing and specifically pertains to those scholars working at the cutting edge of research.

11  Butler, "A 'Bad Writer' "; Gerald Graff, "Scholars and Sound Bites: The Myth of Academic Difficulty," *PMLA* 115 (2000): 1044.

12  Michael Warner, "Styles of Intellectual Publics," in Culler and Lamb, 115.

# Index